Netscape Guide

TO Online ents

& MACINTOSH

OFFICIAL

Netscape Guide
Online Investments

WINDOWS & MACINTOSH

The ultimate reference
for financial resources
on the Internet

An imprint of
Ventana Communications Group

RUSSELL SHAW

Official Netscape Guide to Online Investments: The Ultimate Reference for Financial Resources on the Internet
Copyright ©1996 by Russell Shaw

Library of Congress Cataloging-in-Publication Data

Shaw, Russell.
      Official Netscape guide to online investments : the ultimate
reference for financial resources on the Internet / Russell Shaw.
            p.   cm.
      Includes index.
      ISBN 1-56604-452-9
      1. Finance, Personal—Computer programs. 2. Investments—Computer
programs. 3. Industrial management—Computer network resources.
4. Netscape. I. Title.
HG179.S453 1996
332.024'00285'467—dc20   96-26454
                                                        CIP

First Edition 9 8 7 6 5 4 3 2 1

Printed in the United States of America

Published and distributed to the trade by Ventana Communications Group, Inc.
P.O. Box 13964, Research Triangle Park, NC 27709-3964
919.544.9404
FAX 919.544.9472
http://www.vmedia.com

ABOUT THE AUTHOR

Russell Shaw is a veteran journalist specializing in finance, business, and technology. In addition to *Yahoo! Internet Life*'s popular weekly "Web Wallet" column, he also writes for *InfoWorld*, *WebWeek*, *Financial World*, *Investor's Business Daily*, and *Information Week*.

Acknowledgments

Hearty thanks are bestowed on those who have helped me in this project. Gratitude is enthusiastically expressed to many, including cyberprint agent extraordinaire and multilevel visionary David Rogelberg and equal half Sherry Rogelberg, both of Studio B, for activating my involvement in this book; Bill Machrone of Ziff-Davis and Angela Gunn, Web doyenne of Ziff-Davis's *Yahoo! Internet Life* site, for hiring me to do the weekly "Web Wallet" column that led to this book; plus other *Yahoo! Internet Life* visionaries and creative decision-makers such as Barry Golson, Elizabeth Holzer, Derek Baker, and others for putting up with my bad puns and for letting me keep that way-cool forum.

Muchas gracias also to current and past Ventana staffers and freelancers for their vision and guidance on this book. You've all helped make it better than it would have been without your input. Stand up and be counted: JJ Hohn, Beth Snowberger, Shelley O'Hara, Susan Christophersen, Peter Ferrante, Cheri Robinson, Sherri Morningstar, and Heather Grattan.

And thanks to Netscape co-founder Marc Andreessen, for imagining and then creating innovative browser technology, and to Tim Berners-Lee, for inventing the code that made the World Wide Web and, by extension, books like these, possible. Neither of you know me (not yet, anyway), but let me know what type of Scotch you'd like and it's on the way. It would be karmic justice for helping me change my life.

Hey, everyone! See ya' every Tuesday on the Web at http://www.zdnet.com/yil/content/depts/columns/. Let's have fun and learn from each other.

DEDICATION

Thanks to my family for your love and support. Plus, if it were not for you, I'd have no relatives. To loves who have loved, friends who have helped, and editors who have bestowed their faith in me with assignments. I hope I haven't been too incomprehensible an enigma or too heavy a burden.

Contents

SECTION IV: APPENDICES

Introduction

From investment advice to debt counseling, estate tax primers to venture capital sources, you can find just about any personal finance information source on the Internet. Yahoo, the popular Web index that catalogs World Wide Web sites by subject, currently lists several hundred sources that touch on personal finance topics. But where do you look for this information? And once you find it, how do you make maximum use of what you find?

What if you have a company about to launch an IPO (Initial Public Offering) of stock or a business to promote? How do you make your information available? When the Internet began its explosive growth just a couple of years ago, most of these personal finance sites cost several thousand dollars just to construct. Major corporations either hired several people apiece to build these sites or signed pricey contracts with Internet Service Providers (ISPs) for these services. Now, you don't have to be just a consumer of goods, services, and information. Instead, you can become a provider yourself. For less money than a typical one-month mortgage payment, you can build your own site using one of the Web publishing tools now widely available. With tools such as the Netscape Commerce Server, you'll be able to sell your product or service online, in a secured environment.

WHO NEEDS THIS BOOK?

Almost anyone with a World Wide Web browser and Web access will find the *Official Netscape Guide to Online Investments* helpful. Everyone is a participant in the economy. We all have checking accounts, and most of us have credit cards. We all pay taxes. Then there are automobile and life insurance premiums to fork over, investments to consider, homes to sell.

Web sites abound that either give advice on how to perform these transactions or expose us to vendors who might give us a better deal at less cost for these basic services. This book will describe the available Web sites.

In addition, you can find information in other sections of the Internet called *newsgroups*. A newsgroup is a bulletin board where users can post and respond to messages. There you can find like-minded people and learn from their experiences in the world of money.

As another source, you can look to the major online services such as CompuServe and America Online. These services have personal finance resources of their own. Offline, some highly authoritative CD-ROMs and books are covered as well.

Finally, there are about 17 million businesses in the United States. More than 99 percent of American businesses don't have a Web site. Of those that do, few have had the time or the confidence to investigate the relatively new world of competitive advantages that secured electronic commerce offers. The Internet can take a customer base heretofore limited by geography to a small part of a metropolitan area and expand it across continents. This book covers how to make this transition.

WHAT'S INSIDE?

This book is divided into 4 parts, with 20 chapters and 3 appendices. The parts include "The Basics," "Hot Sites on the Internet," "Other Places for Finance Information," and "Appendices."

THE BASICS

"The Basics" includes Chapters 1 through 4 and covers the skills you need to get started using the Internet.

Chapter 1, "What Is the Internet?" explains the different portions of the Internet, how they differ from each other, what the World Wide Web is, and how and why it is the most navigable resource for personal finance information.

Chapter 2, "What Is a Browser & How Do I Use It?" defines what a browser is and why you need one. This chapter uses the most popular browser, Netscape Navigator, to show how you can search for, pinpoint, access, and process personal finance information.

Chapter 3, "How Do I Find the Information I Need?" shows how to use the major Internet search engines to find the personal finance and investment information you seek.

Chapter 4, "What Financial Information You Can Expect to Find," sketches the big picture of personal finance and investment on the Internet and describes the various types of information available online.

HOT SITES ON THE INTERNET

The next several chapters are organized around different finance and investment subject areas. Each chapter includes an overview of how the area is treated on the Web, as well as some representative Web sites for each topic.

Chapter 5, "Appraisals & Mortgages," describes people who can furnish loans for your home or business, or appraise your home, business, or collectible. In this chapter you'll also discover several sites that gather general real-estate market news and trends.

Chapter 6, "Capital," covers sources of venture capital to help you expand or start a business.

Chapter 7, "Credit & Debt," describes organizations that offer low-interest or secured credit cards and groups doing consumer debt counseling.

Chapter 8, "Entrepreneurship & Consulting Services," includes sites run by people who can help your business thrive and keep it thriving.

Chapter 9, "Insurance," covers advice and sources for all forms of insurance.

Chapter 10, "Investments," describes stock and bond quote services, analysts, brokerage houses, and investment software programs.

Chapter 11, "Malls, Jobs & Services," highlights some of the online shopping areas. Numerous large Web sites function as virtual malls where personal finance vendors have set up shop alongside other types of vendors. Several of the leading ones are described, along with a representative listing of what you can buy there.

Chapter 12, "Mutual Funds," is a guide to Web sites where you can get information about competing mutual funds products, check your existing funds account online, send e-mail for information, or simply learn about this sector.

Chapter 13, "Software," shows you some of the available software. Some personal finance software vendors let you order online; also, freeware and shareware are available. This chapter details what's available both by ordering or downloading off the Net.

Chapter 14, "Taxes," includes online tax databases, news, and information, as well as calculators for various types of taxes, including income taxes, small business, estate, and so on.

Chapter 15, "Miscellaneous," covers other types of finance-related Web resources that don't fit into any of the other categories.

OTHER PLACES FOR FINANCE INFORMATION

In addition to Web sites, you can find other sources on the Internet. This section highlights these sources.

Chapter 16, "Using Usenet," covers newsgroups. More than 30 newsgroups exist that touch on personal finance topics. These are listed and described.

Chapter 17, "Gopher Guide," describes the Gopher resources. Most Gopher resources are university-based, but within this limited universe, more than 20 university schools of business have Gopher servers that provide doorways to relevant information.

Chapter 18, "Extra, Extra: Financial News," highlights relevant news services. Daily business, financial, and political news bears direct relevance to personal finance issues. The leading ones are profiled and the places in which you can find them are detailed.

Chapter 19, "The Online Services," describes other online services. These services not only carry some of the news wires that are described in the preceding chapter but also have their own finance-related discussion groups and forums. This catch-all chapter explores what's available.

Chapter 20, "Offline Resources, On-Target Tools," describes Quicken, Microsoft, and other resources, including their features, prices, and ordering information.

APPENDICES

Appendix A, "About netscapepress.com," explains the resources you can find online at the official Netscape Press Web site.

Appendix B, "Frequently Asked Questions About Online Investing," is a list of questions people most often pose about personal finance sites, tools, and informational resources.

Appendix C, "Other Resources," includes cross-referrals to other print and online sources.

Appendix D, "URLs for Sites Described in This Book," is a listing of Internet addresses for all sites mentioned in this book.

The Glossary defines the key buzz phrases and code words.

REMEMBER THAT THINGS CHANGE

The Internet is a world that changes and expands daily. The *Official Netscape Guide to Online Investments* has information about how you can keep up with these changes on an instantaneous basis. Yet, because things change, there may be Internet sites, newsgroups, or software packages that I've missed. If you have any insights, news, thoughts, admonitions, or praise, I'd welcome e-mail from you.

You can reach me at russellshaw@delphi.com.

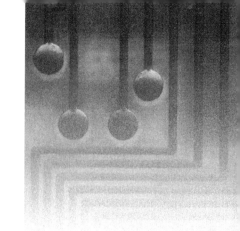

SECTION I:

The Basics

What Is the Internet?

So many companies and so many people are putting up Web sites that the power to publish is now in the hands of the masses rather than just the elite. If the question of the 1980s was, "What's your fax number?," the question for the last half of the 1990s is, "What's your URL?" (Uniform Resource Locator, or Web address). How did the Internet begin? What is the Web? What's the difference between the Internet and the Web? What's a Web address? This chapter answers these questions and more.

This book isn't the only place you can learn this information. Any one of several hundred volumes for sale at your bookstore or your computer outlet would address the nature of the Internet or of its specific functions. Might make for interesting reading, but maybe you really don't care about routers, servers, bits, and bytes. You don't view knowledge about what the Internet is and does as an end in itself, but as a bedrock of information that can help you make money.

This is fine. As a matter of fact, I am in sync with you. Still, a little basic knowledge can't hurt. Think about it. When you were in ninth grade, geometry seemed like something useless, right? Two years ago, when you sat down with your architect and contractor to plan for an extra wing in your new house, didn't that basic knowledge come in handy?

If we agree, let's make a compact, you and I. I'll give you a little bit of Internet 101—with maybe a little Internet 202 thrown in—but only enough so that you'll be better equipped to negotiate this labyrinth of cyberspace without too much hand-holding. After all, you'll want to know where the good mutual fund sites are without being stuck in the online paleontology lab of some obscure Australian university.

Before you get started looking at the various personal finance resources, you should have a good idea of what the Internet and Web are and how they are set up. This chapter provides that introduction. The chapter explains the evolution of the Internet and the different parts that compose this network of networks.

DEFINING THE INTERNET

The Internet is an international web of interconnected government, education, and business computer networks throughout the world. These connections, basically, are actuated through a decentralized Internet "backbone"—hundreds of supernodes spread around the globe that are reception, transmission, and sending points for data from Web servers hooked up to a branch of the network. At this juncture, I'm not distinguishing between a graphic of a smiling stockbroker on some World Wide Web page and a spirited discussion about baseball on some Usenet newsgroup. From a routing sense, all types of transmissions flow from the backbone.

Here's a greatly oversimplified but accurate description of how an Internet transmission works. You put the kids to bed, go to your den, and turn on your computer. You go to a program such as Windows 95 and access the window you've preconfigured to allow you to call your Internet Service Provider (ISP). Your modem dials the number and connects your computer, the *client* computer, to your ISP's *server* computer.

After an onscreen acknowledgment that you're connected, your Netscape browser presents you with a series of alternatives of where you can go next on the Internet. Perhaps you're looking for some specific information about no-load mutual funds but you don't know any Web addresses that you can enter. You do know of the Web search services, of which you particularly like Lycos. You type the Web address for Lycos.

(In Chapter 3, "How Do I Find the Information I Need," I explain how to do a search. Don't be concerned with that right now.) At the moment, we're talking routing. By typing the Web address for Lycos, you've instructed your browser, piggybacking on a connection to your ISP, to comb the branches of the Internet until . . . Eureka! it finds the signature address for the Lycos search engine.

Meanwhile, on the Lycos end, banks of servers in Massachusetts are fielding hundreds of such contacts a second. If the site required a password, the entry procedure would be a bit more complicated, but since Lycos is free, here's what happens. Whichever of Lycos's ports picked up your call is now on autopilot, waiting for you to type **no load mutual funds** in the search field on your computer. Each of those 17 letters has a unique binary code, or a specific combination of "1s" and "0s" that lets both your computer and any computers hooked up to yours know what you've typed in. Your trusty modem accepts the signal from your keyboard, and your browser, now riding the phone connection through your ISP, sends the specific series of binaries to Lycos that tell Lycos's computers what you are looking for.

Lycos, if you're interested, has its servers in Massachusetts and Pennsylvania. Its proprietary technology will, on its own, comb, or "crawl" the Web and look for documents that contain the terms you requested. When it finds them, it excerpts the ones it "scores" the highest and then immediately sends a listing back through the network to your computer in Denver, Denmark, or anywhere else on the blue orb.

You read a list of citations and find a site that you'd like to visit. Click on the underlined hyperlink next to each site that Lycos has listed, and you're there.

How long does a search take? I run this drill several times a day and night. If, to paraphrase an expression that we use in the American South, "the good link's willing and the creeks don't rise," the whole procedure will take a minute or less.

WHO CONTROLS THE INTERNET?

No one entity controls the Internet, although some governments have sought to regulate access to some of its content, and advisory groups exist that draft performance-related recommendations for overall performance.

The lack of control has a set of advantages and drawbacks. The significance that you assign to each will likely be determined by your philosophy and outlook on life. There are many well-meaning individuals who, although genuinely thrilled that the Internet makes the free flow of ideas around borders at lightning speeds possible, are not so happy that even a very few of these places are the stalking grounds for those who would put up graphic photographs of underage individuals in compromising situations.

With luck, this will never happen, but if you find something on the Internet that is highly objectionable to you, there's very little, if anything, that you can do to remove it. A number of online services block certain Web sites or newsgroups, but no number exists for you to call to get something disgusting taken off the Internet. If you notice a strange-looking crowd going in and out of that house down the street and you suspect that X-rated photo shoots are taking place there, you can call your police department or county attorney to investigate. But, should you see such photos on a Web site, that site might be in Finland or Thailand. Your most effective strategy would be to log on somewhere else. And there are plenty of places you can go.

HOW THE INTERNET STARTED

This network started out with a significantly different, and some would say more limited, destiny. Fearing that weapons of mass destruction could cause the communications infrastructure of the United States to collapse, the U.S. Defense Department formed the ARPAnet (Advanced Research Project Agency) project in 1969. The thinking was that a decentralized maze would have a better chance of surviving attack than one with control emanating from hub computers at the center.

Within a decade, other government departments began adopting the same UNIX operating protocols on which ARPAnet ran, and then private sector entities such as educational institutions and large businesses adopted those protocols as well. UNIX and the growth of modems promoted linkages between government agencies and from university to university. The mid- and late-1980s found these links employed to an increasing degree, with a networked culture of fellowship inevitably following.

Sensing the vast communications potential of this new medium, the National Science Foundation acted as a catalyst to bring some organization to this burgeoning online burgh. The NSF funded five supercomputer centers that would formulate a pattern for access and investigate new ways of communication.

The Internet, as it was now known, became more of a civilian entity. Yet communications were mostly limited to textual exchanges using the unpopular and somewhat awkward UNIX command language. Portions of the "old" Internet survive, but to a large extent have been rendered obsolete by the new visual and multimedia World Wide Web.

DEFINING THE WORLD WIDE WEB

Less than a decade past, the year 1989 may seem relatively recent. Yet, considering how people communicated over computer networks, that time was as long ago and far away from the here and now as a grainy old photo from the 1880s is from today's 6-gigabyte capacity digital video disks. In 1989, a team of visionaries at the European Particle Physics Laboratory, or CERN, in Geneva, Switzerland, devised the World Wide Web. The scientists, led by engineer Tim Berners-Lee, were frustrated by the awkward command structure and coldness of the Internet and its immediate predecessor, the then-20-year-old ARPAnet.

There had to be a better way to communicate data over modem lines than the string of horrifying UNIX protocols mandatory at the time. Also, what if a scientist in one nation wanted to show a close-up photo of some microscopic parasite to a colleague in another nation? What was the first scientist supposed to do, photocopy a page from a book and fax it to the colleague?

Led by the hyperkinetic Berners-Lee, the scientists at CERN had a better idea. A string of relatively simple commands called HyperText Markup Language, or HTML, would be devised. The goal was to give visual characteristics to textual documents, thus making the integration of data and images in a stored format feasible. This new format would be the pictorial representation of the Internet. Berners-Lee's creation was called the World Wide Web, or the Web for short—befitting the "parent" Internet's persona as an interconnected, worldwide "web" of computer networks.

The Web was rolled out to the world in 1993. Within a matter of months, a totally unforeseen series of events began to unfold. Quite literally, the world discovered the Web. Automobile marketers, investment advisers, managers of political campaigns, garage rock bands, graduate students in primatology, authors of interactive novels, fourth-grade classes in Wisconsin, television networks, and hobby magazine publishers all started their Web sites.

UNDERSTANDING WHAT MAKES THE WEB WHAT IT IS

The Web is only as compelling as the sites it contains. If you've been only to poorly constructed and ill-conceived Web pages, you're likely to think of this whole phenomenon as just a colossal waste of time. Yet, the well-done sites are what make life online fun and perhaps even profitable.

Most Web sites have a *home page*. This page is akin to the cover of a book. It notes the name of the site and often has several pictures, or *icons*, representing some of the key sections of the site. Ideally, the icons are so recognizable (as in a question mark for the Technical Help section) that no further elaboration is necessary. The icons are, themselves, encoded with hyperlink so that when you direct your mouse or trackball to move the cursor to the icon, your browser accesses the site server on the other end to "turn the page" to the one you want.

Before the graphics-rich Web, Internet sites were text-only. With no icons, your luck in navigation would be entirely dependent on the skill of the indexer. The earlier and still sometimes-used method of displaying textual information on the Web was called *Gopher*, but without icons or any meaningful word-search functionality, finding a term in a 100,000-word Gopher document was a fishing expedition that could take hours. Success wasn't guaranteed. Plus, on Web sites, the ability to visually depict concepts by means of icons or other graphical shorthand cuts down on the number of words, making finding the information that you need easier still.

NAVIGATING THE WEB

To take advantage of the features of the World Wide Web, you need a navigation tool. In 1991, the National Center for Supercomputing Applications (NCSA) in Champaign, Illinois, became the birthplace of the first Web navigation tool, the NCSA Mosaic browser. It was invented by Marc Andreessen, who would leave the NCSA in 1993 to cofound Netscape Communications.

Netscape makes the Netscape Navigator, by far the most popular browser and the one that I cover in this book.

THE INTERNET IS MORE THAN THE WEB

The Web is the most dynamic, energized part of the online world, but it is not separate from the Internet. It's part of the Internet. Other sections of the Internet are better sources for specific types of information and communications than the Web is. This section describes some of the other sources.

GOPHER

As stated previously, Gopher is a text-only representation of the content of an Internet site. The concept was devised at the University of Minnesota, whose mascot for its sports teams is the golden gopher.

If you have one of the early, primitive, text-only Web browsers such as Lynx, or if you don't yet have a Web browser at all and are accessing the Internet through dial-up telecommunications software programs, Gopher will be a blessing to you. Some Web sites are *mirrored*, or copied, on Gopher, whereas, like fans of the LP record album, some locations on the Internet have stuck with Gopher's straightforward, text-only, no-graphics presentation for Gopher menus and Gopher sites (see Figure 1-1). The people who run these sites somehow regard the visual potential of the Web as out of sync with what they want to present to the world. Just as there are flat-earthers, some people even now believe that icons are nothing more than cartoons.

Jibes aside, some kinds of information really don't need pictures. That's why Gopher, which is text-only, is a good place for library catalogs, information about universities, and specialized academic research.

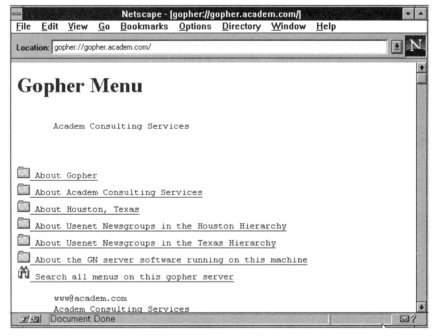

Figure 1-1: *A Gopher menu. (Academ Consulting Services is now found at http://www.academ.com/, a Web address, in addition to this Gopher address.)*

LISTSERV

Listserv is a collection of online forums and electronic mailing lists, some of which are moderated, many of which are closed to non-registrants. A number of places on the Internet can direct you to listservs of interest. Two of these are Web sites that allow for keyword searching of listservs. These are Lizst (http://www.liszt. com/) and TILE.NET/LISTS (at http://tile.net/listserv/).

When you find a listserv that might be of interest, you may be given the opportunity to "subscribe." Don't shy away, because in almost all cases, no money changes hands (except for the money that you'll make by following the financial advice meted out by the experts on some of these lists). It's just that the term *subscribe* is the most accurate descriptor for what goes on.

If you subscribe, you'll automatically get mailings of the postings that other members of the list have sent to it. These mailings are sent to your electronic mailbox as they are received. Instructions may vary somewhat, but to subscribe, most listservs will ask you to enter the word "subscribe" somewhere in the message field.

Some listservs are exclusive clubs, however. Generally speaking, the more academic and arcane-sounding ones may not let you in. You might need to "apply" by stating your credentials to the listserv moderator. On a listserv, a moderator sets the tone of the list, initiates discussions and solicitation of opinions on relevant topics, and, occasionally, screens posted messages before they are "put up."

USENET

Usenet is a compendium of more than 20,000 communities of special interests, ranging from motorcycle enthusiasts to vintage movie buffs. Essentially, Usenet newsgroups are the Internet's take on the old-style, dial-up bulletin boards that have been around for more than a decade. Like bulletin boards, newsgroups allow you to post your opinions on anything, as long as they conform to the group's stated purpose and rules.

These postings are called "threads," which is a fancy term for topic areas. At any one time, some groups can have thousands of postings in hundreds of threads. Figure 1-2 shows a Usenet menu.

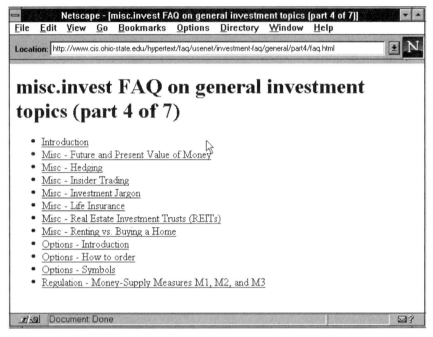

Figure 1-2: *A Usenet menu.*

FTP SITES

FTP stands for *file transfer protocol*, a communications technique that computers use to confer with one another. As an example, a Web site that allows online investing might require you to obtain a Netscape Navigator *plug-in* (extra application program) so that your software can work with that site's. If such is the case, the site might have reserved a few nodes on its server as FTP sites where it makes such applications available for transfer.

Should your site have such a procedure, it will probably furnish you with a generic password that will let you in to the FTP site and tell it to activate the transfer to your computer. You'll download the FTP-delivered missive to your hard drive, and follow the installation instructions.

You can get software updates, including new beta versions of Netscape Navigator, in much the same way. When you visit the Netscape Home Page (http://home.netscape.com/), you're likely to see several announcements of new products. Clicking the desired icon will launch a process that will culminate in an FTP transfer of the desired program or add-on from an FTP site (either at Netscape or at an identical *mirror site* somewhere else), to your hard drive.

INTERNET RELAY CHAT

Internet Relay Chat is a series of "chat" channels. Unlike Usenet, where the communication is done through message posting, IRC dialog takes place in a live, give-and-take mode. If you are on an IRC channel, you can converse with other participants in real-time, rather than simply react to Usenet postings that could have been placed an hour ago, yesterday, or last week.

OTHER SOURCES

In addition, the Internet includes bulletin board services (BBSes) and other services. Not necessarily connected to the Internet, a bulletin board service is a repository of information and communications opportunities, usually specific to a given region or city. Its subject menu is not very deep, however.

Online research utilities such as Dialog and Lexis-Nexis have some of the same information that Web sites do, and may even require similar search techniques. They are expensive but are generally a superior locale than the Web to search newspaper and magazine archives.

GETTING CONNECTED

Parts of life online can be frustrating. An outmoded computer with a slow processor and antique modem can make accessing a Web site an experience akin to watching the grass grow. The best advice that I can give is to come equipped with the best tools possible, as covered here.

In the hardware area, this means at least a 486-66 processor, but preferably a Pentium. "Sixty-six" is a snazzy way of saying you can run 66 million calculations per second. That's not so much if you are loading Web pages while printing out others. You're better off with a Pentium that has the power for at least 100 million calculations for each tick.

Next, you'll need software to access the Internet, as well as a modem to make the phone call. Your online sessions are likely to last an hour or more, so you'll want a dedicated line without Call Waiting. A 28,800 bps (bits per second) modem is mandatory. The World Wide Web can be a crowded, busy place at certain times of the day, so the more telecommunications firepower you've got, the better prepared you'll be to jostle for quick downloads. As for software, you need a browser. Netscape Navigator 2.0 is a browser of choice, as well as the standard that numerous site-builders configure for. You can get Navigator by pointing your existing browser to the Netscape home page (http://home.netscape.com/) and executing a file transfer (as explained earlier), or through your local computer retailer, office supply retailer, or warehouse club.

Finally, you'll need to open an account with an Internet Service Provider so that you can dial into the Internet. Some may bundle their own browser's software into their basic package, but virtually all will allow you to install Netscape Navigator 2.0 into their programs, making that program your gateway to the online world.

You can find Internet Service Providers in several ways. Your computer store probably has a working relationship with several. Most large- and mid-sized cities have Internet user groups whose monthly meeting schedules are printed in daily newspapers, free weeklies, and specialized, local computer publications. If you already have access to the Internet (through a friend, an online service, or at work), you can go to the Web site addresses http:// thelist.com/ or http://www.boardwatch.com/ISP/index.htm for a list of Internet Service providers in your area.

MOVING ON

Now you understand how the parts of the Internet differ from each other but combine to create a persona for cyberspace. And you know what you need to get connected. You're starting to know these waters, but you need a rudder and a compass to navigate the eddies. The next chapter explains how browsers such as Netscape Navigator can help you organize your "surfing" as you look for and organize the personal finance and investment information you want.

What Is a Browser & How Do I Use It?

For access to the World Wide Web—the portion of the Internet where text, graphics, and multimedia come together—you'll need a Web browser. Browsers are software interfaces that take coded documents residing on Web sites all over the world and, through a telephone connection, bring them to vivid life on your computer monitor.

Don't be intimidated. Browsers are inexpensive, easy to install on your computer, and a snap to use. This chapter covers how to get, set up, and use a browser.

FINDING A BROWSER

More than half a dozen Web browsers are out there. Some are included with subscriptions to online services and will cost you nothing extra. A number of them are available through retail channels such as computer superstores, office supply stores, and warehouse clubs. Unless you are buying a browser with a full load of site-construction capabilities, you're unlikely to pay any more than $80, tops. Betas have been known to have bugs, so if you are the cautious type, you might wish to wait for the formal release.

The most convenient way to get a browser is to download one online. Because you'll need Web access first, this approach is a classic Catch-22 situation. You need a browser to get a browser. It's almost like using the equity in a starter home to buy another, larger house.

But after you have a browser, you can then use it to access a newer version. For example, browsers such as Netscape Navigator get updated frequently, so by logging on to a browser company's Web site (for instance, http://home.netscape.com), you can see whether a newer browser is out there. Then, you can download and install it, often for free. Installation instructions are usually attached in a helper file. Many users "graduated" from Netscape Navigator 1.1 to Personal Edition, then to Navigator 2.0 or higher by downloading the new version. Others have made the trip to their local computer retailer and paid a modest $49 or so for the latest release.

GETTING CONNECTED WITH YOUR BROWSER

You use your browser and modem to connect to the Web. The first thing you'll see onscreen is a home page. This is likely to be the "cover page" of the Web site belonging to the Internet Service Provider or online service whose phone lines you are using to reach the Internet. Most ISPs use Netscape Navigator 3.0 or 2.0 (see Figure 2-1) as the preferred browser and are likely to have a customized version of it as their own home page.

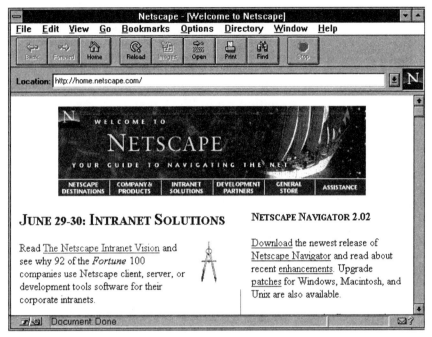

Figure 2-1: *The Netscape Web site home page, as viewed with the Netscape Navigator 2.0 Web browser.*

You use this home page as a starting point on your Web voyage. Some Web site home pages have flashy graphics that can take a good minute or two for transfer between the site's remote computer, or *server*, and your machine. The graphics, which can include corporate logos, snapshots, or illustrations of company products, and whatever other art the page designers can come up with, should give you a hint of what is "inside" the site.

From this starting place, you can then jump to other pages.

MOVING FROM PAGE TO PAGE

To get "inside" to the various pages of the site, you move your mouse or trackball to the particular link you want. These links may be indicated in one of several ways. Sometimes, a photo or illustration has been equipped with linking capability so that, when you use your mouse to move the onscreen cursor or arrow to the picture, that action tells the site's computer to jump to the particular site in question. More often, though, you'll get where you want by clicking on highlighted phrases or words. These words are either underlined, colored, or both (see Figure 2-2).

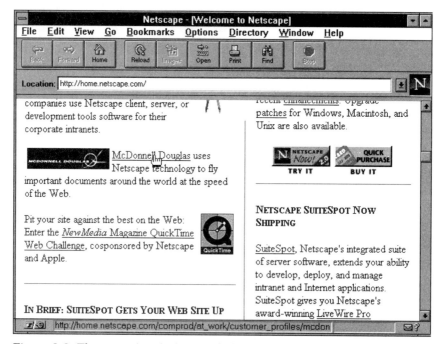

Figure 2-2: *The cursor is pointing to a link from the Netscape home page to the McDonnell Douglas Web site. If this link is clicked, you are whisked from the Netscape site to the McDonnell Douglas site.*

The "language" that makes this all so easily navigable is called *HyperText Transfer Protocol*, or *HTTP* for short. Until the time comes that you are creating Web pages for yourself, you don't need to know a great deal about how it works. The important thing is that it enables you to go back and forth within Web sites and between sites without punching in hard-to-remember sequences of letters, numbers, and punctuation marks that you've long since forgotten even exist.

UNDERSTANDING PAGE ADDRESSES

The easiest way to get to a page is to move there from a link. You can also go directly to a page using the page address. Each page on the Web has a *Uniform Resource Locator*, or *URL*. Of the many tens of millions of pages on the Internet, no two URLs are alike.

Here are some examples of URLs:

http://home.netscape.com/
http://www.whitehouse.gov/
http://www.usadata.com/usadata/index.htm/
http://www.city.net/
http://wings.buffalo.edu/world/

Respectively, these URLs are the addresses of the Welcome to Netscape, Welcome to the White House, USADATA Local Market Data Resource, City.Net, and Virtual Tourist World Map pages.

URLs comprise several sections: the protocol, the server, the domain name, and the path name.

The first section, protocol, tells the browser what section of the Internet to look in for the page that you've identified. Most WWW pages use the protocol *http*. Other sections of the Internet can use such designators as *File* for File Transfer Protocol, *news.* or *rec.* for Usenet newsgroup discussion communities, or *gopher* for text-only files that aren't visually hyperlinked in the way World Wide Web sites are.

After the protocol, you'll see a colon (:), two slashes (//), and the server name. This takes you to the server, which, on the Web, is the *host* machine on which the particular Web site runs or resides. Some Web sites, particularly those belonging to large companies, run their own servers, whereas small- to mid-sized businesses are more likely to contract with a hosting service for switching and other capabilities. They do this because, with the amount of traffic on the Internet, a powerful server is needed to handle lots of access requests simultaneously. If you build your own Web site, you're likely to want to hire a hosting service rather than buy your own server. Leading servers, like Sun Sparcstations, can cost between $20,000 and $30,000 up front.

The third portion of a URL is the domain name. Internet addresses are subdivided into various *domains*, reflecting the classification or activity of the business or institution that put up the site. Examples include the following: .edu, for sites run by or for educational institutions; .gov, for government; .org, mainly for nonprofit organizations; and .com, for commercial enterprises. Except for some consumer-information sites in the .gov or .org domains, most of the Web pages pointed out in this book reside in the .com domain.

The last portion of a URL is the path name. This is usually the specific page of a Web site that has multiple pages.

In a hypothetical example, http://www.genwidget.com/faq/, the "FAQ," or Frequently Asked Questions page, would be on the General Widget site, which is in the .com domain on the World Wide Web and runs on HyperText Transfer Protocol.

USING YOUR BROWSER

You can use your browser in any number of ways to find links on and to Web sites. A good place to start is on the browser itself. Navigator 2.0 has "What's New" and "What's Cool" icons. Typically, these lead to mini-reviews of several dozen "new" or "cool" sites. Written by Netscape staffers, these menus are updated frequently and, of course, contain links to each site.

As another method, you can search for information. Netscape includes a link on its home page to the popular search engine called Excite. You can use this tool to enter words or phrases you want to look for. Excite then displays a list of matching sites, and you can jump from this list directly to the site of interest. The next chapter discusses using search tools in more detail.

DISPLAYING OTHER PAGES

When you see a link that you want to explore, you simply click on that link name or icon, and your browser downloads that page and then displays it. The time it takes to display the page depends on how complex the page is and the speed of your modem. Usually, the browser indicates when it is still busy downloading. In

Netscape Navigator, you can see the stars in the Netscape icon moving. Also, the status bar at the bottom of the screen gives you an update on the size of the document and the bytes transferred. If it's a large document, be patient. The modem and browser are working hard, but unless you are accessing a multi-gigabyte map of the human genome, you aren't likely to overtax your computer to the breaking point.

From that page, you can jump to any links on that page and so on until you find the information you need. You can also use the browser's toolbar (see Figure 2-3) to move back and forth among the pages that you've already viewed.

Figure 2-3: *The Netscape Navigator 2.0 toolbar.*

Use the Back and Forward buttons to move back to the last page you viewed. If you go back, you can also go forward using the Forward button. The Home icon takes you back to the original home page that you saw when you first got connected. You can also access these commands in the Go menu.

In addition, most browsers come equipped with a history list. You can display a drop-down list of sites that you've visited this session. You can click on any of these sites to go directly there. Some less powerful browsers are equipped to go only a few steps back, but Navigator 2.0 allows you to track back through a session across more than a dozen pages.

If you want to go to a particular page and you know its address, you can use the Open button to call up a specific Web page using its address or URL. Click this button and then type the URL in the text box and press Enter.

Use the Stop button to halt loading of a Web page. For example, if you clicked a link by mistake, click the Stop button to stop. Or, if a page is taking too long to download, click Stop to halt the download. When you click Stop, you don't terminate your connection. Instead, you simply stay on the current page and quit downloading the new page.

WHAT REALLY HAPPENS WHEN YOU MOVE TO A LINK

When you've powered up a link, essentially what you've done is tell your browser software that is piggybacking a ride on your modem to access the Internet and pull up the Web (or other document) site page. Encoded with the knowledge of how to reach the domain, and then the server, on which the file is located, the browser seeks it out. Greatly simplified, it "asks" the server at the remote location to dish up, or "serve" it the given page. Assuming that the server is not too busy, it should do just that. Your modem then carries the message. The browser then translates the programming languages in which the site is written, and delivers it to your screen in a visual format that you can understand and will, it is hoped, be appealing to the eye as well as the mind. As the transfer is made, a status indicator at the bottom of your screen tells you how far along the loading is. If you see a designation that says Received 72,408 bytes, of 134,556 bytes (total file size), you're more than halfway there. If the Internet has no traffic jams, the countdown should be relatively continuous until the file transfer is done and you've pulled down the desired pages for viewing and navigation.

SETTING BOOKMARKS

If you find a site that you like, you may not remember how you got there and you may not want to have to write down the URL of all the sites that you have found useful. Instead, you can save these addresses in the form of a bookmark so that you can easily return to them.

On Netscape Navigator, the Bookmarks menu lets you flag individual Web pages for later viewing—either during the same session or during a future one. You can add pages to your list of bookmarks using the Add Bookmark command. Any sites that you add will always be available each time you start Navigator. If you are using more than one browser, however, keep in mind that these bookmarked archives are not normally interchangeable.

To view a page that you've saved, use the View Bookmarks command. You see a listing of your marked items. To go to one of these sites, click on it. A cool thing about the Navigator 2.0 Bookmark function is that the title of each clipped page is listed by descriptor, as well as by the URL, which is indicated on the bottom of the page. You can also open Bookmarks by selecting "Go To Bookmarks" and then selecting the desired bookmark from the dialog box. Regardless of the way you go about it, the browser "remembers" the URL, though, so when you click on it, the retrieval process is launched.

On most browsers, the order of bookmarked items lists the most recently created marks at the end of the bookmarked file menu. With Netscape Navigator 2.0, you can reorder the lists.

Other browser applications allow you to change the colors and type sizes of onscreen displays, capture files to disk, and turn off the automatic loading of images. To turn off images in Navigator, open the Options menu and uncheck the Auto Load Images menu selection. This change is especially helpful if you have a 14,400 bps or slower modem and don't have the time or patience to watch graphically rich pages come to life on your monitor at an arduously slow pace.

SEARCHING FOR TEXT ON A PAGE

In Netscape Navigator, you can use the Find command to move quickly to a particular section of a page. This command does not let you search for other Web sites, but does let you find specific words or phrases on the section of the site that you are now looking at. Large sites can contain several thousand words of text.

To use Find, follow these steps:

1. Click the Find button.

2. In the Find What text box, type the word or phrase that you want to find.

3. Select the direction Up or Down.

4. If you want to find only text that matches the case as you've entered it, check the Match Case check box.

5. Click OK.

If you have a different browser, follow the steps for that browser to find information on a Web page.

PRINTING A PAGE

If you want to have a hard copy of a Web page, you can print it. If you have Navigator 2.0, you can use the Print button in the toolbar. Or, open the File menu and select the Print command. When you select Print (see Figure 2-4), you can choose which pages to print as well as the number of copies. Select the options that you want and then click the OK button.

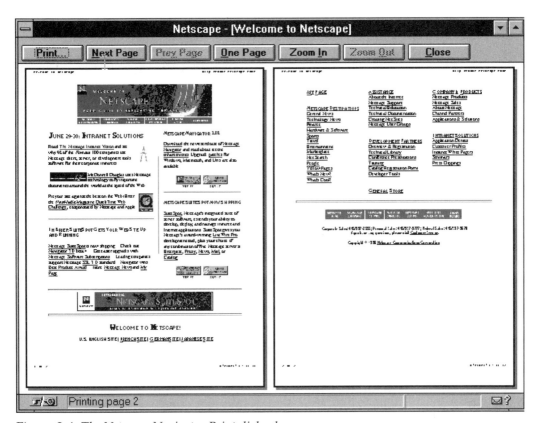

Figure 2-4: *The Netscape Navigator Print dialog box.*

A final tip: Not all browsers send the entire complement of graphical content to your printer. Netscape browsers do. Many dot-matrix and even some inkjet printers might not have the internal memory to process every visual artifact that the browser sends it from the page. Here are some short-term solutions:

- Capture the document as a text file on your word processing program and use its own print program to give you a hard copy. The best way to do this is by capturing the document as a text file, using your browser's Save As command.

  This approach has its intricacies. Your browser will likely append the term ".htm" to your file. Later, if you call up the file through your word processing program, it will read the file not as you saw it on the Web page, but as text, along with the *source code* that the designers of the site used to program the various visual elements. A better idea would be to use your browser's Open File program to retrieve and then display the downloaded file. You can even do this offline. You might not see every single icon, but you'll come a heck of a lot closer to the real thing.

- Free up as much memory as you can by closing any unrelated applications.

- Print only one page at a time.

A better solution is to buy a newer, more powerful printer.

FILLING OUT FORMS

Much commerce on the Internet is done via forms. The majority of these are created in the Common Gateway Interface (CGI) standard, which lets external programs interact with HTTP-reading servers and then with browsers.

On a business site, CGI-powered forms (see Figure 2-5) are often used to send and receive information to and from recipients, such as yourself. Web sites that require registration or that poll your opinions on a given topic via a check box format are likely to be using CGI. Most browsers understand and are able to translate a CGI document upon reception as opposed to transmission.

If, for example, you are using a CGI to apply for a money market account, you'll fill out the requested information in the appropriate boxes and then follow a procedure that will launch a secured transmission of the data over the Internet from your computer to the bank's or brokerage's server.

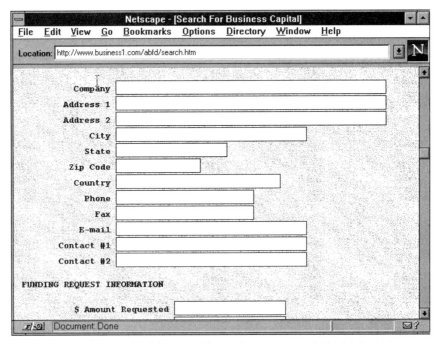

Figure 2-5: *A CGI-enabled form can be used to contact a Web site for information or to complete an application.*

Going Other Places With Your Browser

In addition to Web pages, you can access other sections of the Internet with your browser. You can access Usenet *newsgroups*, collections of online communities with common interests, through news servers. (Your Internet Service Provider will know the name of your news server. Chances are that your ISP has already set it up so that the browser will automatically go to the correct place. Here are the steps to follow if you are using Netscape Navigator:

1. Open the Options menu.

2. Select the Preferences command and then select News.

3. Type your news server's name in the NNTP server field. NNTP stands for Network News Transport Protocol, the language that the Internet uses for newsgroups.

4. Click the OK button.

Usenet is a realm unto itself, but it does share some attributes with the Web. Usenet has more than 20,000 newsgroups, divided into subject areas such as alt., comp., rec., and sci. "Alt." is short for "alternate," "comp." for "computer," "rec." for "recreation," and "sci." for "science." The newsgroup alt.business.import-export, for example, contains discussions of international trade issues. Individual topics within this subject field are divided into threads.

The first time you access a newsgroup, your news server will ask whether you want to "subscribe" to it. Don't worry; no money is changing hands. That's just the server's way of asking whether you want to add it to your Usenet hotlist. Don't confuse this hotlist with your Web bookmarks. Some of the intent may be the same, but Navigator stores it in a different area.

To access that newsgroup again, you can follow these steps in Navigator:

1. Open the Directory menu.

2. Choose the Go To Newsgroups command.

You see a list of all the groups to which you've subscribed. You can add your own comments (messages) to the group. Here are the steps that you follow in Navigator to add comments:

1. Go to the File | Mail Document mail item and call up the Send Mail/Post News dialog box.

2. In the message field, you can either compose your comments on the spot, or else attach comments that you may have written earlier on your word processing program.

Sending E-mail

Many Web sites have mail-to's, which are hyperlinks that bring up a given e-mail address on the screen. This might be the address of the Webmaster, customer service, or an officer in the company that put up the Web site. If you select this option, Netscape Navigator displays a dialog box for creating the message (see Figure 2-6).

Netscape calls up a field that allows you to attach a message you may have created offline on your word processing package, or that you wish to compose at the moment. Perhaps you want to respond to an offer. Here's how to do so.

Ideally, you have prepared for this by asking your Internet Service Provider for the name of your Simple Mail Transport Protocol (SMTP) server. Once again, this probably has already been set up by the ISP.

After you obtain this information, key in the name of the server in the Options | Preferences | Mail menu item area. You then will be given the opportunity to customize your settings on this menu. These settings allow you, if you choose, to be automatically or periodically signaled when an e-mail message comes in and you are online—even if you aren't in the mail area.

After you've made your choices, click on OK to accept.

The next time that you boot up your browser, it should be able to send and receive e-mail messages.

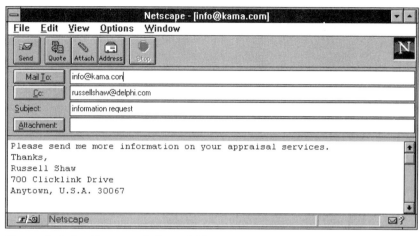

Figure 2-6: *Sending e-mail through Netscape Navigator.*

MOVING ON

You've now configured your browser and have a good idea how the various sectors of the Internet differ in presentation and content. The next chapter will tell you how to find that content and surf through terabytes of data on the Internet to locate the personal finance–related information you seek.

How Do I Find the Information I Need?

With the popularity of the Web comes complexity. Most experts predict that the Web will have several hundred thousand URLs, more than a million images, and at least a terabyte of text before the millennium turns. A terabyte worth of text is about 175 billion words, more than in 35 million 50,000-word books. Stacked, a terabyte of characters would stretch 110,000 miles high, or almost halfway to the moon.

So, how do you navigate through this thicket to find exactly what you want? To start, you have to figure out what you want to find. What is your goal? What do you want to accomplish? Perhaps you are unhappy with the 19 percent interest rate that you're paying on your MasterCard, and are looking for a resource that will tell you where you can do better. Or maybe you want to compare floor plans for a remodeled kitchen. If you are starting a new business, you might be looking to find a source of venture capital. As another reason, say that you're a student and want to incorporate photos of the 1995 collision between Jupiter and a comet in your high school science report. You can find all this information and more on the Web.

By knowing how to search, where to search, and what to search for, you can turn the Web from a seemingly incomprehensible sea of URLs to a quality-of-life enhancer. This chapter covers all you need to know about finding information on the Web.

To understand how much the Web can help you, consider an example. Say that you are planning a ski trip to Colorado. Without the advantages of the Web, you might start by looking in the phone book for the phone numbers of some travel agents and then making some calls. After enduring much phone tag, the fifth agent you talk to asks you to come to the office so that she can give you some brochures. In between dropping the kids off at soccer practice and running to the pharmacy, you fight for the last parking spot, wait 15 minutes to see the agent, and finally get your brochures. The only trouble is, the brochures are a year out of date. The resort that you picked out just added meeting space and has repositioned itself as a conference resort. You don't know that, and neither does the agent.

With the Web, you can use your PC or Mac to access the icon for your World Wide Web browser. A connection is initiated, and within seconds, you are on the Web. You use your browser's search tools to search for information on "ski Colorado." In less than a minute, a menu of Web sites comes up, along with a brief descriptor of each. You can also tell from this list which of these sites have photos as well as text. A mouse click, and you're transported more than a thousand miles from your den in some subdivision to a ski resort 10,000 feet up near the Continental Divide. All the information about the resort is up-to-date.

Two weeks later, you and your significant other are toasting a good day of schussing the slopes with a bottle of vintage burgundy.

SEARCHING THE WEB

Before you learn how to find what you want, it's important to have a grasp on what is available *to* find. The Internet has better places than the Web to meet people or text-search an academic journal from May 1994. But for almost anything else, the Web is the place to look.

When you look for sites on the Web, a search engine is your road map. Although they differ in presentation and depth of content, most search engines work the same way. Server computers housed in the corporate headquarters (and other sites) of the leading search engine companies comb, or "crawl," the Web each night looking for sites that have been added or changed in the past 24 hours. When you launch a search, the search engine crawls its repository and finds sites containing the words you requested.

After the basic retrieval is done, most engines "rank" the top 10 or 25 sites that you've requested. The ranking is not done by quality, but by objective criteria such as the following:

- Where in the text the matching phrase first appears (sooner, or higher, is better).

- How often it appears (more is better, because frequent appearances indicate that the site regards your phrase with more importance than the ones that are ranked lower).

- How close within the document identical citations appear to each other.

Here are the leading search engines: their Web addresses, their chief characteristics, and how they can help you find what you are looking for.

ALTAVISTA

http://www.altavista.digital.com
AltaVista is the largest search engine with the most Web pages. If you are looking for an obscure reference deep within a Web page, this is the place to go. On the negative side: citations are not ranked in the order of relevancy (such as how many times the word or phrase that you requested appears), and lots of extraneous citations are often pulled up.

EXCITE

http://www.excite.com
Excite is a very fast search engine that will retrieve and rank your

citations quickly and clearly. It offers a "concept" search function that, to me, seems oblique and incomprehensible, so stick to the keyword search choice.

INFOSEEK

http://www.infoseek.com
InfoSeek is absolutely the best searching tool for business information. An enhanced version searches not only the Web but also daily business wires and several specialty business and financial publications. It's like having a library on your desktop.

LYCOS

http://www.lycos.com
One of the oldest and most visited engines, Lycos excels in its citation phrasing. Some search engines will give you only the title and a one-sentence summary of the sites they retrieve, but Lycos usually furnishes a paragraph. This way, you'll have a better idea of whether you want to jump to that site. One negative is that some citations still pull up even after their Web pages are taken off.

OPEN TEXT

http://www.opentext.com
The most flexible of the search engines, Open Text allows you to search on both a "simple search" and a "power search" level. Power searching lets you specify several phrases while excluding certain keywords. If, for example, you key in the search terms "bond" and "interest rates" but don't want to retrieve any documents where the phrase "municipal bonds" are mentioned, you have the option to do that here.

WEBCRAWLER

http://www.webcrawler.com
WebCrawler is fast, friendly, and visually attractive, but not especially comprehensive. A good engine to practice on, though.

YAHOO

http://www.yahoo.com

Yahoo (see Figure 3-1) is not really a search engine but is more like a table of contents that specifies Web sites through category and subcategory listings organized like a tree—stem, branches, twigs, and leaves.

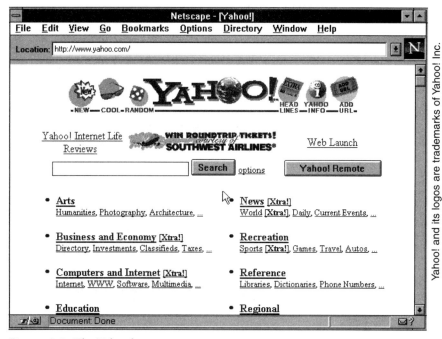

Figure 3-1: *The Yahoo home page.*

The information assembled on the Web is best perceived as a series of domains. That's what the inventors of Yahoo had in mind when they went "live" on the Web in 1994. The subindexes change frequently but the main subject areas are far less likely to.

Think of the home page Yahoo index as a table of contents. Here are some key areas, with further descriptors for each:

- *Arts*   Humanities, Photography, Architecture
- *Business and Economy*   Business Directory, Markets and Investments, Classifieds

- *Education* Universities, K-12, Courses
- *Health* Medicine, Pharmacology/Drugs, Fitness
- *Recreation* Sports, Games, Travel, Autos
- *Science* Computer Science, Biology, Astronomy, Engineering

The Web isn't as complex as it seems. In fact, it's user-friendly.

PICKING A SEARCH ENGINE

Now that you know what's available, you need to decide which search tool would work best for you. Dozens of search utilities are available to scour the Web, but no two are the same. They differ in many ways:

- The number of sites they list.
- How deep into a site's text they scour to perform the search field.
- How often they update.
- Whether they charge a fee or are free.
- Whether non-Web or even non-Internet searching is available.
- How you perform a thorough search.
- What you get as the result of a search.

HOW MANY SITES ARE LISTED?

Some search engines, such as AltaVista and Open Text, aspire to list every word on every Web site. Lycos, another powerful search tool, doesn't list every word, but catalogs virtually every Web page. There's a wow factor, but this can lead to a lot of irrelevant "hits." If, for example, I'm looking for places from which I can download info about or even a copy of Java (a Web authoring tool), a search on a complete index might come up with references to coffee, or that Indonesian island paradise. This is mostly a good thing when you are not sure exactly what terms would give you the results you are looking for.

Size matters in some things, but not necessarily in search engines. What's more important is how flexible its search routine alternatives will be, how quickly it will find the information for you, and how clearly it will present them. Yahoo is probably the best place to find whether a site exists or not, but I prefer Open Text, InfoSeek, and Lycos for executing a search in which I'm using a key phrase, such as "Portland mortgage financing," to see whether any sites exist that mention that phrase.

How Deep Is the Search?

A given Web site can have hundreds of pages and more than 100,000 words. The deeper into a site you go, the more the information may be arcane or repetitive. That's why some search engines, such as Yahoo, excerpt from and are searchable only from home page text or the first 100 words of the entire document. Others, such as Excite's Magellan, Lycos's Point, and the independent iGuide, review Web sites via a one-star to four-star formula. These reviews are combined with a search engine that doesn't provide complete Web hunts but enables you to search for reviewed Web sites based on the type of site it is and the rating points it has earned.

If you are not seeking specific information that might be on only one site, you might try the review sites first to get a good idea of what some quality presentations are. Looking for a mutual fund site where you can learn the basics and apply online? All three review services allow you to keyword search. Because they don't force you to drill down through several subject trees until you reach the search function, Point and Magellan are a bit easier to use.

How Often Is the Information Updated?

At least in theory, most engines use automated robots or spiders, which are computer programs that scour the Web daily in search of new sites. Some engines update daily and also allow for people to add their own sites. Each should state its updated policy on its Frequently Asked Questions (FAQ) page. This feature is usually reached through the Help or Customer Support icon on the home page.

How Much Does the Search Engine Charge?

The earliest Web search engines were operated by university computer departments and thus were subsidized. Now most engines are commercial and have to pay their own way. Most do this by selling advertising on their main pages, but a few others charge by the hit as the non-Internet research utilities do.

Can You Search Non-Web Areas?

You might think that the information you want is on the Web, but there could be Gopher or Usenet sites that contain the data you desire. All the Web search utilities will find text-only Gopher sites. AltaVista and Excite let you tailor your search to Usenet or the Web, and Yahoo's search results integrate Web URLs with newsgroup headings.

How Do You Perform Complex Searches?

Search engines generally allow you to specify several search terms. Some are equipped for Boolean searching, an example of which would be terms interlinked by conjunctions, such as "Java AND applet, BUT NOT coffee." Others allow you only to string terms together without separation. Here, you'd go "Java applet." Again, Open Text is best here.

Here's how to search for "Java applet" on Open Text:

1. Choose the Power Search option.
2. You'll be given a delineator choice—"and," "or," "but," and so on. Choose "and."
3. In the first search field, type **Java**.
4. In the second field, or box, type **applet**.
5. To the right on the second line, type **Not** as your delineator.
6. Then, in the third field line, type **coffee**.
7. OpenText will then pull up a list of Web documents with the terms *Java* and *applet*, but not the word *coffee*, in the text.

WHAT YOU GET FROM THE SEARCH

Most search tools give you the top 10 or 25 hits, scored by proximity indicators. If, for example, search engine Lycos finds *Java* and *applet* listed right next to each other in four documents (see Figure 3-2), those documents would score the highest and be cited first. The next two documents might find those two terms separated by one word, and so on.

Figure 3-2: *Searching on Lycos for* Java *and* applet *yielded these results.*

PERFORMING A SEARCH

Search tools are easy to access:

1. Simply enter the URL of the search engine that you'd like to use.

2. A home page with a Search icon should appear.

3. Type the terms for which you want to search. Until you become practiced at this, be as general as possible. Make sure that your spelling is correct.

4. You'll see a list of citations. Each citation will be under-lined or linked. If you see one that looks interesting, click on the link. You'll be whisked to that site.

If you don't see what you want, your search terms may have been either too general or too specific. Say that you are thinking of starting a biotechnology company in Los Angeles and are looking to the Web for venture capital sources. Entering **venture capital** and **California** might have brought hundreds of citations. Typing **venture capital**, **southern California**, **funding**, and **new biotech-nology companies** should deliver far more specific results.

If you have a computer that can support graphics, a modem, an account with an Internet Service Provider, and browser software such as Netscape Navigator, you're just a log-on away.

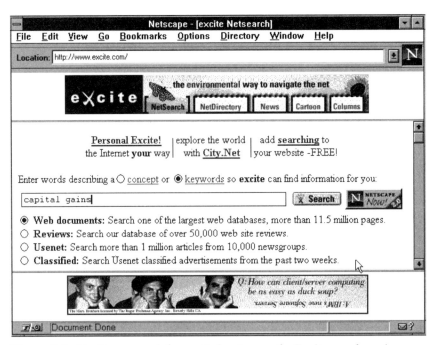

Figure 3-3: *Starting a search for* capital gains *on the Excite search engine.*

Use the Excite search engine on Navigator to find Web sites with the term *capital gains* in the text (see Figure 3-3). Then, click on the site with the highest, most relevant point score (see Figure 3-4) and see what information you can find (see Figure 3-5). Then, use the Netscape Navigator Find command on the toolbar to search the local file that you now have on your screen, and look for the term *tax shelter* (see Figure 3-6).

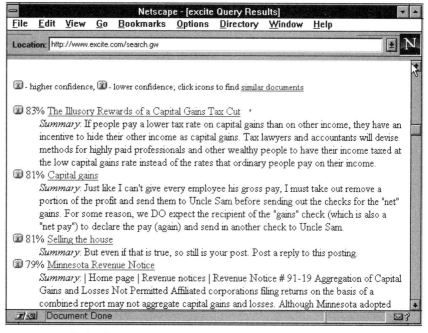

Figure 3-4: *"The Illusory Rewards of a Capital Gains Tax Cut" rated highest in an Excite search for the term* capital gains.

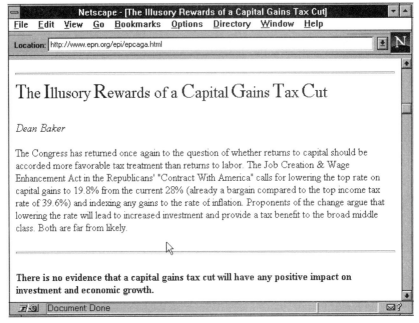

Figure 3-5: *By clicking the link in the search results table, I have now arrived at this page.*

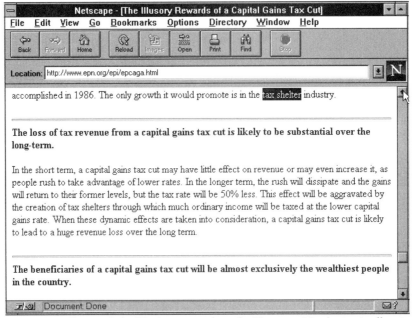

Figure 3-6: *I've used the Find command on the Netscape Navigator toolbar to locate the term* tax shelter *in the document shown.*

USING USENET NEWSGROUP SEARCH TOOLS

Although some of the search engines will clip Usenet citations, none specializes in this section of the Internet. Deja News, the preeminent newsgroup-only search tool, does. Are you looking for a specific discussion thread or topic but aren't sure what newsgroup to find it in? Deja News (http://www.dejanews.com) lets you search back several months across more than 15,000 newsgroups (see Figure 3-7). You can specify that the citations it finds be ranked in chronological order, grouped by writer (the engine lists the e-mail address of each postee), or by newsgroup itself.

Figure 3-7: *The Deja News search page.*

To do a Deja News search, enter the URL http://www.dejanews. com, and the Deja News home page will appear on your screen.

Most searching needs can be satisfied by using the standard search form. Type a search term such as **actuaries**, and a list of all newsgroup postings for the last two months that contain the term will be retrieved and displayed.

Power searching lets you configure the citations that you get in chronological order, by newsgroup, and by the Internet address of the person who posted the message. Use power searching if you want to limit the citations that you get to only one newsgroup, such as alt.misc.invest.

Use Deja News to search Usenet for the phrase *capital gains* in the text. How many citations did Deja News find?

SEARCHING GOPHERSPACE

Because text-only Gopher applications hit their zenith before the Web and its powerful search tools emerged, this section of the Internet did not spawn the all-seeing, all-knowing engines that the Web did. Gopher searches never expanded beyond title words of documents. This means that searches are only as effective as the individual operators and indexers of Gopher sites are.

Within these severe constraints, the best Gopher search tool is Veronica. To reach Veronica via Navigator, log on to a search utility such as Excite and type the term **Veronica** in the search field. A listing of servers throughout the world that house Veronica will be displayed. You get to them the same way you access Web sites, through click-and-point.

Access Veronica to find Gopher files with the phrase *capital gains* in the title. Go to the keyword search option. Then, click on the first file cited, or the one that looks the most relevant to you.

MOVING ON

Now you know how to search. But what are you looking for? In the next chapter, you'll look at the kind of personal finance information that you can find in your searches.

What Financial Information You Can Expect To Find

4

The Internet has several hundred personal finance–related World Wide Web sites with more than 50 Usenet newsgroups and 20 Gopher servers significantly dedicated to this topic. Because the Internet is a living, growing thing, sites are likely to be coming soon whose depth of functionality and utility can't even be envisioned now.

Unless you know exactly what site you are looking for or what search term you want to use to look for a specific topic, the best way to survey what's available is to get a comprehensive online overview of the personal finance resources, as covered here.

 ## WHAT YOU CAN FIND ON THE WEB

The Web offers the widest number of resources on personal finance. You can find information ranging from insurance to mortgages and from employment to taxes. Before you get into the specific information covered in Section II of this book, "Hot Sites on the Internet," read this chapter to get an overview of the type of information you can expect to find.

Note that this chapter uses Yahoo, a popular search tool to highlight some of the topics. Yahoo is more of an index to the Web than a full-blown search engine. If you want to take a look at these categories, start at http://www.yahoo.com. Then, select "Business and Economy"(see Figure 4-1). The list of Business and Economy sites is further broken down on a subdirectory page (see Figure 4-2). Keep in mind that Yahoo isn't the only way to access and find these services. Far more thorough searches are possible on engines such as Excite, Open Text, Inktomi, Lycos, InfoSeek, and AltaVista.

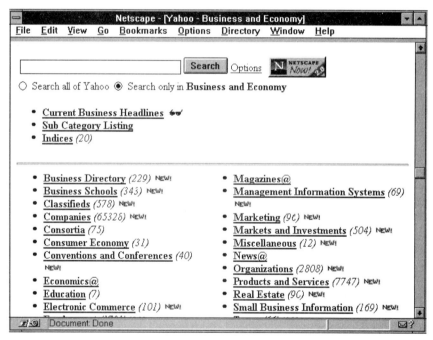

Figure 4-1: *Yahoo's Business and Economy page.*

Also, Yahoo doesn't always list every resource or categorize it in the way you might expect, but its simple structure provides the best teaching tool for illustrative purposes here.

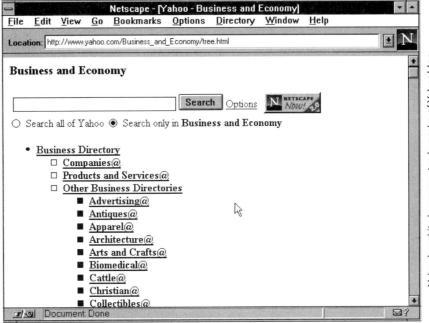

Figure 4-2: *Yahoo's Business and Economy subindexes.*

BUSINESS SCHOOLS

It's easy to find information on business schools. The list in the Yahoo index isn't a storehouse of personal finance information sites so much as it is a potential repository of sources. A number of colleges of business are listed, many of which offer either for-credit or noncredit courses in personal finance topics.

Many university professors supplement their income as business consultants. If you find a college listed in your area, you might want to give its business school a call and find out whether any of its professors do the type of consulting that would help your business—or know of someone reputable and authoritative in the community who does.

CLASSIFIEDS

If you want to trade merchandise or a service with someone else, try some of the various classified areas. Yahoo's Business and Economy/Classifieds subdirectory is further divided into more than 20 subject areas. Most aren't directly relevant to the topic, but the Barter and Business Opportunities areas stand out.

ACCOUNTING SERVICES

Another resource is the collection of various accounting services provided on the Web. To find this type of listing in Yahoo, look in Business and Economy/Companies/Financial Services/Accounting (see Figure 4-3). Here you can find several dozen subdirectories, including the largest collection of tax preparers with Web sites. You can also find listings for accounting organizations and accounting software packages.

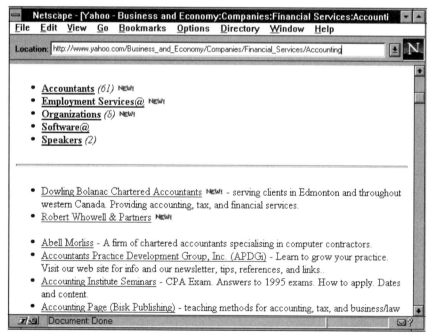

Figure 4-3: *Yahoo's Business and Economy/Companies/Financial Services/ Accounting subindex.*

BANKS

Only a small percentage of the U.S.-based banks with a Web presence actually permit anywhere near the full suite of functions that you can perform by walking into your standard, brick-and-mortar financial institutions. The percentage of banks with actual, online transactional capability will rise as the decade draws to a close, however.

In Business and Economy/Companies/Financial Services/Banks (see Figure 4-4), you can find links to the online pioneers as well as to the banks that choose to restrict their Web presence to the online brochure mode.

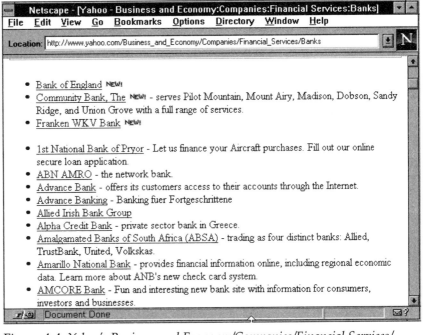

Figure 4-4: *Yahoo's Business and Economy/Companies/Financial Services/ Banks subindex.*

Insurance

Life, health, casualty auto, and specialty insurance companies as well as a large collection of independent agents—these are all on the Web, along with the inevitable cache of consumer advice sites, insurance tutorials, and prequalifiers.

To find this listing in Yahoo, use the category: Business and Economy/Companies/Financial Services/Insurance.

Economics

If you believe that the oft-volatile nature of our global economy can be felt clear down to Main Street, you might want to read some of the think-tank pontification on where the world's money supply is headed. A good starting place is Business and Economy/Economics in Yahoo.

Electronic Commerce

Interested in digital money? Electronic data interchange? You can find information relating to electronic commerce on the Web. If you are using Yahoo, try the category Business and Economy/ Electronic Commerce. If you are interested in setting up an online store via the Netscape Commerce Server, some excellent information is available on the future of digital money.

Employment

You can also find hundreds of career advice sites, job listings, resume services, and individual resumes of job seekers. Being employed is often the first requisite toward having a secure personal financial status, so this might be the first, best place for you to go. In Yahoo, start in the Business and Economy/Employment category.

MAGAZINES

In addition to the services offered, you can also find news and current information, such as through business magazines on the Web. In the category Business and Economy/Magazines, you can find links to publications with a Web presence. Several of these sites run personal finance articles, which are sometimes loaded onto their Web sites. Some of these include:

- *Barron's* magazine
- *Business Opportunities Handbook*
- *Financial Planning Online*
- *Income Opportunities*
- *Internet Investors Journal*
- *Money* magazine
- *Nest Egg*

MARKETS & INVESTMENTS

Looking for investment opportunities? You can use the Web to find information on bonds, brokerages, and mutual funds. Within Yahoo, look at the Business and Economy/Markets and Investments category. Here you'll find the following subcategories:

- *Bonds*   Several bonds sites are listed, including those that offer detailed research reports, analyses, and end-of-day price quotes for bonds from all over the world.

- *Brokerages*   Discount brokerages, full-service houses, capital managers, and commodities traders are listed here. This subject is discussed in detail in Chapter 10, "Investments."

- *Mutual Funds*   (See Figure 4-5.) Basically, three types of sites are linked here: general information services with basic- to intermediate-level information on mutual funds; mutual-fund rating surveys that provide comparative performance statistics for groups of funds; and, most important, the funds themselves. Many major mutual funds have links here that, when accessed, give you basic company information and provide an electronic mail interface where you can enter your contact information.

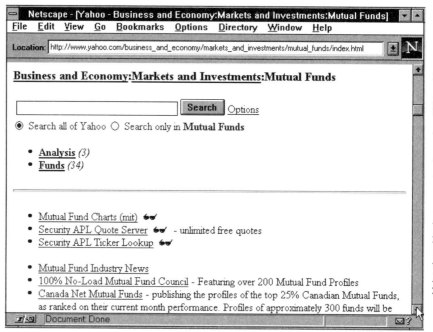

Figure 4-5: *Yahoo's Business and Economy/Markets and Investments/Mutual Funds subindex.*

■ *Newsletters*   Much of the well-considered, informative material that you'll need for investing comes from the newsletter community. Here's where you can read stock market and individual stock pricing projections and forecasts, real-time market analysis and commentary, and strategy tips ranging from cautious investment for retirement-planning to the highest-return speculative commitments. I discuss some of the best resources in Chapter 10, "Investments."

■   *Personal Finance*   (See Figure 4-6.) The portfolio-expand-
ers, the money-loaners, and the money advisors—both of
the human and the cyber variety—lurk here. There are
electronic debt calculators, investment primers, business
law and personal finance tutorials, automobile financing
companies, and providers of mortgage loans. A larger,
more conclusive listing of mortgage loan companies is
available under the Real Estate directory of Business and
Economy, which I'll get to very shortly.

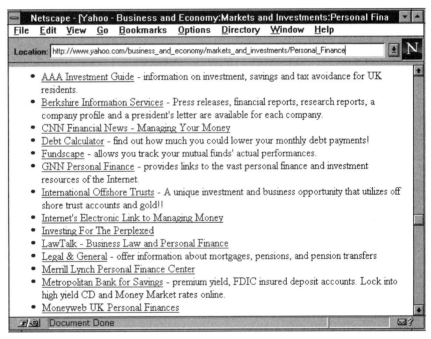

Figure 4-6: *Yahoo's Business and Economy/Markets and Investments/Personal
Finance subindex.*

BUSINESS NEWS

The Web has several respected sources of business news, including *Business Week*, the *Economist* magazine, and the *Financial Times* of London. *Corporate Financials Online*, a real-time business and company news source, is also on the Web. The *Wall Street Journal* also has a subscription service on the Web. You can find links to these magazines in Yahoo's Business and Economy/News/Business category.

PRODUCTS & SERVICES

Looking for a particular service? Check printing? Appraisal? You can find a wide variety of financial services on the Web. Use the links in the Yahoo Business and Economy/Products and Services/Financial Services subindex. Here you'll find listings for appraisal companies, banks, check-printing firms (where you can order personal or business checks cheaper than what your bank charges for them), issuers of secured credit cards, factoring firms (companies that write loans against your documented receivables), and offshore tax shelter specialists.

REAL ESTATE

You can find three basic types of sites that are useful if you are buying or selling real estate. Several sites survey lenders across the United States and post average rates by market on a daily or a weekly basis. Mortgage calculators take your projected interest rate, size of your mortgage, and length of terms and give you a base monthly figure on how much it will cost you. Chapter 5, "Appraisals & Mortgages," addresses this topic.

Then, most important, many hundreds of mortgage companies are on the Internet. Some will even prequalify you online, although most ask you to fill out a form that you e-mail to them through a Common Gateway Interface (CGI) featured on your Netscape Navigator browser.

To start, try Business and Economy/Real Estate/Mortgage Loans. The most complete list of Real Estate sites isn't here, however, but in Business and Economy/Companies/Financial Services/Financing: Real Estate.

SMALL BUSINESS INFORMATION

In addition to real estate information, you can find sites that provide practical advice and inspiration to entrepreneurs, people looking to buy franchises, and folks looking to run a business from their home. I detail dozens of these sites in Chapter 8, "Entrepreneurship & Consulting Services."

TAXES

On this subindex (see Figure 4-7) you'll find tax forms, tax calculation programs, and tax advice, as well as the Web sites for several organizations that would like nothing better than to drastically reform, or even do away with, the U.S. Tax Code. Chapter 14, "Taxes," should give you the close-up profiles you'll need before you click on.

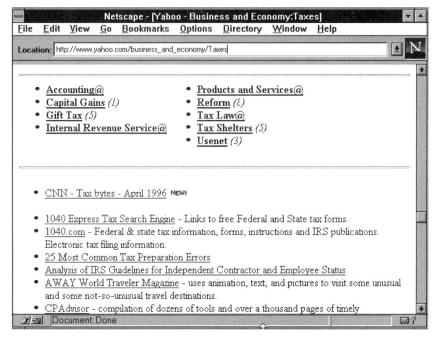

Figure 4-7: *Yahoo's Business and Economy/Taxes subindex.*

WHAT YOU CAN FIND ON THE ONLINE SERVICES

Chapter 19, "The Online Services," provides further details, but here, in capsule form in the following sections, are the personal finance information highlights of the four major proprietary commercial online services.

AMERICA ONLINE

The nation's fastest-growing online service throughout much of the 1990s, America Online has many informative topic areas, heavily weighted toward investment topics. These include a site run by the American Association of Individual Investors, the

Fidelity Online Investors Center, *Investor's Business Daily*, Merrill Lynch, Morningstar Stock and Fund Reports, UST Securities, Vanguard Online, and *Worth* Magazine Online. For more consumer-oriented financial repartee, Consumer Reports, the superb Motley Fool investment information area, and *Money* magazine's current content, chat areas, and searchable archives from older issues can be found here. Several personal finance chat rooms are available on AOL as well.

COMPUSERVE

The hub of CompuServe's money management content is in its Personal Finance Center. There are forums, or discussion groups, on investments, taxes, and the wise use of financial-management software.

There's also a rich haul of company information, such as the Hoover Company Research Database (also on AOL), the pricey yet thorough InvesText Brokerage Research database of stock analyst opinions, historical information about the stock prices and earnings records of individual, publicly traded companies, and several mutual fund and commodity newsletters.

MICROSOFT NETWORK

The Microsoft Network, a dial-up online service that may be converted to a subscription-based Web site in the near future, has several financial resources, including the MSN Investor, a stock-quotes service. You can also find information about companies in the Hoover's Business Index and tax information from the Internal Revenue Service.

PRODIGY

Prodigy doesn't have as extensive an informational archive as America Online or CompuServe, but its transactional gateways are the best. Bill Pay USA allows you to cut checks online and saves you that long wait at the post office. Online Trading provides a secured environment for 24-hour trading with a leading discount brokerage house. Strategic Investor has stock selections, analyst reports, price histories, and projections. You can do online banking with Wells Fargo Online. You can also find several personal finance chat rooms, as on the other services.

WHAT YOU CAN FIND IN USENET NEWS-GROUPS

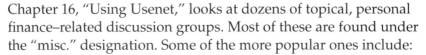

Chapter 16, "Using Usenet," looks at dozens of topical, personal finance–related discussion groups. Most of these are found under the "misc." designation. Some of the more popular ones include:

- *misc.entrepreneurs*   Discussion of operating a business (see Figure 4-8).
- *misc.invest*   About the investment and handling of money.
- *misc.invest.real-estate*   About property investments.
- *misc.jobs.resumes*   Resumes are posted online.

Another interesting newsgroup is *alt.invest.penny-stocks*, which, as you may have guessed, contains discussions about investing in low-cost stocks.

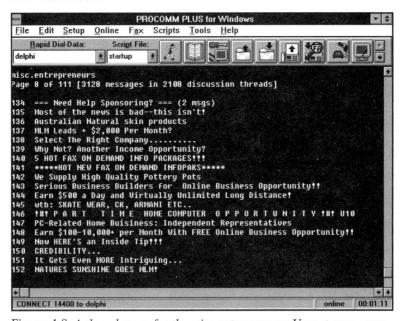

Figure 4-8: *A thread menu for the misc.entrepreneurs Usenet newsgroup.*

The more-limited "relcom." hierarchy in Usenet has several discussion areas appealing to those with an interest in personal finance. A few of these include:

- *relcom.commerce.estate*   About real estate.
- *relcom.commerce.money*   About currency values and trading issues.
- *relcom.commerce.stocks*   Covers a broad range of stocks and bonds topics.

The "clari.net" hierarchy in Usenet is a link to real-time newswires that frequently carry news impacting personal finance issues.

If your Internet access provider or online service allows a clari.net gateway access, you can find archived stories under this type of group, with interests such as the following:

- *clari.apbl.biz.briefs*   Hourly business newsbriefs from the Associated Press.
- *clari.apbl.biz.headlines*   Headlines of top business stories.
- *clari.apbl.reports.dollar_gold*   Daily gold and dollar prices.
- *clari.apbl.reports.economy*   General economic reports.
- *clari.apbl.reports.finance*   Reports on the money supply.
- *clari.apbl.review*   Daily review of the news.
- *clari.apbl.stocks.analysis*   Market analysis from the insiders.
- *clari.apbl.stocks.dow*   Dow Jones averages.
- *clari.biz.economy*   Economic news and indicators.
- *clari.biz.economy.world*   Economic stories regarding non-U.S. countries.
- *clari.biz.features*   Business feature stories.
- *clari.biz.urgent*   Breaking business news.
- *clari.living.consumer*   Consumer issues and products.
- *clari.news.usa.gov.financial*   U.S. fiscal and financial policy.

WHAT GOPHER RESOURCES YOU CAN FIND

Gopher, the text-only Internet interface that predates the World Wide Web, grew up as more of an academic research archive than a mass communications medium. For this reason, the culture of this dominion is still stilted toward library catalogs and archived papers on arcane topics. Yet, a few germane sites have popped up here, including those run by the Small Business Administration and TEXAS-ONE, which maintains a catalog of services for Texas small businesses.

MOVING ON

Now you know where to find all kinds of personal finance information such as stock reports, consumer credit applications, insurance quotes, and tax advice. Starting with the next chapter, "Appraisals & Mortgages," most of the rest of this book gives you a detailed close-up of the dozens of resources available in several key subject areas, both on the Internet and the online services, and offline in popular CD-ROM and software packages.

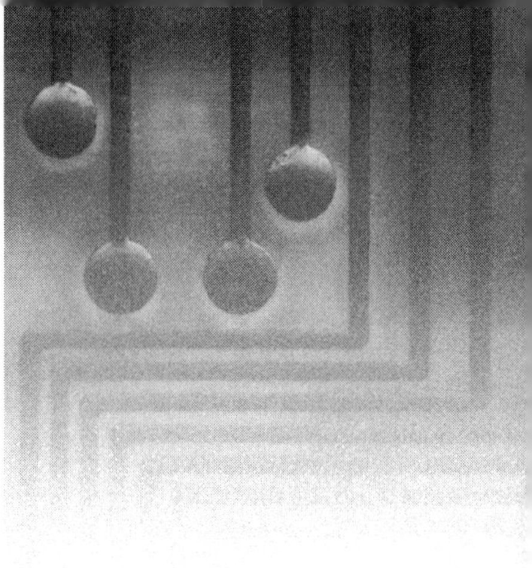

SECTION II:

Hot Sites on the Internet

Appraisals & Mortgages

The real estate profession is no stranger to computing. In fact, real estate agents, mortgage brokers, and loan officers have been using online databases and communications tools for at least a decade.

Back when the Internet was the exclusive province of high-level academic researchers, Realtors all over North America were tapping into lists of available homes for sale. Theirs was one of the first nontechnical professions to employ online computing technology on a widespread basis. If, back in 1986, you were house hunting for a three-bedroom home with a swimming pool in suburban Chicago, a Realtor would take some basic information from you and then launch a query to see whether any homes on the market matched your request.

In the mortgage lending industry, the flow of information was similarly one-sided. If you were looking at getting a mortgage financed, you would call a loan officer at your local bank or mortgage broker, who would then drop a brochure in the mail. If you were selling your home, you'd call a recommended appraiser. Applicants did not have the tools available to process that information on their own, to peruse homes for sale, to compare and evaluate the experiences and pricing structure of relevant service providers.

Slowly, the Web is changing the way the public receives information about home appraisals and mortgages. You still can't tap into a national database and see photos of every home for sale or rent, but that will come soon. Until that day, the Web's best utility will be as a digital window shopper. It sounds limited, but as anyone who has ever been in the housing market knows, the process temporarily takes over your life. Anything that saves you even a few hours of time is a blessing.

WHAT MAKES A GOOD APPRAISAL & MORTGAGE SITE

Information is the plasma that flows through the blood of the real estate industry. I am talking about up-to-the-moment statistics about loan rates and terms, which can change daily. It's no mystery why Realtors were among the first professionals to buy cellular phones. They were using computers to exchange data while most of us were still working with electronic typewriters and the U.S. mail.

A good real estate site should take the instantaneous information paradigm and bring it to its URL. Here are some features that these sites should have:

- Content, which may include average mortgage rates in a city, state, or even the nation, must be updated frequently.

- If it's a site run by an association or federation of professionals such as appraisers or Realtors, it should have a search function to look for practitioners.

- Should you want to contact a member broker or appraiser directly, a mail-to for each online professional is a must.

- Jargon is sometimes unavoidable, so a glossary is a big help.

- Links to other sources, such as Chamber of Commerce or economic development Web sites, are also helpful on sites where people contemplating relocation may look.

APPRAISAL & MORTGAGE SITES

In this section, you'll visit some housing-related sites that may help you find an appraiser, calculate your mortgage, or even apply for one.

NATIONAL DIRECTORY OF MORTGAGE BROKERS

http://206.86.104.2:80/loans
Before you go to any mortgage Web sites, I recommend that you try this site. This site is worth frequent and extended visits, not just for its national mortgage loan search capabilities, but for an extended primer that will walk you through the thicket of jargon having to do with the world of housing loans.

Your first stop in National Directory should be "Common Mortgage Terms & Common Mortgage Questions." Some 37 terms are explained. Bless their collective cyberhearts, because in no case did National Directory's jargon interpreters need more than a paragraph to explain buzzwords that are each worth a full chapter in real estate financing texts. Thankfully, they also avoided the *Webster's Dictionary* trap of using another variant of the same word to define the original.

For example, take a look at how National Directory explains complex terms such as Adjustable Rate Mortgages (ARMs), Balloon Loans, and Graduated Payment Mortgages. Before you apply for a home loan, you'll find that it's in your best interest to understand each. All the definitions on this page not only tell you what the expression means but also how it affects or benefits you.

Adjustable Rate Mortgages: "A type of mortgage loan that usually has a term of 30 years where the interest rate fluctuates and depends on a particular interest rate index. The advantage of this type of loan is that lenders typically offer initial discounts (called teaser rates) on the interest rate index making the loans less expensive than a traditional fixed rate mortgage. In addition, the loan payment goes up and down depending on the actual financial conditions of the economy which can be an advantage if interest rates remain constant or decline during the life of the loan.

The disadvantage of this type of loan is that your exact payment over time is unpredictable and can increase."

The advice here is right on the money. Your financial advisor may tell you that ARMs are not good strategies for the risk-averse.

Balloon Loans: "A type of mortgage loan that is exactly like a traditional fixed rate mortgage except that it becomes 100% due after a specified amount of time has elapsed. When the loan matures, you must pay the loan off in cash (Balloon Payment) or refinance. The advantage of this type of loan is that the initial rate is usually lower than a normal fixed rate loan. The disadvantage of this type of loan is that you may have to refinance or pay off the loan if you do not sell the home by the time the loan matures."

Here is another example of this site's superb ability to objectively discuss complex issues. Balloon Loans are highly controversial. Some people affirm that a Balloon Loan helped them make the leap from a small starter home near a college to a three-bedroom suburban cul-de-sac. There are those folks, however, who dread an impending payment on a Balloon Loan.

Graduated Payment Mortgages: "A type of mortgage where the monthly payments start low but increase by a fixed amount each year for the first five years. The payment shortfall or negative amortization is added to the principal balance due on the loan. The advantage of this type of loan is a lower monthly payment at the beginning of the loan term. The disadvantages are typically a slightly higher rate than traditional fixed-rate mortgage loans and lenders usually require a larger down payment. In addition, the negative amortized amount increases the balance due on the total loan which can be a problem if the value of the home declines."

Two other value-added pages on the National Directory site are a checklist of documentation that you should bring to your loan application appointment and a table of qualifying ratio standards insisted upon by the Federal National Mortgage Association ("Fannie Mae") and the Federal Home Loan Mortgage Corporation ("Freddie Mac"). These two entities sound like characters from a country music song, but far from it. These entities purchase loans from the original lending institution. Even if a local savings and loan approves your mortgage application, it may eventually be sold to Fannie or Fred Loans. For Fred loans, the PITI (Principal, Interest, Taxes, and Insurance) plus long-term installment debt can't exceed 36 percent of your household's gross monthly income. Fannie loans are a bit stricter, with general loan guidelines at about 33 percent.

Figure 5-1: *The National Directory of Mortgage Brokers has a searchable list of national members.*

If you think you qualify, it's time to use the site's search function to find a broker in your region (see Figure 5-1). Then, after you've made contact and scheduled an appointment, run the Print command from the spreadsheet and bring several records with you when you see your mortgage banker. National Directory suggests complete banking information, credit card numbers, all the information on current outstanding debt that you can possibly gather, as well as a list of assets, such as cash, furniture, cars, and insurance policies in force.

AccuComm

http://www.he.net/~accucomm/

Some of the information included at this site is frankly a bit scary. Much of the text is devoted to a discussion of what errors may pop up in ARM-based loan calculations.

"The federal government agrees that ARM miscalculations pose a serious problem in the mortgage industry," AccuComm writes. "The government commissioned three studies in 1991, by the Federal Deposit Insurance Corporation (FDIC), the Office of Thrift Supervision, and the National Credit Union Administration (NCUA), which produced some surprising conclusions. According to these results, 38% to 46% of mortgage lenders have been making errors in their management of ARM loans. The FDIC found that 29% of the ARMs that have come under the control of the Resolution Trust Corporation (RTC) have errors in them. The Office of Thrift Supervision, which oversees federal savings and loans and savings banks, found errors in loans made by 34% of the 95 savings associations that it studied."

Estimates are quoted noting that back in 1993, $23 billion of the $603.5 billion then outstanding in ARM loans was owed to homeowners in the form of overcharge refunds. About half the 22 million ARM loans in the United States reportedly have some element of miscalculation.

It would have been easy for this site to start pointing fingers and accusing the mortgage financing industry of malfeasance. Yet, as you learn from reading further, the main culprit seems to be the mushrooming popularity of ARMs and the numbing complexity of financing choices. Too often, this results in loan officers overwhelmed not only by an increased workload but also by the challenges of keeping abreast of a constant stream of new interest rate indexes and plans. To be in sync with new products such as, for instance, seven-year fixed-rate periods within an ARM, standard calculation practices may have to be revised. But, in a Catch-22 situation, the workload generated by intense consumer interest in these new attractive alternatives eliminates the discretionary time that a loan department might need to crunch the numbers necessary to revise its loan numbers accordingly.

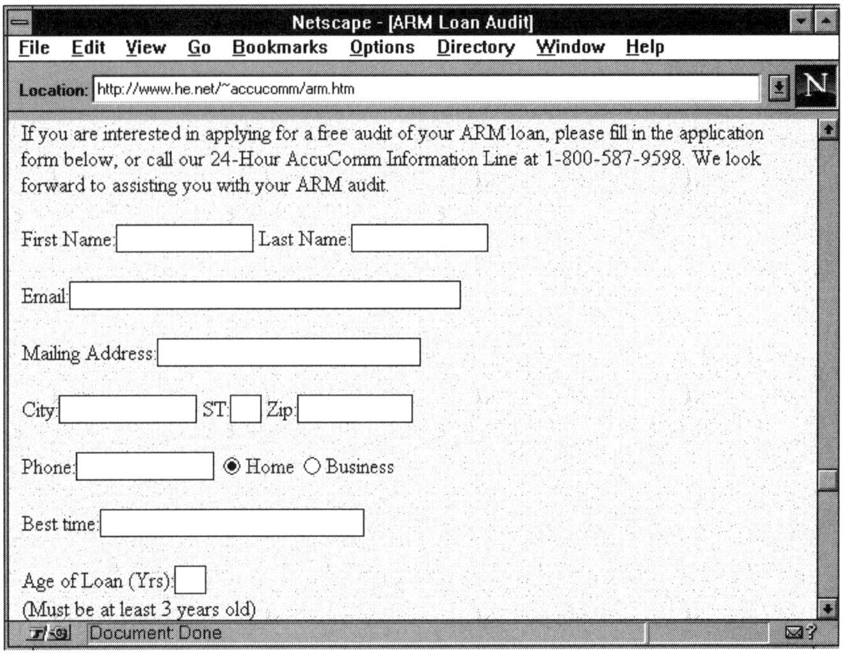

Figure 5-2: *This site tells you whether you're being charged too much for your Adjustable Rate Mortgage.*

Faced with this possibility, consumers may wonder, "Has It Happened To Me?" That's actually the title of the like-named AccuComm site article's most useful and important section (see Figure 5-2). Five red flags are mentioned, including a scenario in which "the loan has been sold one or more times. Incompatibility in mortgage servicers' software systems can introduce errors during the changeover."

The best problem-solving strategy for Web sites is for them to offer their own diagnostic services as a remedy for a problem. The e-mail link here is more than just a thrown-on mail-to without any embellishment. "I've got questions. Please call me," the mail-to says. The mail-to should trigger a reply to your questions. If the site has its customer service act together, it should send an automatic response back to your electronic mailbox acknowledging that your query has been received. Then, no more than a week or two later, the actual explanation should await you.

"I've got questions. Please call me." This book isn't the proper forum for road tales, but yes, I as well as you have heard those words before. And not necessarily in cyberspace.

Appraisal Institute

http://www.realworks.com/
This is the Chicago-based professional guild for real estate appraisers, the professionals who take detailed measures of a house's worth before a sale can be made or a loan is approved. You, your Realtor, or your mortgage loan officer may be about to hire one. Just what are you getting for your money?

A somewhat self-promotional but tightly written explanation of the process appears on the Institute's main page:

"Because much private, corporate, and public wealth lies in real estate, the determination of its value is essential to the economic well-being of society," the Institute writes. "It is the job of the professional appraiser to determine these values by gathering, analyzing, and applying information pertinent to a property.

"Unquestionably, the professional opinion of the appraiser, backed by extensive training and knowledge, influences the decisions of people who own, manage, sell, purchase, invest in, and lend money on the security of real estate," the document continues. "And because the appraiser is trained to be an impartial third party in the lending process, this professional serves as a vital 'check in the system,' protecting real estate buyers from overpaying for property as well as lenders from over lending to buyers."

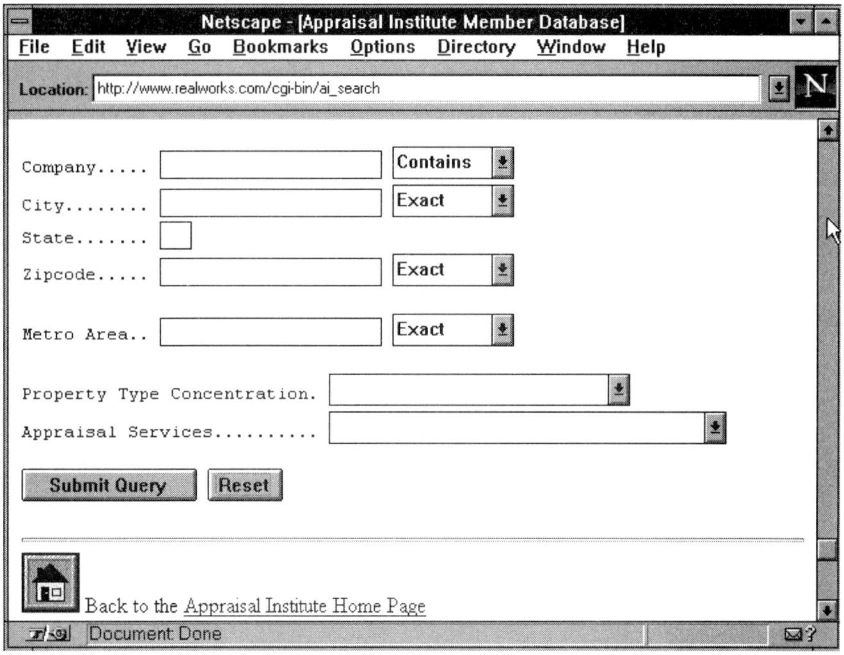

Figure 5-3: *Use the Appraisal Institute search form to find a real estate appraiser in your area.*

Appraisers judge homes, right? Of course, but as you learn on the site's checklisted Services Provided section, they do a lot more than just collect fees of $175 and up for their most common purpose. Appraisers also work on Business Valuation studies and provide both Zoning and Expert Witness testimony. The Appraisal Institute is also involved in public outreach, providing a search form (see Figure 5-3) so that you can look for an appraiser in your state or city.

The Institute's site also furnishes a free Adjustable Rate Mortgage Loan Audit, which is described on the page of the same name. It also has a link to AccuComm, whose suite of services is described earlier in this chapter.

If you require even more info, the Appraisal Institute has more than 60 books and 5 regularly published magazines available for a fee.

ERC

http://www.erc.org
The Census Bureau estimates that the average American changes addresses 11 times in his or her lifetime, so relocation isn't limited to high-rung corporate transfers. Relocations can be trying times. The process will also have a major impact on your finances.

The Employee Relocation Council (ERC) is a research organization and think tank devoted to the topic. The site has several useful areas, all reachable from the home page.

If you are about to undergo the relocation experience or feel the possibility developing, the ERC's On-line Research Center site has several areas that will be worth your time, including:

- "ERCs Crystal Ball: Current and Future Trends," an examination of business and socioeconomic events affecting the relocation industry.

- "Law and Government Relations," a regularly updated posting on new or revised Internal Revenue Service rulings affecting relocation.

- "Relocation Tax and Legal Information," a chart listing how relocation to and from each of the 50 states may affect your state income tax liability there.

- "U.S. Domestic Relocation Information," which gives relocation industry policies and statistical studies.

"Domestic Relocation" notes that, in 1995, it cost an average of $44,920 to relocate a current, homeowning employee and $35,902 to bring in a new hire owning a home in a different city. For those same companies, the average cost to move renters was $12,366 for current employees and $8,948 for new workers.

When you find yourself in a negotiating mode with a company about something as sensitive as picking up some of your moving costs, having a good idea of what you and the company are dealing with would be helpful. More information may help your position. Also, coming across as a person who does fastidious research will only help your standing as a valuable member of the team.

If you want to delve even deeper into the subject, ERC's Domestic Relocation Publications page lists several association publications for sale. Two are absolutely essential for anyone about to be relocated or thinking about initiating the relocation process. "Relocation Assistance: Transferred Employees" touches on topics such as "Shipping Household Goods," "Temporary Living," "Househunting Trips," and issues involved with subsidies paid for "Purchase Closing Costs."

For the entrepreneur or executive considering whether to relocate an associate to headquarters or out to a branch office somewhere, the site also offers what it calls "The Primer: a Guide to Employee Relocation and Relocation Policy Development." This volume touches on recommended policies about assistance offered for moving services, home inspections, and "Househunting, travel, temporary living and return visitation trips."

These and several other ERC tomes can be ordered either by phone or via an electronic mail link from the site.

ERC charges for most of its information but does make very basic information about state tax deferrals for relocation available on a chart. More substantive data about housing-related moving-expense deductions is available in "Relocation Law," an ERC document that can also be ordered from a mail-to. Tax information is available for free on its site.

FINANCENTER, INC.

http://www.financenter.com

If you are buying a new home, you may be debating whether to choose a 15-year or a 30-year mortgage loan. A shorter-term mortgage will, of course, pay off your home loan more quickly but will demand more from you each month. The lengthier payment terms will produce additional tax savings.

The Financenter site automates this wrenching decision process for you, describing typical 15- and 30-year mortgage payment models. A browser such as Netscape Navigator 1.1 or above has the capability to read tables on which much of this information is supplied.

On the site's "Comparison: 15 Year and 30 Year Loans" section, a "Schedule of Payments, Interest and Tax Savings" page describes scenarios for different years in each loan life. The basic model used for each chart is a $100,000 mortgage. After the third year of a $100,000 15-year note for which the monthly payments are $857, the remaining amount owed will be $86,710. This compares to $96,417 outstanding on a 30-year note. Other comparative data for 15-year and 30-year mortgages, respectively, are the following: Yearly Principal Paid, $4,709 and $1,272; Yearly Interest Paid, $5,580 and $6,312; Cumulative Interest Paid, $17,577 and $19,172; and Yearly Tax Savings, $2,881 versus $3,159.

In terms of the principal, your loan may differ. For more specifics, you may want to try one of Financenter's several online mortgage calculators. The following paragraphs take a look at four of them.

The "15 or 30" calculator asks you for inputs such as percent Interest Rate, dollar of the loan amount, years to repay the loan, Discount Points, Origination Fee, and miscellaneous costs (see Figure 5-4). In this field, you type your combined state and federal income tax rate, the appraised value or purchase price of your home, your yearly property taxes, the amount of your annual homeowners insurance, and the number of years it should take before you either sell the property or retire the loan.

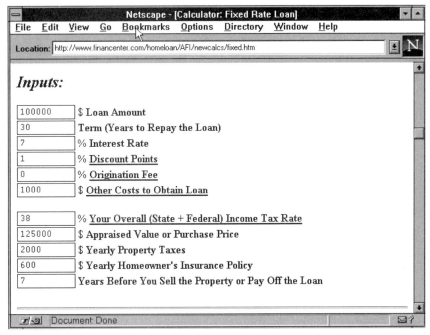

Figure 5-4: *Financenter's calculator shows the "real" costs of a typical mortgage loan.*

The resulting display furnishes estimated monthly principal and interest, taxes, and mortgage insurance. These are combined to give you a total monthly payment as well as your total cost if you paid off the entire mortgage immediately (well, there's always the lottery).

These scenarios will be operational only if you can get the mortgage in the first place. The Financenter page, "Estimating the Amount for Which You Qualify," will help you there. Income inputs requested by this online calculator include your monthly salary or wages before taxes, average monthly overtime or commissions, and average monthly dividends or interest, as well as alimony, child support, pension, social security, or other income, if relevant.

Next, the calculator requests information on your monthly obligations, such as credit card payments, auto, student, or (existing) real estate loans. Finally, it queries you on a hypothetical interest rate and term (years to repay the loan).

You know that two different people will not necessarily respond the same way using the same set of facts. That's why Financenter provides "conservative" and "aggressive" borrowing amount estimates for down payment amounts, loan amounts, and monthly payments with taxes and insurance.

If it appears that you'll be able to borrow enough to finance a mortgage on that dream home, you'll have to manage the payments for several years—at least. The "How much will my payments be?" page has a payment calculator virtually identical to the one in the "15-30" section. It, too, gives you projected monthly principal and interest, taxes, and insurance.

As anyone who has bought a home knows, closing costs are one of the necessary evils. The site can also help with a "Closing Costs When Purchasing" online calculator. This is a sophisticated offering, asking for inputs such as discount points, origination, escrow, survey and recording fee costs, and any transfer or other special taxes that may apply. Don't forget to type an amount for a Termite Infestation Report. The site notes, by the way, that such reports are "Not required at higher elevations." Results supplied include fees, property taxes, prepaid interest, monthly principal and interest, taxes, and insurance.

Financenter is not a mortgage company, but its site does provide such a link. If you are still interested after reading this information, you can apply online for a mortgage through American Finance and Investment, Inc., Fairfax, Virginia.

GOLDEN APPRAISAL SERVICES

http://www.GoldenGroup.com

Dozens of locally based appraisal companies have Web sites. Some are just advertisements for their services. The basic content model here is a brief description of what they offer, a bit about their previous experience, and then, of course, how much they want to help you. If you're lucky, the site has an e-mail link at the end of the text.

Such pages are mere presences that do not maximize the potential of the Web as a communications and transactional medium. After searching for a metro-based site that pushes the envelope at least a little bit, I was pleased to find Burbank, California–based Golden Appraisal Services (see Figure 5-5).

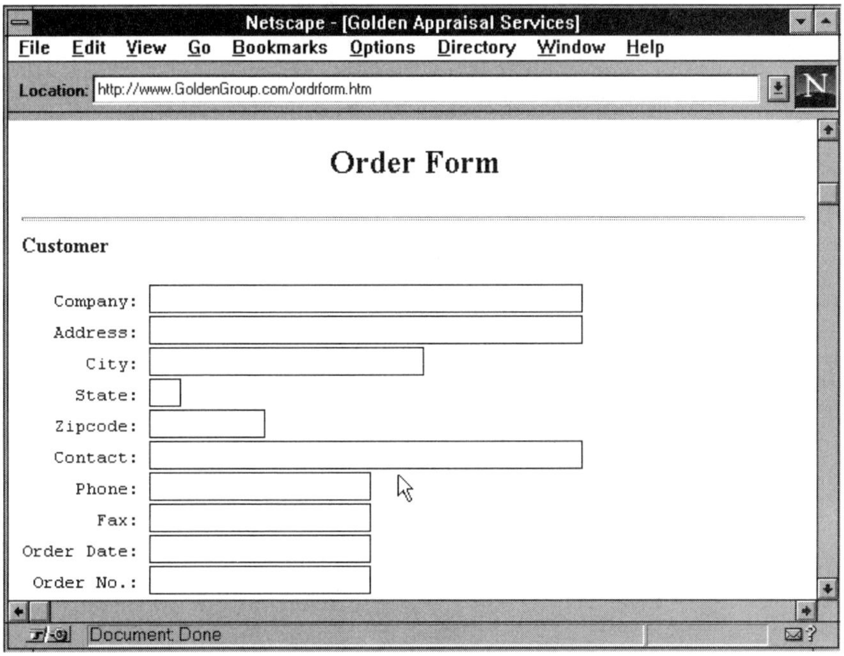

Figure 5-5: *This site lets you preorder an appraisal online.*

The best way that an appraisal company can take advantage of its URL is by introducing a time-saving element into the preappraisal, preparation stage. In this vein, Golden's site offers an especially thorough online Order Form (shown in Figure 5-5) where you type key information and e-mail it to the company.

After the perfunctory name and address, the information fields cover topics such as room count, the year the house was built, lot size, and garage spaces. The appraisers at Golden also want to know whether you have an attached garage and whether a pool, spa, or both grace your lair.

Too many Web sites fear that price quotes will scare away visitors. At best, I find this specious reasoning. At worst, it's a deceptive practice. Kudos to Golden for putting up one of the most complete services price lists I've seen on any kind of Web site. Prices are quoted for drive-by appraisals—there really are such things—expanded drive-bys, and extra amenities such as flood certification. Just in case you're wondering, Golden's base rate for an appraisal of a home in the $450,000 range runs about $375.

HOMEBUYER'S FAIR

http://www.homefair.com
This site offers several useful places to go, including Fair Mortgage Qualification Calculator, Intelligent Mortgage Agent, and Mortgage Finance Resources.

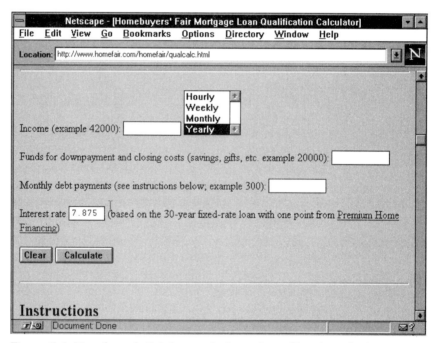

Figure 5-6: *Homebuyer's Fair has a calculator that will project whether you qualify for a mortgage.*

Homebuyer's Fair Mortgage Qualification Calculator (see Figure 5-6) is one of the easiest to use. Mortgage calculators are, in essence, online spreadsheet programs that will compute monthly mortgage payments based on equity, length of mortgage, down payment, interest, and points. The calculator asks you to input your income, the amount of funds you have available for down payment and closing costs, your total monthly debt payments, and a projected interest rate. You simply e-mail this data to Homebuyer's server.

Based on the data that you submit, Fair Loan gives you your projected maximum qualification amount. What really makes this site worth a call is the primer about how mortgage applications are processed. It is strictly elementary stuff, but highly practical.

The most practical advice: "The ratio of your monthly mortgage payment plus nonhousing debt to your monthly income must be no higher than 36 percent. Again, you will find lenders who will stretch this ratio. If your monthly debt is greater than 8 percent of your monthly income, then by reducing your debt you could afford more house."

The tutorial also recommends that your down payment be at least 5 percent of the mortgage, and cautions that you need to have enough money to cover closing costs as well as the down payment.

Running only on JavaScript-enabled browsers such as Netscape Navigator, the Intelligent Mortgage Agent is another online program for which you submit data and get a recommendation back. The first two questions help the online calculator define some basic parameters. It asks whether the loan amount you need is over $207,000, and it also wants to know what percent down payment you intend to make. The brains behind this silicon loan officer work for Premium Home Financing, a national mortgage broker firm.

The Agent assumes that you will stay in your new home for enough years to cover the accrued closing costs. Just as in the "real world," it also lowers closing costs for more expensive loans. After answering several more questions, the Agent computes a table that lists the recommended (mortgage loan program) name, points, and rates.

Homebuyer's Mortgage Finance Resources page offers a handy

table with descriptions of these and other calculation tools, including Refinance and Rent-Buy Calculators. It also provides links to several articles on mortgage topics, including an informative discussion on the pros and cons of 15-year versus 30-year notes.

MORTGAGE MARKET

http://www.interest.com/
A service bureau specializing in mortgage-related information, Villa Park, Illinois–based Mortgage Market Information Services, Inc., has a fully keyword-searchable site with a rich library of breaking mortgage news, frequent updates on average rates for all 50 states (see Figure 5-7), and links to mortgage lenders who have their own Web sites.

Figure 5-7: *Search average mortgage rates in your state with this tool.*

From the home page, you can go to any of four sections. These are Banking, Consumer, News, and Newspapers. The last section provides links to Web sites of several newspapers, where you can read the real estate classifieds or general business news. If you are thinking of moving to another area of the country, these links are especially helpful.

A rich library of individual mortgage loan companies awaits you on several of the state menus. These listings offer brief descriptions of each linked company, including basic contact information, the types of loans they offer, and loan rate ranges.

MORTGAGE RESOURCE CENTER

http://www.mortgageselect.com
Staying current on the latest home lending regulations is a must for all borrowers. Mortgage Resource Center, Inc., in Eagan, Minnesota, offers several free and fee-based regulation information services (see Figure 5-8).

Figure 5-8: *Learn about mortgages and shop for one from the Mortgage Resource Center site.*

Every business day on the AllRegs section of its Web site, MRC posts new regulation announcements made by the Federal National Mortgage Association ("Fannie Mae"), the Federal Home Loan Mortgage Corporation ("Freddie Mac"), the Government National Mortgage Association ("Ginnie Mae"), the Federal Housing Administration, and the Veterans Administration.

Many of these announcements are arcane bureaucratspeak but several may affect you. These topics can range from new information that lenders can provide, to borrowers inquiring about the ownership of their mortgages, to policy revisions pertaining to lender selection of property inspectors. These text-searchable abstracts stay posted for 90 days.

These postings are archived as summaries and are furnished for free. You can also access MRC via an onsite mail-to to sign up for an e-mail news service that automatically routes summary updates to your electronic mailbox as they are received by MRC.

For complete texts, a subscription to Mortgage Resource Center is required. After your membership is processed, you can log on to get the enhanced information you need.

MOVING ON

For most people, a home is the biggest investment they'll ever make. Starting and capitalizing a business can cost more than even a pricey mortgage, though. As you'll see in the next chapter, entrepreneurs who are looking for funding and advice on starting or expanding a business will also have to play the loan game. The next chapter highlights Web sites that can help you do just that.

Capital

Ever since childhood, when perhaps you ran a lemonade stand and delivered newspapers, you've wanted to run a business of your own. For whatever reason, you didn't follow that path, but now, recent developments have awakened the urge. You've picked up a great deal of business sense in your successful career, but all you need is money and the motivation to disregard the torpedoes and strike out on your own. The United States has 12 million small- to medium-sized businesses, with about 17 million total businesses. Who's to say they know any more than you do?

Some of us will make changes in our lives only when we read the writing on the wall. If that's the case, resources that you can find on the Web might be able to help you turn angst into action.

It's Saturday morning in any one of several thousand basement workshops in North America. You're feeling a little guilty about missing your 11-year-old son's soccer practice, but this is about the only time that you have to perfect what you hope is the brilliant invention you've been working on. The stakes, it must be said, might be higher than simple ego fulfillment. The company where you work as a systems engineer just reported a flat sales quarter last week. You've heard rumblings that there may be some consolidations of sales offices as well as research and development. You never thought you'd be downsized out of the position you've done so well in for the past six years, but, realistically, you have to consider the possibility.

Two other people with whom you work have the same fears. One is an engineer like yourself; the other is a sales and marketing genius who could sell space heaters to Virgin Islanders. Yet, between the three of you, precious little discretionary working capital exists and you don't have many connections with corporate decision makers who might be willing to fund a start-up or buy you up outright.

Well, money is available, and it's in the venture capital community. Some $7.5 billion in venture capital funds were committed in 1995, according to the Price Waterhouse LLP Venture Capital Survey (see Figure 6-1), which, along with more than 55 companies looking for projects to fund, has a Web site.

Figure 6-1: *The Price Waterhouse Venture Capital Survey.*

Some trends evident in the last few years should dispel some stereotypes. You may think that the balance of this money goes to well-pedigreed, high-tech concerns in Silicon Valley. But of 1995's outlay, only 17.1 percent was for software corporations, and 22.5 percent of the total was expended in Silicon Valley. Other strong segments were general technology (such as electronics and bio-technology), health care, and consumer goods, whereas the South-east, New York, and New England's combined outlay exceeded Silicon Valley's by more than $700 million.

Even more important for you, about 40 percent of all companies receiving funding and 31 percent of all funds allotted were primarily to small, start-up, or early-stage companies. This is indicative of an upward trend that's been going on for the past several years, says Price Waterhouse, whose survey is endorsed by two entrepreneur-friendly associations you ought to know—the National Venture Capital Association and the National Association of Small Business Investment Corporations.

WHAT MAKES A GOOD CAPITAL SITE

"Promises, Promises" may have worked as the title of a Broadway show tune but it's not a feature of a good capital site. These companies can take your business to the next level, but an element of trust is necessary at the outset.

Here are common attributes you should look for in these sites:

- *Credibility*   The company should not make any exaggerated claims that one touch from them will make you rich.

- *Biographical Information*   Each principal's experience should be listed in a conclusive biography. This will give you clues about a company's strengths and weaknesses.

- *References*   Are the company's recent or existing clients willing to be contacted for a reference? If so, names and phone numbers should be listed.

- *Methodology*   The company should provide a clear explanation of how the evaluation process works and how much the partners will want to be involved in your company's day-to-day operations if they invest.

- *Specialty* What type of companies are the investors interested in? Start-ups? Growth? Both? What industries are they looking at? High-tech? Biotechnology? Umbrella factories?

- *Project lists* Wherever possible, these sites should contain a table of projects funded, the amount provided, and the use that the investment was put to (plant expansion, research and development, etc.). Tables allow for quick but thorough review and should be readable through a compatible browser such as Netscape Navigator.

BEFORE YOU BEGIN: DO YOUR RESEARCH

Before you let your eagerness get hold of you, however, a little preparatory research will serve you well. You owe yourself the task of researching the answers to three basic questions:

- *What are venture capitalists looking for?* Many specialize in only a few areas, such as biotechnology or computer software. If your idea is a bit different, you might be better off affiliating with a generalist.

- *Who is funding what?* This is one field in which you'll do better to follow the road *more* traveled. Companies who have already funded projects in the field that you are contemplating might be more predisposed to talk to you, and later, with you.

- *Are you ready?* Are you a risk taker? Can you handle not getting a paycheck every other Friday? Are you equal to obfuscation, unreturned phone calls, a significant amount of patronization? Please realize that, in venture capital as in other business dealings when someone has a resource you wish to utilize, courtesy is not the same thing as commitment. If you can't tell the difference, you're a kind but overly trusting soul who could use a major reality check.

FINDING A VENTURE CAPITALIST

If you're toying with the notion of starting or growing a business, venture capital may be the answer. To would-be and existing entrepreneurs, a sympathetic venture capitalist must seem like an angel. An angel who swoops down from some blessed place, writes a check in the six or seven figures, and frees the aspiring tycoon from the vagaries of subservient corporate life to one where he can ride his or her better idea to fame and riches.

So much for movie fantasy. Yet, if the chasm between daydream and fulfillment can at times be bridged by hard work and preparation, the fact is that venture capitalists *do* exist. The hardest part is finding them. Just maybe, the Web is the place to look.

At this writing, at least 70 venture capital–related sites are on the Web. Most of them are direct links to sources, with clicks to these sites generating home pages with descriptions of projects sought, and either phone numbers or mail-to's for more information.

Finding a venture capitalist is like computer dating, but with a lot more on the line. So let's examine some venture capital sites on the Internet and see what they offer.

CHECKING A VENTURE CAPITAL META DIRECTORY

A venture capitalist funds you because he wants to make money with you, not because he likes you. If you want to proceed from that truth, I counsel hitting one or more of the several venture capital *meta* Web directories. A meta directory simply means a directory of directories, or, in this case, a compendium of several venture capital resource listings.

Rather than hit dozens of individual venture capital sites from the get-go, you'll probably find that a meta—some of which have substantial search engine power—is a good initial time saver.

Depth of information varies, but the way that metas work is more or less the same. You'll likely be given a choice of business and industry you are in or would like to be in, asked for the state or region you are based in, and how large of an investment you seek.

Some of these sites require secured registration first, but the few minutes that you spend in this process will in most cases make you privy to some pretty darn impressive information-crunching power.

This section covers some of the best venture capital directories.

America's Business Funding Directory

http://www.business1.com/
Like many Web sites that contain information about capital, this site (see Figure 6-2) covers more than venture capital. It lists funding sources for equipment leasing, accounts receivable factoring, import/export funding, and Small Business Administration Loans.

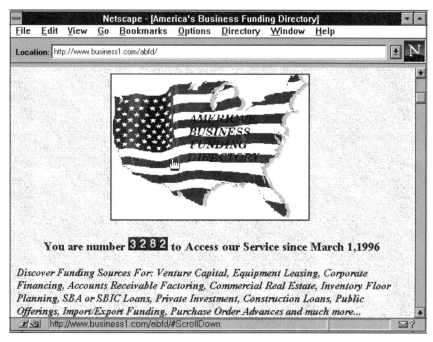

Figure 6-2: *America's Business Funding Directory's home page.*

You start your search from one of six home page toolbars, all of which are useful:

- *Don't Delay, Start Today*   A general guide to the site and how the information it contains may be helpful to you.

- *Capital Funding Search* (See Figure 6-3.)   A place to fill out specifics of your funding needs through a Common Gateway Interface form. Along with your Netscape-secured $99 that you authorize to be charged to your credit card, your answers are e-mailed to the Funding Directory. Within 48 hours, your funding request is matched up against the listed criteria of 10,000 funding sources, and a list of candidate funding companies is e-mailed back to you. The $99, which includes your classified advertisement reached via the site's Looking for Money Classifieds toolbar, is fully refunded to you if you score no "hits."

- *Funding Source Updates*   A list of sources with new information, such as revised criteria, successful new start-ups they'd like to brag about, and new venture capital companies.

- *"Raining Money": The Book*   A book about how to obtain venture capital; the book can be ordered through the site.

- *Looking for Money Classifieds*   Classifieds that either you place on your own or are offered as part of requesting a Capital Funding Search.

- *Business Promotion Resources*   Links to Web sites that will promote your business after it is up and running—presumably with the help of the venture capitalists identified through America's Business Funding's search service. And what a complete search service it is! After some basic contact and financial information, you are offered more than 40 "funding types," including construction loans, initial public offerings, recapitalization, syndication, and turnarounds. More than 30 business sectors are listed, including construction, electronics, entertainment, health and fitness, mobile home parks, and retail. The $99 sounds well worth it.

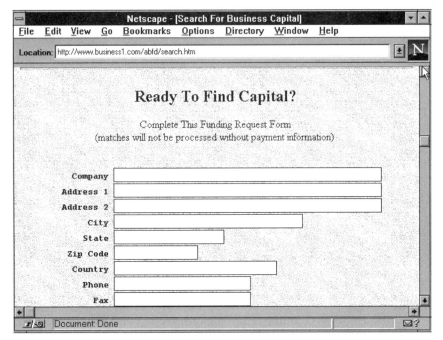

Figure 6-3: *America's Business Funding Directory search page.*

AMERICAN VENTURE CAPITAL EXCHANGE

http://www.businessexchange.com

The strength of this directory is not so much in its depth of information (see Figure 6-4) but in the several flexible ways that it allows you to place your "Venture Seeking Capital" listing. Start-ups are welcome.

For $295 a year, you get to write a one-page summary of your company or proposed business venture and then describe it by what you perceive to be its attributes, its financial projections, the qualifications of your existing or proposed officers, and the capital needed.

After payment is secured, AVCE puts your ad on its Web site, dial-up bulletin board, and newsletter. You have your choice of 13 industries that include real estate development, retail/wholesale, service, consumer products, and agriculture. You can specify eight different Capital Needed ranges, spanning from under $50,000 to $5 million and greater. The site also has a Level field where you can check under Start Up or Expansion.

Figure 6-4: *The American Venture Capital Exchange home page.*

CORPFINET DIRECTORY OF VENTURE CAPITAL FIRMS

http://www.corpfinet.com

Because it is only one section of a far broader index of corporate and commercial finance sites on the Internet, CorpFiNet's Directory of Venture Capital Firms (see Figure 6-5) isn't as complete as some of the other metas but arguably is the most focused. All the sites here have Web links from which you can click to the venture capital firm's site directly.

This site lists companies by such key criteria as the amount of Capital Under Management, industries in which a company specializes, location, and investment stage. You can sort results in alphabetical order, by location (such as cities, alphabetized within an individual state), or size of assets under management. Each subject field offers a pull-down menu of several choices. If you are just launching, use the Investment Stage box to look for the ones that specify start-up.

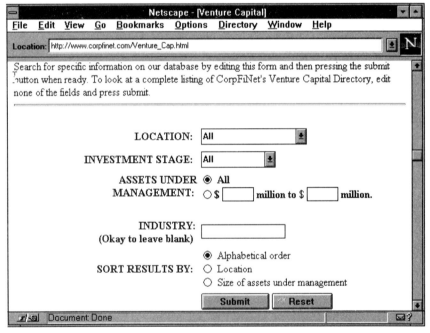

Figure 6-5: *CorpFiNet's Directory of Venture Capital Firms.*

FINANCEHUB

http://www.FinanceHub.com/
Another useful directory is InterSoft Solutions's FinanceHub (see Figure 6-6), which has more than 80 venture capital links in its field of several hundred financing sources. Of the seven home page links, the two that will be of greatest value to you are Investment and Venture Capital. Clicking on Venture Capital brings you to an easy-to-use search form where you can look for listed firms

through a keyword (such as **telecommunications**) or through a list of five funding amount criteria, ranging from "under $100,000" to "over $10 million." The site also features a handy browse function to cruise through new venture capital listings, such as those added within the last month.

Figure 6-6: *The FinanceHub home page.*

FinanceHub's content reflects a business philosophy with which I heartily agree. The site gives you enough of a hint of its database's power by allowing you basic searches for free, but it charges for more detailed search tasks. This is good: too many Web sites of all types make you pay up front before they give you even a scintilla of search information.

FinanceHub's Investor Seeker Database has more than 11,000 listings of firms that might be interested in putting capital into your business (see Figure 6-7). For less than $250, FinanceHub promises to get back to you within 48 hours with a list of investor firms that is annotated with contact names, the amounts the firms fund, the types of deals they are looking for, their geographic areas of interest, and the documentation they'll need before they talk with you seriously. And, oh yes: FinanceHub guarantees money back immediately if the search that you request doesn't pinpoint at least four sources.

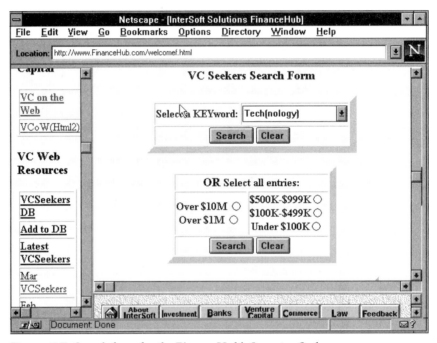

Figure 6-7: *Search form for the FinanceHub's Investor Seeker.*

PRICE WATERHOUSE LLP NATIONAL VENTURE CAPITAL SURVEY

http://www.pw.com/
Here you can find an exhaustive database culled from public information sources. This database lists hundreds of recent venture capital investments alphabetized by industry and funder, and ranked by amount. This list will help you determine who is funding your would-be competitors in the industry into which you might wish to enter or expand. Most of the larger transactions

listed are buyouts or expansions, transactions that venture capitalists have been known to do.

This site is exquisitely rich in detail. It opens with a map of the
United States divided into 15 regions. Each of the regions is
highlighted with a different color showing the amount of venture
capital invested in firms based in the given area. The next two
fully clickable search areas let you look for investor companies
and venture capital firms by industry and state. Most major
industries that support venture capital are listed, including biotechnology, business services, electronics, hardware, medical
instruments, pharmaceuticals, and software. You'll also find a
category for "miscellaneous" which, given the ever-widening
scope of entrepreneurial ingenuity, is a necessity.

Clicking on any of these hyperlinks produces a list of firms with
a track record of subject area interest and regional relevancy. This
list shows you who is getting funding and who is making it
available.

RLS, INC.

http://iplex.com/rls
The business model for this venture capital directory is a bit
dissimilar to the others discussed here. Like the others, the database of more than 1,000 venture capitalists here can be searched by
amount of capital needed, funding stage, type of project, and
geographic location. Tampa-based RLS (see Figure 6-8) promises
five sources if the funding amount requested is more than
$200,000. If not, the search fee of $99 will be paid back. Also, RLS
charges no search fee if the amount of funding sought is more
than $1 million.

You won't pay that much up front, but you will if RLS's com-
puterized fishing expedition is successful for you. Unlike the other
metas, RLS collects a modest finder's fee that decreases with the
size of the amount financed through sources that it locates for you.
If $25,000 through $499,000 is found, the fee is 5 percent. This
percentage declines steadily so that the second $1 million, over
and above the 2.0 percent charged for the first million, is assessed
at 1 percent, and everything greater than $2 million is levied at 0.5
percent. Thus, the fee for a $1.5 million capital investment from a

single source would be around $35,000. This fee, which may be tax deferrable, might be well worth it given the time and energy that you'd have to expend identifying and prequalifying these capital sources on your own.

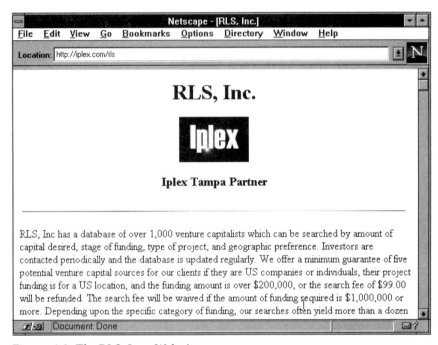

Figure 6-8: *The RLS, Inc., Web site.*

Getting Capital for Existing Businesses

The highest-profile venture capital companies may not want to talk with you unless you have a proven track record as a smaller company but want to grow your going concern. Yet, several reasons exist for checking out some of these sites. First, although they don't specialize in capital for start-ups, several companies have good advice for new companies. Second, reading their management philosophies will give you a good grasp of how the game is played at a higher level—one to which you aspire. And, finally, you may be the CEO or CFO of a growing company that could use additional capital.

With this in mind, read this section to find some useful higher-end capital resources sites on the Web.

ACCEL PARTNERS

http://www.accel.com/
A great place to get started would be at Accel Partners, whose investment interests lie across a broad range of companies, including telecommunications, multimedia, health care information systems and services, and software. More than 30 companies in which Accel has invested over the years either have gone public, have merged with public companies, or are still owned in part by Accel. A list of these companies is provided on the Accel Investment Stock Quotes page accessed through the Portfolio Home Page icon, with same-day trading quotes delivered through a link with Time Warner's Pathfinder service.

That information should serve as a motivator, but as a start-up you might be more interested in Accel's "Advice to First Time Entrepreneurs: Evaluating a Venture Capital Firm to Meet Your Company's Needs," which you can get through clicking on the Resources page. This treatise provides some clear guidance about what venture capitalists want and what rings their bells.

Accel's basic, but wise words: "Your process of selecting a venture firm is, therefore, much more analogous to the selection of key managers in your company than it is to the selection of a bank for a loan. With a banker, the appropriate question is 'How much money will he give me?' With a venture firm, the right question is 'How much money will he make me?'"

DRAPER FISHER ASSOCIATES

http://www.drapervc.com
Draper Fisher is based in the heart of Silicon Valley and specializes in software company investment. But even if that's not in your area of interest, don't overlook this site. There's simply no better

tutorial on the Web for the "good grasp" aspects of venture capital decision making that respected firms such as Draper Fisher use as part of their modus operandi.

Two gold mines of information exist here. The How to Reach Us page, accessed through a home page icon, contains far more than just a "click here" mail-to. The real value here is a seven-point recommendation of what a business plan prepared for any capital-lending firm should include. This is useful, important stuff, which includes:

- Investment Size and Structure Requested
- Description of the Product or Service
- Brief History of the Company
- Business and Marketing Strategy
- Analysis of the Market and the Competition
- Resumes of Key Management (Highlighting Industry and Market Expertise)
- Current Financial Statements and Projections

By going to the specified page and clicking on the Add Book-mark choice found in Navigator's Bookmarks menu (which is found on the top toolbar), you can bookmark Draper Fisher's Operations and Strategy page (see Figure 6-9). Not only that, but print it out and take it with you wherever you go, because this is a unique, inside look at the eight-step internal deliberation process that Draper Fisher (and many of its competitors) puts every serious venture capital application through. Each of these steps, including market evaluation, reference checking, risk evaluation, and potential customer contact, is examined in detail.

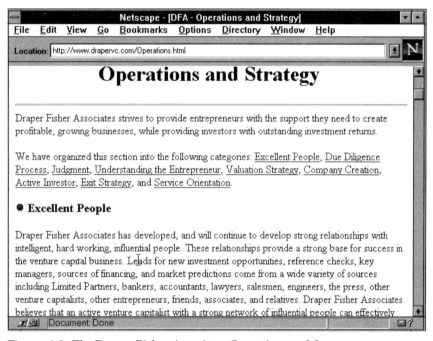

Figure 6-9: *The Draper Fisher Associates Operations and Strategy page.*

OLYMPIC VENTURE PARTNERS

http://product.com/olympic

Billing itself as the leading technology-oriented venture capital firm in the Pacific Northwest, Olympic Venture is interested in already existing but early-stage, young technology companies west of the Rockies. On its Web site, which is far sparser in information than Draper Fisher's but succinct enough to convey the message, Olympic Venture lists venture capital firms involved in the backing of new or growing companies in the software, life sciences, multimedia, communications, health care, and environmental sectors. Links are provided to the Web sites of more than a dozen companies that it has helped start.

Olympic Venture's When and How page affords a concise glimpse at its decision-making process. In essence, a "point partner" is appointed as your primary contact who, during the familiarization phase, begins to involve the other two partners in increasingly serious funding discussions as the project's feasibility goes up. Decisions, which typically take about two months, are made by committee.

SIERRA VENTURES

http://www.sierraven.com
If you're looking for capital, you may be under the mistaken notion that those who might lend funds to your start-up company will need nothing more than a good quarterly balance sheet and some periodic check-ins to keep them happy. Far from that, as you can read on the Sierra Ventures Web site.

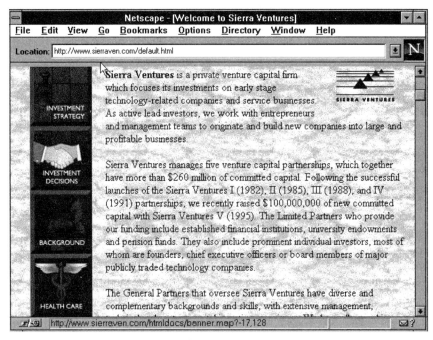

Figure 6-10: *The Sierra Ventures home page.*

Like numerous other venture capital firms, Sierra Ventures will want to be closely involved with the running of your business. Sierra's five icons on its home page are Investment Strategy, Investment Decisions, Background, Health Care, and Information Technology. Each takes you through various aspects of how the company operates and the kinds of enterprises it is interested in funding.

On the Investment Strategy Page, the statement "We Are Active Lead Investors" is made in bold type for all to read. This, we are told, means developing the product, service, and business strategies, as well as identifying and recruiting members of your company's Board of Directors. Yet, for this hands-on involvement, you get access to Sierra Ventures's professional services networking capabilities, as well as its philosophy of "patience" that can last several years.

Click on the Investment Decisions icon to try a brief tutorial about how to approach Sierra. It's basic but useful: "A good plan describes the company's product or service, backgrounds of the members of the management team, target market, competition, business strategy, company history, current capital structure, past projected financials, and the financing required."

COMMERCIAL FINANCE ONLINE

http://www.cfonline.com/
Commercial Finance Online operates several mailing lists targeted for people with interests in banking, leasing, business investing, import/export financing, business trade opportunities, and venture capital. Much of the traffic on the venture capital list consists of discussions with others who are seeking funding, have been denied funding and want to commiserate, or have gained funding and want to share their perspectives with others.

It's easy to subscribe to the Venture Capital Mailing List server. Just go to the Venture Capital listing on the Commercial Finance Online page and enter your electronic mail address in that field. You'll now be part of one of the Internet's "communities," one of the main elements that make the Internet so popular.

MOVING ON

For some of us, obtaining capital is a remote dream, far removed from our everyday concerns. Getting a lower-interest rate credit card and paying our debts are more immediate needs. That's why I've devoted the next chapter to credit and debt.

Credit & Debt

On any given day, the chances are pretty good that you'll have unsolicited credit card offers in your postal mailbox. In cyberspace, the world of credit is a buyer's market. Given the capability of the medium to visually present information in an enticing form, the Web is a natural medium for introductory credit card offers, many of which are bound to sound like an infinitely better deal than the 17.65 percent Annual Percentage Rate (APR) banking relationship that you're stuck with now. You can find this type of information on the Web easily, as covered here.

Although such deals—which aren't necessarily misleading—proliferate on banking sites, a number of resources will tell you how to manage credit, how to get out of debt, where to shop for the lowest-interest Visa or MasterCard, and finally, how to start repairing your credit by getting "secured" plastic. This chapter also covers these sites.

What Makes a Good Credit Site?

A credit site worth doing business with ought to have three basic attributes, what I call the "three Cs": credibility, clarity, and content. This section covers these attributes so that you can evaluate the sites you visit.

I'll talk a bit about each of the three Cs:

- *Credibility*   The site should not use too many superlatives but should contain a sober discussion of the product offered, its positives, and its negatives. Also, the potentially hidden catches should be spelled out at the outset. If a bank is offering a card at an introductory 6.9 percent interest rate that will rise to 17 or 18 percent after the first year, it should say so plainly, in clear view. Fine-print disclaimers are fine, but not enough.

- *Clarity*   Does the site allow for smooth navigation? Are all the major features indicated with clearly defined icons or links on the home page? Are all the features where they need to be, or is Help in the "contact us" page, not on tech support? Is there a search engine to comb the site?

- *Content*   Is the site updated frequently? Few things are more irritating than going to a site and reading about a promotion that expired five weeks ago. If it's a bank site, is there a searchable list of branches, with postal addresses and phone numbers? Are there links to other sites, with financial information? Does the site let you apply for a credit card online, or look up your checking balance?

Before we visit some credit-related sites, let's explore the three Cs in even more detail.

Credibility

Staying away from sites that have a carnival barker or huckster atmosphere is a good idea. If you were to transcribe into words the loud late-night ads of some stereotypical used-car salespersons, you would hear most of their sentences ending in exclamation points(!). You can pick up on the signals that, transmitted in text, indicate that the person doing the selling is emphasizing style over substance:

too many exclamation points, too many bragging words such as *only*, the frequent appearance of YOU in all capital letters. Overemphasis on style means, in too many cases, that the substance is not there. For instance, I have a problem with the American Express and Discover Card Web sites because they are too oriented around periodic promotions and short on value-added information.

Credibility has a lot to do with a tone that is measured, without hype or dumbing-down. Like many things, you'll know it when you see it.

CLARITY

Credit sites constructed with clarity have a definitive home page that tells you what is on the site, and they have accurately named subtopic titles that reflect what you'll find discussed when you click on the given link. (A pet peeve: too many home page site directories use undecipherable, cutesy icons to indicate what's available. Icons are cool, but they should say what they mean underneath them.)

Because credit, like many other disciplines, comes with its own jargon, a clear and cogent Frequently Asked Questions (FAQ) page also is mandatory. A glossary helps, too. Finally, similar to the best voice-mail systems, there should be a way to get a live person, either through a clickable mail-to that will let you send an e-mail function (see Chapter 3, "How Do I Find the Information I Need?" for help on sending messages) or through a phone number to dial for customer support.

CONTENT

Give me information. For example, perhaps I am looking at a bank that I have never heard of. I want information on that bank. Where is it based? How large is it? What other services does it offer? Does it provide links to other sites, such as credit bureau tutorials, automobile loan rates, mutual fund quotes, and detailed information about Individual Retirement Accounts? After all, credit and debt are major factors in our financial lives, but they must exist in symbiosis with our overall personal financial profile. Sites that realize this are useful.

A Rant

In this book, I really try to keep the soapbox oratory to a minimum, but sometimes I just can't help it. One way to ruin the party before it starts is to make you, the Internet accessor, do all the work. Some sites—personal finance and otherwise—make you download and then configure specialized files and programs to read the information on the site. I have no problem with providing links to RealAudio or Shockwave for extra, multimedia experiences, but asking someone to download a 200,000-byte Adobe Acrobat .PDF file just to read the text strikes me as a bit disingenuous. Unless you are desperate, it won't be worth your time to hassle with all this stuff. Go to sites that have done most or all of the work for you.

CREDIT & DEBT SITES

Credibility, clarity, and content. Keeping these goals in mind, let's go out on the Web and see what we can find.

MASTERCARD INFORMATION CENTER

http://www.mastercard.com/
Because virtually all the credit cards issued by U.S. banks are likely to be through Visa or MasterCard, it isn't surprising that these two familiar associations have put up their own sites with links to banks that issue one or two of these cards. These sites are likely to have links to several types of Visas or MasterCards, so this is a good, general place to start. The MasterCard Information Center, which is clickable from the MasterCard home page (see Figure 7-1) is your launch point for information about credit card services and vendor partners.

Figure 7-1: *MasterCard's Information Center can be reached from its home page.*

This page links to several banks both within and outside the United States that offer the familiar plastic with the red-and-yellow-circled logo. Several of these bank links satisfy my demanding three Cs standard. After you've visited the MasterCard site, you'll have learned a lot more about how you can apply for credit, how you can manage your credit well, and where you can apply for it.

ADVANTA NATIONAL BANK

http://www.edvance.com/
This site contains a standard Common Gateway Interface application form that asks you to type the basic application information and then uses your Netscape Navigator secured protocol and electronic system to send your credit application request to the bank.

Convenient, yes, but nothing special. Not until you get to an online U.S. Savings Bond Calculator (see Figure 7-2), which Advanta put on the site to tout its offer of a free $50 Series EE Savings Bond after you've charged more than $2,500 on your EDVANCE MasterCard. You could charge a hot new car stereo system and earn the savings bond with one signature, but that wouldn't be exactly prudent, right? The online calculator agrees, preaching by inference a gradual approach. When you provide information by typing the total monthly average balance of your credit card, the APR, the amount that you typically charge per month, and the annual fee, you'll be given a projected target date of when you will have earned the bond.

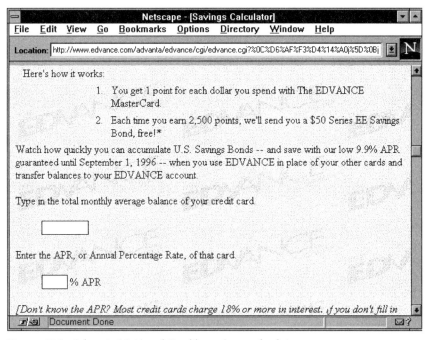

Figure 7-2: *Advanta National Bank's savings calculator.*

AT&T UNIVERSAL CARD

http://www.att.com.ucs/

Far more than just an online application center, this complete site has an In The Know submenu (see Figure 7-3) that whisks you to several basic information fields of use. For example, "What Your Credit History Says About You" explains what credit grantors such as AT&T Universal look at when they access your credit file after they've received your application. Much of this information, such as place and length of employment, you'll already know. But are you also aware that grantors consider the number of accounts you have, when they were opened, what your current balance is, and how many times you've been late?

Also, you might not realize it, but if you are denied credit, you are entitled to a free credit bureau report. That's why the inclusion of the toll-free numbers for the three major credit bureaus is a useful feature here.

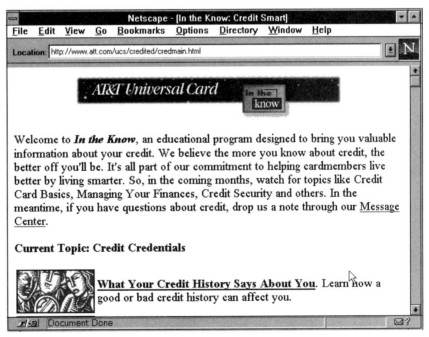

Figure 7-3: *AT&T Universal Card's In The Know page.*

AT&T Universal's Glossary is also welcome. Many of the terms are self-explanatory, but a few will straighten out inevitable confusion. Do you know, for example, what *nominal APR* is? For the record, it is "the contractual interest rate applied to your account. This rate," the Glossary says, "may be changed once in each calendar quarter." You'll find a link to "cardmember Agreement" for more information.

At any given time, substantive cross-promotions occur between the AT&T Universal Card and its long-distance phone services. A series of links on the Universal Card home page take you to some of these subject areas.

BANK OF AMERICA

http://www.bankamerica.com/
On the Bank of America Web site, clarity is served by eight well-defined subject areas. Some of these are Personal Finance, for your personal profile; BA Today, for corporate news; Economics, for general economic news and analyses of import to investors, savers, and borrowers; and Special Offers, for you-guessed-what.

Personal Finance (see Figure 7-4), a feature under the Personal area, has links for MasterCard, Visa, and Personal Loan applications, as well as Home Banking. This page also has a Personal Investment Profile, which routes you to a 12-question, multiple choice self-examination of your investment philosophy. More about this useful feature is provided in Chapter 10, "Investments"; I've mentioned it here to promote the notion that the best credit and debit sites treat the topics as a subset of a broader subject range.

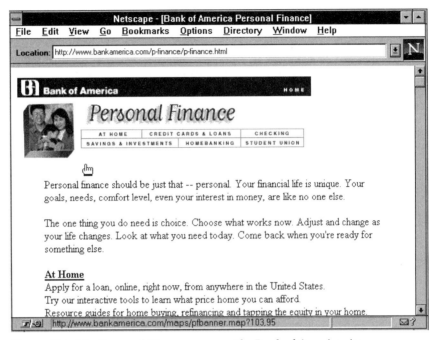

Figure 7-4: *The Personal Finance page on the Bank of America site.*

Just about all the pages on Bank of America's site have bottom-screen hot button links for Contact, Personalize, Help, and Search. Sites such as Bank of America's that are fully keyword searchable deserve bonus points.

FIRST CONSUMERS NATIONAL BANK

http://www.FCNB.com/
Like an increasing number of banks these days, Beaverton, Oregon–based First Consumers has no branches in the standard sense. Instead, it operates what is known as a "credit bank," which is a credit-granting and payment-processing center. Such "banks" may not have tellers, but instead focus almost exclusively on credit cards.

First Consumers has taken the credit card market and carved out a useful niche as one of the leading issuers of secured cards. These cards, attractive to people with past credit problems, most often allow for a credit limit equal to or not much greater than the collateral you have in a savings account with that issuer. If, for example, your car was repossessed three years ago but your credit has been good for the last two years, you'll have trouble getting an unsecured card. Institutions such as First Consumers may be an option for you.

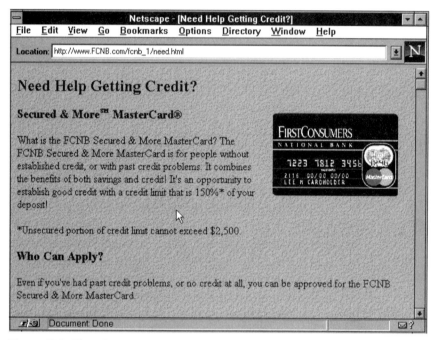

Figure 7-5: *First Consumers National Bank offers secured credit cards.*

Several dozen banks offer secured plastic, but First Consumers's Web site is one of the few to devote significant space not only to an online application but to explaining how you can use this new tool to repair your credit (see Figure 7-5). Some of the places to hit are Building Good Credit, Make Credit Your Ally by Building A Strong Financial History, and Take Charge Of Your Finances. Under Credit Management Tips, you're instructed to Keep A Log of All Your Charges, Balance Your Checkbook Every Month, and Review Sales Drafts Carefully Before You Sign Them. Common-sense advice, but a little online hand-holding never hurt anyone.

FIRST UNION BANK

http://www.firstunion.com/

The Web site for this growing North Carolina bank isn't as comprehensive as some others in terms of outside links or hand-holding. For depth of information about specific services, however, this site, which the bank calls First Access Network, is deserving of plaudits.

First Access's online application links (see Figure 7-6) are constructed for several of First Union's MasterCard, Equity Loan, and Consumer Loan programs. Those people who are reluctant to convey confidential applications over a modem will find a concise explanation of the security used, as well as the Web server technology provided by Netscape and Open Market. Anyone intrigued by the topic or needing the comfort of details before going ahead will find links to the Netscape and Open Market sites.

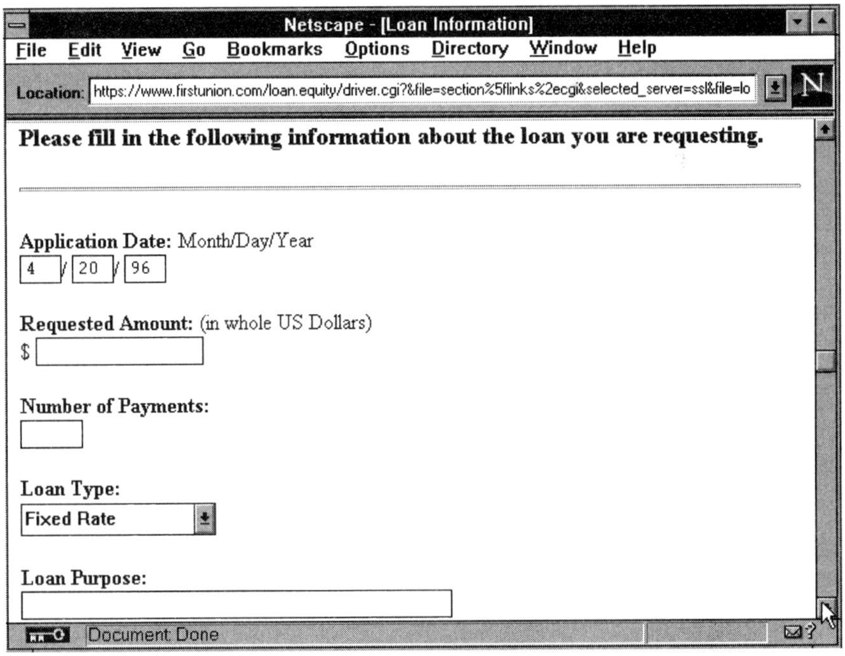

Figure 7-6: *First Union Bank's Equity Loan page.*

Now one of the 15 largest commercial banks in the United States, First Union provides online applications for Visa, MasterCard, lines of credit, and balance transfers, as well as for specialty products such as its Secured MasterCard and its Hornets MasterCard (named for pro basketball's Charlotte Hornets, which, not so coincidentally, are based in First Union's headquarters city). Each of these product listings has links that provide an attractively laid out summary of benefits arranged in check box format. For example, First Union's Gold Card offers automatic automobile rental insurance, emergency cash and card replacement, and credit lines starting at $5,000. And, yes, you can apply online.

WELLS FARGO BANK

http://www.wellsfargo.com/
Wells Fargo's site, as of this writing, is more of an account informational and transactional platform than a place for financial information or counsel. Still, the site has four redeeming virtues:

- You can fill out and electronically submit an application for a checking account (see Figure 7-7). When your application is approved, you are mailed back a PIN number, which you can then use to check your balances online.

- The site gives you substantial information on how your session is encrypted to ensure security.

- The site allows an interface to download your transaction details to any one of several financial management software packages, including Quicken.

- In 1996, Fargo bought First Interstate Bank, thus expanding its area of in-person operations from its California base to 10 other Western states.

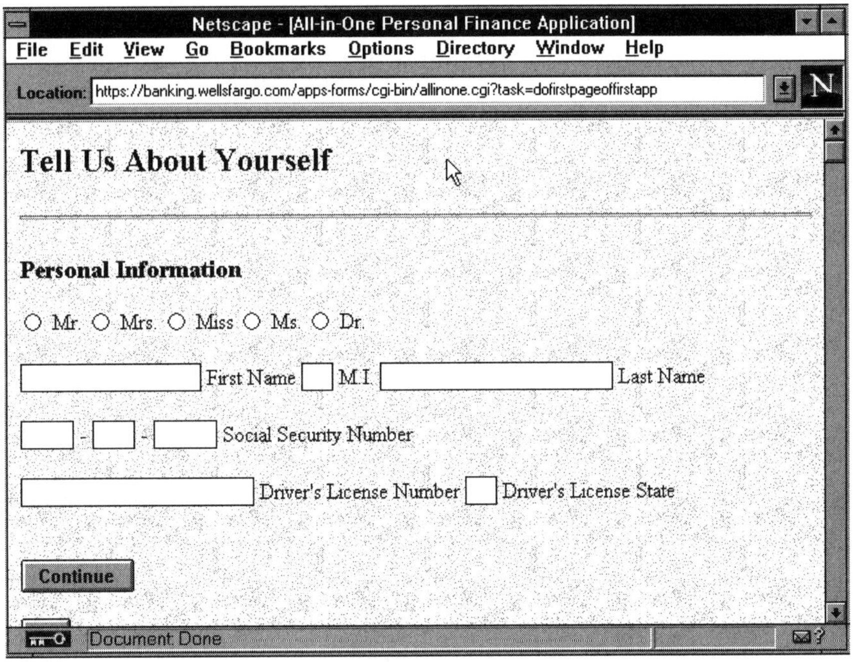

```
╔══════════════════════════════════════════════════════════════╗
║ ──      Netscape - [All-in-One Personal Finance Application]  ▼ ▲ ║
║ File  Edit  View  Go  Bookmarks  Options  Directory  Window  Help ║
╠══════════════════════════════════════════════════════════════╣
║ Location: https://banking.wellsfargo.com/apps-forms/cgi-bin/allinone.cgi?task=dofirstpageoffirstapp  ▣ N ║
╠══════════════════════════════════════════════════════════════╣
║                                                                ▲ ║
║  Tell Us About Yourself              ▷                           ║
║  ────────────────────────────────────────────────────────────   ║
║                                                                  ║
║  Personal Information                                            ║
║                                                                  ║
║  ○ Mr.  ○ Mrs.  ○ Miss  ○ Ms.  ○ Dr.                            ║
║                                                                  ║
║  [                   ] First Name [  ] M.I. [              ] Last Name ║
║                                                                  ║
║  [     ]-[   ]-[     ] Social Security Number                    ║
║                                                                  ║
║  [                     ] Driver's License Number [  ] Driver's License State ║
║                                                                  ║
║  [ Continue ]                                                  ▼ ║
╠══════════════════════════════════════════════════════════════╣
║ [▫◯] Document: Done                                        ✉? ║
╚══════════════════════════════════════════════════════════════╝
```

Figure 7-7: *Wells Fargo's site allows you to apply for a checking account.*

The encryption tutorial is one of the easiest to understand of any Web site I've visited. It explains that your social security number or personal financial information is disguised, and it provides a link to the Netscape Commerce Server site for more information. On the Wells Fargo site, you can even find out how to tell whether your session is encrypted. I can't resist quoting here: "When the key icon at the lower left corner of your screen becomes solid, and a blue line appears at the top of the browser's screen, everything is encrypted. The icon appears broken when not in use."

VISA WORLDWIDE

http://www.visa.com/
By almost any objective yardstick, I find Visa Worldwide's Visa Expo site to be inferior to MasterCard's. It doesn't have as many bank links or as much "bet you didn't know that" information.

What you will find is lots of promotional information about how many merchants worldwide accept the Visa Classic Card (more than 12 million at last count), and, in nonspecific superlatives, just how great the Visa Gold Card is. On the Visa Classic link, you can view and listen to a recent Visa ad. This might be a fun place to give the multimedia capabilities of your computer a spin, but it doesn't add much to the depth of your knowledge about credit and debt.

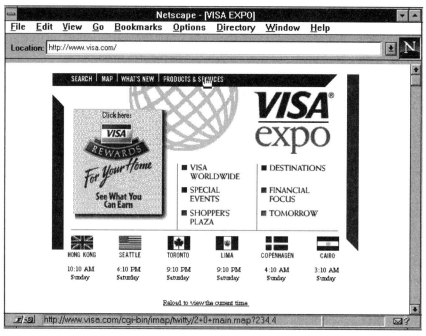

Figure 7-8: *Visa Worldwide's Web site is heavy on promotional information.*

You can find some useful nuggets scattered throughout Visa's site. It has a navigable and user-friendly search facility (see Figure 7-8) that prompts you for your country or zip code and then tells you what Visa-compatible Automatic Teller Machines might be nearby. To access this function, click the Personal Services link on the home page. When you're on the Personal Services page, you'll see an underlined hyperlink to the ATM search function.

You can use Choices & Decisions, a program that contains credit card and loan worksheets, to help you figure out "the impact of credit card and loan interest on the price of any of your purchases." To get to this page, start at the Visa Expo home page. Then click on the Financial Focus icon. Read the README file and then download Choices & Decisions through another link. A simpler navigation model would have been to house the number-crunching abilities for Choices & Decisions on the Visa server, where you could then access it.

NONBANK CREDIT & DEBT SOURCES

You can find several worthy places on the Internet that concentrate far more on telling you about credit than setting you up with credit. Two that truly stand out are the sites maintained by the RAM Research Group and the TRW Information Services site, operated by one of the three major credit bureaus.

RAM RESEARCH GROUP

http://www.ramresearch.com/
This site is one of the most comprehensive Web sites I've seen anywhere. It has 11 major subject areas, each of them highly navigable. Several are likely to be of interest to anyone who has or wants credit. Some of the linked features on RAM Research Group's site include:

■ Your Direct Link to the Best Credit Card Offers is a hyperlink to selected bankcard issuers' Web sites (see Figure 7-9).

■ Tracking Bank Credit Cards for the American Consumer ranks credit cards by interest charged. Cards are ranked by interest rate and annual fee, if any. The issuing bank is listed as well as whether these cards are available nationally or just in states or communities where the bank maintains branches.

- Complete Databank of U.S. Bank Credit Card Issuers lists more than 10,000 banks, savings and loans, credit unions, and other entities that issue cards.

- The Payment Card Research Engine can be used to search credit-related newsletters as well as much of the information available elsewhere on the RAM Research Group site.

Figure 7-9: *RAM Research Group's Your Direct Link to the Best Credit Card Offers provides access to Web sites of banks that issue low-interest credit cards.*

TRW INFORMATION SERVICES

http://www.trw.com/

The main mission of a credit bureau is to catalog your credit history, details of which are used by bankers, automobile dealership finance managers, mortgage loan officers, and others in assessing your credit worthiness. (Not, as you may think, to make your financial life difficult.) If you have had problems, learning more about what credit bureaus are, how they operate, and what your rights are would help you. You can find this information on the credit bureau sites on the Web.

The three main credit bureaus in the United States are Trans Union, Equifax, and TRW Information Services. Equifax's Web site is a bit thin, but TRW (see Figure 7-10) wins the quality race here by more than default. It's not especially deep, but it does provide brief and succinct answers to questions such as "How are credit granting decisions made?" (character, credit capacity, and existing credit), "How does divorce affect a person's credit?" (greatly depends on circumstances), and "What should I do if I find an error in my credit report?" (contact the bureau and explain the error on forms the bureau provides).

Figure 7-10: *The TRW Information Services home page.*

WORD OF ASSURANCE

Ever heard of a *firewall?* Web sites use these software programs to act as gatekeepers between the publicly accessible content on the site and the internal, confidential material contained on internal or proprietary corporate systems. If you're concerned that someone will use a credit bureau Web site to gain access to your credit report, don't be. The firewalls used by the bureaus are supremely impenetrable. The three or four incidents a year when a system is crashed have nothing to do with the Web; they usually happen when a merchant with a password to get into a TRW or Equifax database sells the password to an unauthorized third party, such as a private detective agency or suspicious ex-boyfriend. All three bureaus monitor accesses constantly and, with no questions asked, will deactivate passwords of said transgressors. So don't worry.

CREDIT SCORING

http://pages/prodigy.com/ID/vcr/Score.html

If the world of credit is still arbitrary and still a bit evil to you even after all the Web sites you've visited, you have a place to go where you can vent your frustrations. Credit Scoring, an article on the Victims of Credit Reporting Web site, explains how grantors feed numerical criteria into computers that then rate your application. Some 85 percent of all credit granting decisions are made in this manner. This site also has a link to the Federal Trade Commission Web site, which has press releases of the regulatory body's 1992 decision permitting these practices.

Kudos to this site for calling credit scoring the arbitrary, judgmental practice that it is. Most credit scoring systems give bonus points for lengthy employment, not being self-employed, and significant time at current residence. In light of today's entrepreneurial economy, in which an increasing number of upwardly mobile folks are self-employed or work on a series of high-dollar employment contracts rather than having a 30-year career with one firm, Credit Scoring's objections are right on the mark.

BANKRUPTCY: THE FINAL OPTION

http://www.law.cornell.edu/uscode/11/
Should all your avenues to work out your debts be exhausted, bankruptcy may be an option. You can find the complete text of the United States Bankruptcy Code under the keyword searchable Title-11 Bankruptcy Section of the U.S. Code site maintained by Cornell University Law School. You can find detailed explanations of terms that are commonly discussed but incompletely understood, such as Chapter 7 (Liquidation), Chapter 11 (Reorganization), and Chapter 13 (Adjustment of Debts of an Individual with Regular Income).

MOVING ON

Maybe you are planning to use the credit you've earned to start an entrepreneurial venture. The next chapter, "Entrepreneurship & Consulting Services," looks at sites maintained by people and organizations that can advise you how to start a business, restore a floundering one to health, or keep a thriving, ongoing business sound.

Entrepreneurship & Consulting Services

If you've been able to start a business, how can you ensure its success? Well, nothing is certain in this world, but several heads—especially if they contain the brains of expert, experienced consultants—are better than one.

Consultants sometimes get a bad rap. Sometimes that's because they tell people what they don't want to hear. A consultant can be criticized if he becomes a timid "yes" man, and seen as too critical if she dissects your business plan with a meat cleaver. A classic "damned if you do, damned if you don't" scenario, but almost entirely undeserved.

If you are a mature adult, you'd better realize that, by odds alone, people exist with more experience than you in the field you are in. The Web is a great place to find, and even prequalify, this expertise.

First, a reality check. For a starting or a growing business, getting a loan from a venture capitalist, your bank, or a rich family relation won't be enough. You might enjoy an inner gleam when someone invests money in you, but without a well-executed business plan, that loan will quickly stop being a doorway to your dreams. Instead, it will be a monkey that will stay on your back for all your living days—and perhaps beyond.

Finding a reputable, knowledgeable consultant to help you hone your commercial vision is far more than simply a matter of two heads being better than one. Nor is the strategy a mere hedge against the possible hidden truth that, somehow, your idea isn't right for the business sector you will compete in, the city or region where you propose to base your enterprise, or the time of year you are planning for your big rollout or expansion.

The sad truth is that four out of five businesses fail during their first year. Undercapitalization and inexperience are frequently cited as the causes, but they are more the symptoms. The real reason is unchecked ego.

In my long career as a business journalist, I've written hundreds of detailed stories on companies that have been derailed by entrepreneurial ego. I've even seen ego at work in the would-be ventures of friends and relations. It's a powerful motivator, but ego can also be blindingly corrosive.

An inescapable paradox is at work here. Wanting to become an entrepreneur in the first place takes ego and a disproportionate sense of one's own worth. You spend hundreds of hours honing the concept with supportive friends and maybe a few potential clients. As the sweetness of each new "sounds great" comment rings in your ears, the effect accumulates like too much candy on your teeth. Add to this the endless stream of rosy, hardly objective "you can succeed, too" booster testimonials in self-help business books and magazines. Gradually, you build an impenetrable wall of ego-driven pride in your idea. You become impervious to the suggestions of objective outside sources.

These sources "just don't get it," you think. Truth is, *you* don't. Six months later when the start-up funds have run dry and the cash flow is sparse, the Chapter 11 or Chapter 13 bankruptcy reorganization ads on late-night cable television are no longer anathema. Just try borrowing more money when you are already hocked to the gills, with red ink on your ledger and nothing but empty promises from sales prospects that may never materialize.

Why bother risking your finances and your life to your ego when you can get objective information and advice from qualified and experienced management and marketing consultants? Many honest, battle-tested practitioners of this craft would be perfectly willing to help you, and hitting the Web is a great place to look for them.

WHAT SHOULD A GOOD CONSULTING SITE OFFER?

Too many entrepreneurial advice sites are out there that, in essence, say something vague, such as, "We have years of experience helping start-up companies. Our staff is willing to help you." Add to this the bubbly endorsements from clients who, for all you know, might be the consultant's cousins. These sites are a waste of time. Plainly, they were thrown up in haste, with minimal effort. Do you really want people with that type of *Cliff's Notes* approach to business advising you on your affairs of commerce? No. The first thing to look for when you evaluate a site is substance. That is, specific information about what kinds of services the site offers. Where have the principals worked before?

Several world-class consulting firms specialize in work for multinational corporate giants. Most of these consultants have Web sites, but because they aren't that interested in small, growing companies, this chapter doesn't list them all. Instead, I'm more concerned with experts who either specialize in or devote significant resources to helping you, the entrepreneur.

Keep in mind that you should not visit these sites expecting to find all the answers you need. Some business-oriented Web sites, such as those concerning investment or credit, are by design more amenable to quantifiable, statistical, or trend line data. Entrepreneurship advice, though, is a highly subjective field in which large storehouses of information are not nearly as relevant as a description of what kind of services a company provides and how it prefers to work with you to design a program that jointly fits its expertise and your needs.

For this reason, consulting and entrepreneur-oriented sites are low on data and high on what I respectfully call the "this is what we can do for you" message. On some other kinds of sites, such a message can indicate an overly promotional persona, but not on these. I have no problem with such content; it's in the nature of the subject matter.

CONSULTING SITES

This section covers entrepreneurial and consulting service Web sites that can give you information, point to more resources, or hook you up with the right people.

AMERICAN MANAGEMENT ASSOCIATION

http://www.tregistry.com/ttr/ama.htm

Partly a professional affiliation and partly a learned society, this group is the official organization for the study of management techniques. Its primary interface with the public is a curriculum of more than 200 conferences a year on 11 management and leadership skills. The curriculum is skewed toward skills appropriate for corporate-jungle survival rather than entrepreneurial start-up, but the skills taught would be useful to any businessperson. You can use this site to find information on the seminars.

As listed on the site, some of the topics include Executive Effectiveness, Fundamentals of Sales Management for the New Sales Manager, Management Skills for Executive Secretaries and Administrative Assistants, Successful Managerial Skills for Black Managers, and Developing High Performance Teams. Each of the main course listings has a hot link that routes you to further information. Unit One of the Executive Effectiveness Course, for example, is described as a seminar that enables attendees to "find out how others actually see them in action, use new insights to improve their management style, build on their strengths and work on their weaknesses, and clarify their career objectives and create an action plan." If you have questions or want to order more information about American Management Association products, you can use the e-mail link (see Figure 8-1).

These courses are not cheap. Executive Effectiveness will set you back $3,335 if you are not an American Management Association member, or $2,900 if you are. Yet, these seminars can be a great place to network as well as to sharpen your skills.

The only problem I have with this site is that not a lot of substantive information is available. Putting some course curricula highlights on the site—rather than just a rundown of what taking each course will do for you—would have been useful.

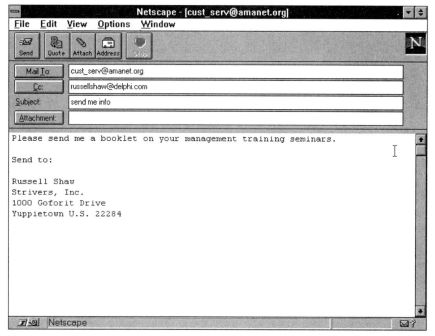

Figure 8-1: *The American Management Association offers an e-mail link for its products.*

BIRMINGHAM BUSINESS ASSISTANCE NETWORK

http://www.tech-comm.com/customer/bban
This site will be of direct help to you only if you plan to start a business in the Birmingham, Alabama, metropolitan area. So, why write about a site like this? Throughout North America, a growing number of regional or local economic development authorities or private consortia are putting up Web sites that act as clearinghouses for office space, labor, and financing for entrepreneurs. This simple yet well-organized site typifies the best.

Birmingham Business Assistance has no direct electronic mailback and no links, but lists a to-the-point rundown, without being too showy or shrill, of the services provided by the network. This means management assistance, help in identifying financing alternatives, and a Business Incubation Center to house offices of brand new companies. BIC tenants have access to copy and fax machines, computer stations, a receptionist, janitorial service, and clerical and word processing services.

As a nonprofit corporation, Birmingham Business Assistance Network is subsidized by the City of Birmingham as well as by investments from the private sector.

BBAN sounds like a great idea. If you, as an entrepreneur, would like such an entity in your community, visit the BBAN Web site and familiarize yourself with its offerings. Then, contact someone through the site for advice on how to spark the establishment of a similar group in your area.

CEDAR CONSULTING, INC.

http://www.cedarconsulting.com/
This Los Angeles–based management consultancy doesn't have a lot of administrative how-to advice on its site. I've decided to list it because it goes into exquisite detail about the types of services it offers and how it works with its clients to configure a consulting regimen topical to each business circumstance.

A division of accounting firm Muso & Co., Cedar's professional services include business systems analysis and design, proposal requests and evaluations, business systems and accounting audits, and professional financial management services. On the site, these services are described within the parameters of how the company works with new clients. You can get to each feature from the home page (see Figure 8-2).

For example, the "preparation and planning phase" is described as part of Cedar's "Creating the Vision" process. "During this preparation and planning phase," the site says, "we will perform a detailed requirements analysis as well as review your existing business processes and organization. This is also your opportunity to design the systems that will support your vision of an outstanding product or service. Next, our consultants will prepare a systems configuration and develop a plan for data conversion and implementation with your team. This plan, together with the approval and commitment of your executive management, will be the blueprint to building an effective and productive business management system."

Like some other entrepreneurial Web sites, Cedar has no Common Gateway Interface for mail-to's, but does provide phone and fax numbers for you to request more information or direct contact.

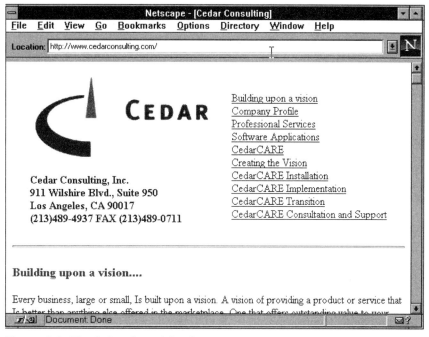

Figure 8-2: *The Cedar Consulting home page.*

CEO Resource

http://www.ceoresource.com/ceo/
The heart and soul of this very useful site is a series of pop quizzes that are designed to gauge your need for business advice. The counsel is provided by the Goodman Group, Inc., a Dallas-based consultancy aimed at the business owner and entrepreneur.

Quizzes can be not only fun but useful. The home page starts with a warm-up quiz, including questions such as "What do you do when there is not enough of you, or not enough time, to do everything that is necessary for you to run your company?" and

"How often do you really spend time on the bigger picture of what you want and where you are going? Your own personal needs as well as your company's goals?" Even if you never visit CEO Resource's site, these are applicable soul-searching questions to which you should devote some thought.

The two most useful CEO Resource site quizzes are "Agenda for the Future of You & Your Company" and "How Fast Are You Burning Cash?" Each quiz is self-administered, without a specific scoring system. The answers are designed to give you a perception of where the challenges and potential problems lie for your business. You can then attach this information to an e-mail mailback provided at the end of each quiz. You'll be sent introductory literature or contacted by phone if you convey a wish for this in your e-mail.

Arranged in a multiple choice format, the "Future" quiz asks you questions such as where your growth needs lie (expansion, new branches or stores, franchising, downsizing), and what your most pressing financial issue is (cash flow, profitability, capital formation, banking/credit, or financing).

The sobering "Burning Cash" quiz (see Figure 8-3) requests that you estimate your monthly fixed costs for 24 items, including computer supplies, furniture/fixtures, equipment leases, rent/utilities, taxes, travel, and total salaries. Then, after adding up all these costs, you are asked how much merchandise you need to sell or clients you need to see in a given month to get you to the profit point you want. Presumably, a Goodman Group consultant will be happy to guide you to that place.

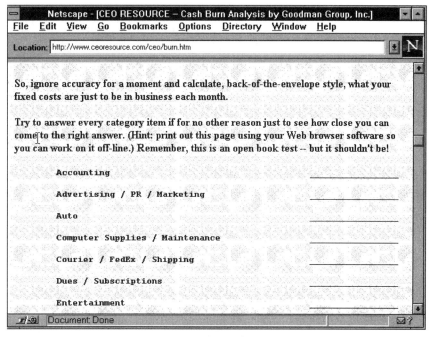

Figure 8-3: *CEO Resource's "Burning Cash" quiz.*

ERNST & YOUNG LLP

http://www.ey.com/
Outstanding for its simple yet informative navigability, the E&Y
site is probably the most straightforward of any provided by a
major worldwide consulting firm. The home page starts out with
some basic information about the U.S. practice, such as the industries it covers, the expertise it offers, and the locations where it
does business. The site is organized a bit like a digital bulletin
board with company news (dates and times of upcoming seminars), new services, and top-level hires, as well as several publications of interest to the entrepreneur. Unfortunately, none of the full
studies is available online; you'll have to request those.

Utilitarian information for the start-up resides in the site's
Center for Business Innovation section. Under the Electronic
Commerce link (see Figure 8-4), you read that the Center, in

collaboration with the Ernst & Young Center for Technology Enablement, will study this issue and presumably be equipped to help clients determine the applicability of specific Electronic Commerce strategies to their business. "Information technology is radically changing the relationships between a business and its customers, including the very form and substance of commerce. . . . What forms of electronic commerce create the most value for businesses and clients? What technologies enable the greatest commercial value? Under what circumstances is value created? What business strategies maximize the value generated through electronic commerce?" E&Y is developing expertise in these issues, which it will be happy to share with its clients.

Such a site content strategy provokes a debate. How much actual information should be put online? Is the site primarily a promotional doorway to a potential consultant-client relationship?

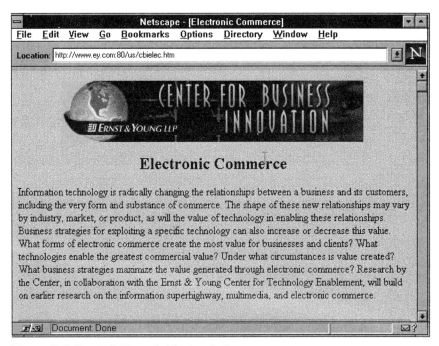

Figure 8-4: *Ernst & Young's Electronic Commerce page.*

MC 100, INC.

http://www.mc100inc.com/

The site offered by Madeira Beach, Florida–based management consultants MC 100, Inc., has more informational content than most management consulting firms. The site has a boilerplate mission statement, a client profile, and a brief "consulting method" description. The real value-added data is deeper into the site.

For example, The Edge is a page that contains links to several articles by MC 100 CEO Robert H. Smith. To Mr. Smith's infinite credit, the links lead to full-text postings of the works. Some of the more interesting-sounding titles available here include "Strategically Focused Improvements: How the Best CEOs and Companies Get Better," "Strategic Business Reengineering: Leadership and Enlightened Common Sense," "Shifting Into Overdrive: Strategic Business Planning for the Growth Company," and "The CEO Advisor: Miscellaneous Questions and Answers From Assorted Issues."

MC 100 also has a 10-question litmus test (see Figure 8-5) designed to rate your company's managerial fitness. The quiz is called Ten Tough Questions, but the queries are more a matter of truthful conscience than of brain-racking. Some of the questions include, "Is your company having difficulty in responding to market or industry changes?"; "Are customers complaining about quality, missed deadlines, or errors?"; and "Are competitors targeting your market, key customers, or employees?"

If you answer "yes" to 4 or more of the 10 questions, MC 100 advises you to get a checkup real quick. "Your company is in serious difficulty, probably in a turnaround situation, and decisive corrective action is needed now. It may already be too late," you're warned.

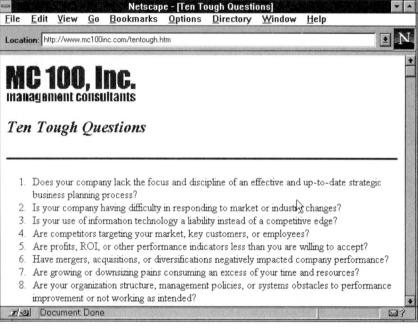

Figure 8-5: *MC 100, Inc.'s Ten Tough Questions page.*

MCKINSEY & COMPANY

http://www.mckinsey.com/
In the highly competitive yet tightly knit consultancy community, McKinsey & Company is generally regarded as the leading strategic counseling company in the world. With 67 locations around the planet and a collective resume that includes top-level interactions with a significant number of the world's largest corporations, McKinsey is the Tiffany of consulting firms. Its consultants have written more than 90 books on management, the titles of which are listed on the McKinsey site.

Does this relate to you if you are wanting to, say, open a specialty chemical distributorship in Wichita? It might. Some of your prospective or existing clients may be divisions of companies whose top administrators receive daily guidance from McKinsey execs. Knowing the traits of those who pull the strings is a good idea. Also, familiarity with the world-class, highly regarded McKinsey consulting modus operandi is useful when you are looking for a consultant more accustomed to working with smaller businesses your own size.

Like consultants of all sizes, McKinsey doesn't "take over" or "dictate to" companies but rather "works with" them. On the McKinsey Working Methods and Principles page, to which you can jump from the home page, the firm notes that its "efforts are collaborative, leveraging the clients' knowledge of their businesses with our knowledge of problem solving, the industry and relevant new technologies. Whenever appropriate, we ask that client personnel be made available to work with us as full- or part-time members of the study team."

PERSONAL PROFILING FOR CAREER PLANNING

http://www.win.net/~comp1/
This company, which has the same name as its Web site, isn't a management consulting firm so much as a human skills development company that offers customized training literature for your enterprise. If your company is a start-up or a young, growing concern, PPCP's kits, tapes, surveys, and booklets will probably be useful.

The site has full electronic mail capability for ordering this information. Some of the published material, which can be reached from the home page (see Figure 8-6) includes a Coping and Stress Profile, a Discovering Diversity Profile, and a Time Mastery Profile.

To get an idea of the information included, take a look at the Time Mastery Profile. This 36-page booklet and 12-page self-scoring questionnaire "measures responses related to time-related behaviors in 12 categories by having the user indicate strong or mild agreement or disagreement to various statements. The user then adds up the scores for instant results. Using the scores, the user determines an overall time mastery level and prepares a graph that shows which behavior categories offer the most opportunity for improvement. The workbook then helps the user prepare an action plan for personal improvement."

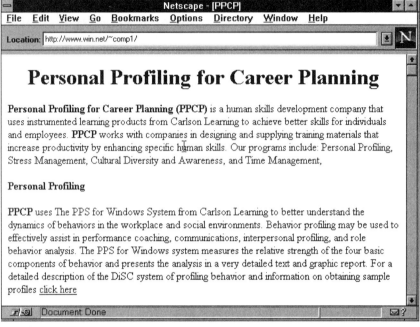

Figure 8-6: *Personal Profiling for Career Planning's home page.*

SMI CONSULTING SERVICES

http://www.xmission.com/

For a young, growing business, some of the critical skill sets are sales, marketing, organizational development, and planning proposals for potential clients, partners, or investors. SMI Consulting Services provides expertise in all of these areas and has an especially thorough Web site that describes how the company works with clients to hone skills in each of these subjects. It's a must for consultancy sites and a welcome feature here: an e-mail link for direct contact (see Figure 8-7).

Under presentation planning, the site offers strategy development lessons that consist of an analysis of "key issues, your features, benefits and proofs, and your competitors' strengths and weaknesses, [as well as] determining or reviewing your specific key messages and making sure they are consistent with your overall strategy." With the help of practice sessions, attention is also paid to presentation delivery.

Proposal planning covers such regimes as strategy review and consultation, analysis of key issues, and writing and editing text. Sales and marketing competency studies cover fields such as assessment of managers, designing of customer surveys, and quantitative measurements of sales effectiveness.

Professional competency studies, according to SMI, "develop a framework that explains what competencies are required for a person to perform a job at a prescribed level of proficiency. It is considerably more difficult to develop an adequate and accurate understanding of the competencies required for high performance in professional positions than in simple production line positions."

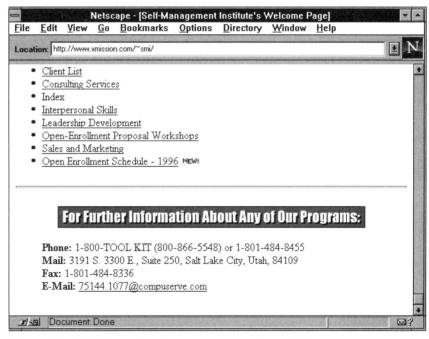

Figure 8-7: *SMI Consulting Services's electronic mail link.*

The Small Business Advisor Newsletter

http://www.smartbiz.com/

This site is a billboard for a monthly newsletter that features advisory articles on topics such as finance and cash flow, human resources, insurance, law, management, marketing, operations, technology, and tax matters. The site provides a list of articles contained in recent issues. Many of these, such as "Advertising Within a Small Budget," "Home Office Tax Deduction," and "Women as Entrepreneurs" seem perfectly tailored for the small-business person.

The Small Business Advisor Newsletter would be a more rewarding experience if at least some of the content were put online. You can, though, get two free issues (see Figure 8-8) by clicking on the site's mail-to link (at http://www.smartbiz.com/sbs/n7a.htm).

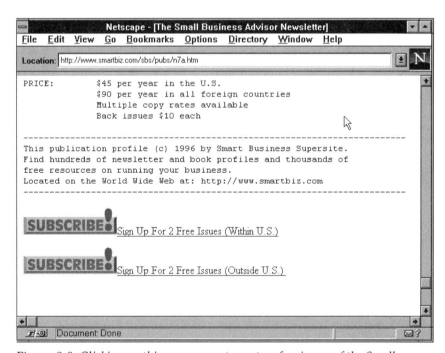

Figure 8-8: *Clicking on this page can get you two free issues of the Small Business Advisor Newsletter.*

WILSON INTERNET SERVICES

http://www.wilsonweb.com/

Dr. Ralph Wilson, president of Rocklin, California–based Wilson Internet Services (see Figure 8-9), takes a unique approach by imparting well-considered consultant advice in one particular area—whether entrepreneurial companies should have Web sites and what such a site can do for your business. Because you're already reading this book and are coursing through this chapter, I'm assuming that you not only are intrigued by the content that you can find on the Web but are perhaps even somewhat interested in establishing a presence there. Wilson gives some of the most carefully thought-out pros and cons that I've seen about whether a business needs a Web site, or at least an Internet presence.

On the pro side, you can do niche marketing through Usenet newsgroups and listservs, expand your customer base from a locality or region to the world, and communicate inexpensively and directly with your customers. On the con side, Wilson warns that a high-traffic Web site is very expensive to develop, and that something of value, such as information, should be added or people won't visit. Essentially, he's saying that even if you build it, they may not come. He adds that electronic commerce should not be taken haphazardly and requires a product such as the Netscape Secure Commerce Server "to offer buyers a sense of security."

Practicing his "value added" advice, Wilson also has a fascinating treatise about why people visit some Web sites and not others. He breaks it down to four prime motivations: information, entertainment, economic, and social. He goes into considerable detail about each of these motivations and then gives some closing strategic tips. Written in a studied but friendly tone, the advice is remarkably free of ill-conceived salesmanship. If only the message on every Web site were so similarly and elegantly crafted.

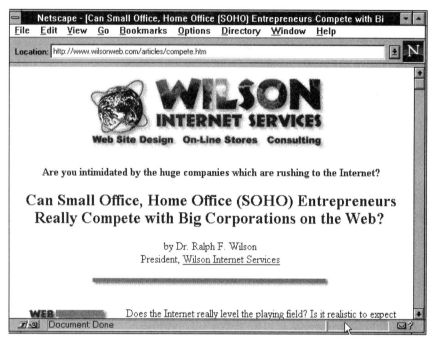

Figure 8-9: *Does your new business need a Web site? Wilson Internet Services may have the answer.*

MOVING ON

The consultants have spent a day at your brand-new company. In the middle of the night, your warehouse suffers a robbery, or an accumulating snowpack causes your roof to collapse. Or, your husband or wife calls and says your car has been in a fender bender and needs a $1,500 body job. Not only do you need to plan intelligently for personal or business success, you must cover yourself against commercial or personal calamity. In the next chapter, "Insurance," you'll find some Web sites that will help you do just that.

Insurance

Beatle John Lennon once said that "life is what happens when you've made other plans." That truth is exactly why you should carry comprehensive insurance on the material things that you hold dear, from your home to your health. Few responsible people would differ with that imperative, but many would say that shopping for insurance can be a hassle. Here's where the Web can help—with basic as well as detailed information. This chapter covers the insurance sites worthy of your attention.

WHAT MAKES A GOOD INSURANCE WEB SITE?

The Web includes many hundreds of sites that deal with insurance. The best of them satisfy at least a few of several following attributes:

■ They concentrate on direct insurance topics, not overly emphasizing the investment or financial-planning aspects of insurance.

- They avoid jargon. Where jargon is necessary, they explain the terms clearly.

- They have a search function that enables you to find agents in your city and state.

- They have an electronic mail-to you can e-mail for more information.

- They have a list of tips that may lower your premium; for example, which cars are safest or how to safeguard your valuables against theft.

- The tone is helpful instead of the vapid "Hi, here we are and we'd love to help you with your insurance needs" language that you see on some sites.

INSURANCE SITES

You can find many types of specialty insurance around, but I've decided to concentrate on the basic forms. This section covers insurance companies that tout their life, health, casualty, or auto insurance plans on their Web sites.

AccuQuote

http://www.accuquote.com/

Numerous Web sites take the information you input and then search for the lowest insurance rates. Dozens of other sites offer impressively comprehensive fonts of general insurance tutorials. AccuQuote, a service provided by Northbrook, Illinois–based independent insurance brokerage Byron Udell and Associates, is one of the few insurance Web sites that does both.

A good bit of self-promotion on the home page belies the fact some truly useful information resides here. Start with an online calculator page titled "How much life insurance do you need?" The calculator crunches the "breadwinner's" annual income, age, percentage of income required by dependents, number of years that you want your beneficiaries to receive this income, the average future annual inflation rate, and the annual interest rate that your beneficiaries would earn on the insurance death benefit proceeds. It then gives you an amount for recommended coverage.

If you haven't quit smoking by now, the AccuQuote Examples of Savings page will give you a good financial incentive to do so. From a database of 270 searched insurance products, a 45-year-old nonsmoking male in excellent health seeking 10-year level-term insurance would pay an average $1,200 yearly premium (see Figure 9-1). In contrast, a cigarette-smoking male of the same age would be assessed $2,625 yearly, and a cigar-smoking male would find himself $3,530 poorer on average (see Figure 9-2).

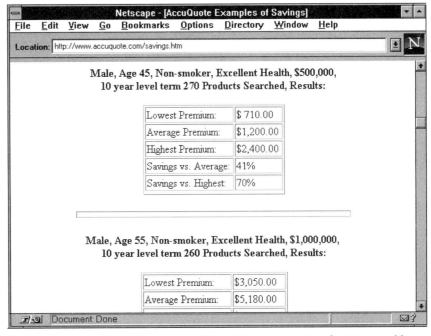

Figure 9-1: *AccuQuote has averaged typical insurance rates for 45-year-old nonsmoking males.*

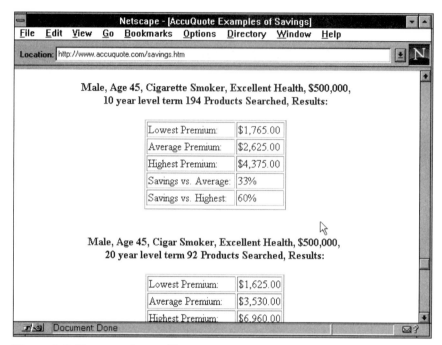

Figure 9-2: *If you smoke, you'll pay.*

Like any complicated topic, insurance has its own jargon. That's why AccuQuote's Basic Types of Life Insurance page is valuable. On this page, you can learn the difference between term life, whole life, universal life, and survivorship life. In case you're interested (and you should be), term is a cashless value insurance that covers only the risk of death for that year. It's "pay as you go." True to the name, whole life insurance is for the lifetime of the policy holder. An investment vehicle as well as a type of insurance policy, universal life has built-in flexibility due to changes in interest rates. According to AccuQuote, survivorship, or "2nd-to-die" life insurance, will "allow the insurance company to delay the payment of the death benefit until the second spouse's death, thereby creating the dollars needed to pay the taxes exactly when they are needed. This coverage is widely used because it is generally much less expensive than individual coverage on either spouse."

Finally, AccuQuote has an excellent Frequently Asked Questions (FAQ) section that explains important issues such as what financial criteria to use to select a safe insurance company, and the difference between standard and preferred rates.

AID ASSOCIATION FOR LUTHERANS

http://www.aal.org/

In North America, a large number of insurance policies are written by affinity organizations. These can be entities whose membership is drawn heavily from specific occupations, trade associations, labor unions, demographic constituencies, or religious groups. A good example of the latter is the Aid Association for Lutherans, a self-explanatory entity that for more than 90 years has been helping Lutherans obtain business, disability, health, and life insurance at rates generally below the national average.

On the AAFL site, each of these services is discussed concisely, usually in one or two pages. The Appleton, Wisconsin–based organization has struck a happy medium between overly superficial topical brevity and lengthy discourse. Webmasters on other sites should take a cue from AAFL's ability to impart and organize the basics in a diligent but to-the-point fashion. Each of the pages has links for Information Requests (see Figure 9-3) as well as a mail-to for general electronic correspondence.

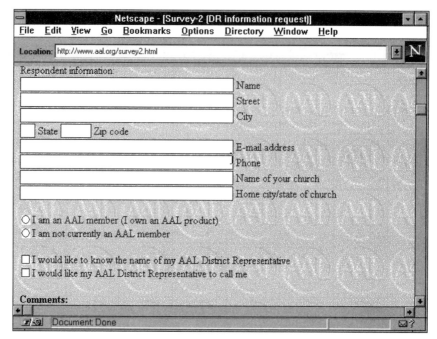

Figure 9-3: *Aid Association for Lutherans allows you to request more information.*

The Business Insurance page has explanations of buy-sell insurance, nonqualified deferred compensation, key person insurance, and "split-dollar arrangements." Key person insurance compensates for the loss of a key employee, as well as for time spent looking for a replacement for that person. Split-dollar arrangements are compensation plans that insure individuals that you, the business owner, deem important to the success of your enterprise.

The Disability Income Insurance section is primarily devoted to a description of the Aid Association's three major Earning Power Protection plans. Earning Power Protection Plus provides a disability income during both your earning and retirement years. Earning Power Protection for Homemakers is touted as one of the few policies in the country that provides insurance protection for homemakers who become disabled. Earning Power Protection for Business Expenses pays a monthly benefit to cover your business expenses should you become totally disabled due to an illness or an accident.

Another page, "Life Insurance Products for Lutherans and Their Families," summarizes the nature of benefits afforded to holders of AAFL's adjustable, whole-term, and modified survivor life insurance policies.

CNA INSURANCE COMPANIES

http://www.cna.com/
Chicago-based CNA's Web site is a little thin on substantive information but gets pluses for simplicity and navigability. The home page (see Figure 9-4) has four icons, including springboards for Financial Info (about the company), Products, Feedback, and Other Links.

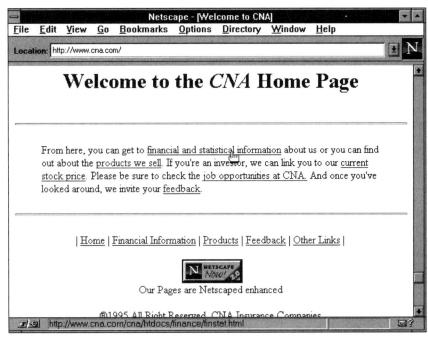

Figure 9-4: *The CNA Insurance Companies home page.*

Unless you are buying CNA's stock or need to be reassured about an insurer's financial strength before you buy a policy, the Products page is probably the only one you'll care about. On this page, you get attachments to more information about individual and property insurance, as well as commercial insurance and risk management services.

The Individual Life Insurance page is threadbare, with a basic listing of offerings. To its credit, it offers a mail-to available for comments and questions.

CNA's site has less information than most, but that isn't a sin if you are going to the Web to search for an insurance policy and you don't want to read through a treatise first.

GARY & TONY'S ONLINE INSURANCE

http://www.studentinsurance.com/
You might be wondering why a company whose name sounds more like that of a pizza parlor than an insurance firm is included. I have two good reasons. First, this was one of the first Web sites put up by an independent insurance agency—a vital segment of the business that is too often overlooked. Second, these guys have figured out a niche that is chronically underserved by the conglomerates.

That niche is Student Select, a private health insurance plan for the collegian. To get to this page, click on the icon from the site's home page. As Gary and Tony say, "Did you know that many of the college health insurance policies offer 'bare bone' benefits that may not cover you in case of a large, unexpected expense?"

Circumstances that could lead to noncoverage are explained. The page then provides thorough details of Student Select. Events and procedures such as surgery, anesthesia services, emergency care, X-rays, and ground or air ambulance service are covered, but pregnancy, mental illness, and substance abuse usually aren't.

After reading this, you can fill out an online application (see Figure 9-5) and specify your desired deductible and payment mode.

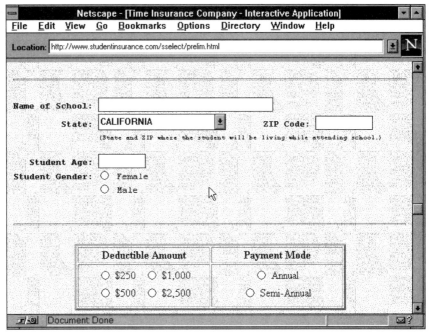

Figure 9-5: *An online health insurance application on Gary and Tony's Online Insurance site.*

ILLINOIS DEPARTMENT OF INSURANCE

http://www.state.il.us/ins
Every state government in the United States has an insurance department. The folks there have a thankless task. Staffers are likely to be reviled by a citizenry that thinks the agency is literally or figuratively in the pocket of powerful insurance giants, whereas the companies and their agents are routinely frustrated that the department never seems to grant them the kind of rate hikes that the companies believe they need to remain profitable.

Figure 9-6: *Illinois' Department of Insurance site has information about shopping for car policies.*

As the saying goes, if you are attacked from opposite sides, you are probably somewhere in the middle. This means that, in more cases than they are given credit for, insurance regulators serve the civic good.

Another way to serve the "civic good" is to offer a Web site with a whole bunch of very helpful information on it. That's exactly what the Illinois Department of Insurance has done (see Figure 9-6).

Most of the beneficial information on the site is about auto insurance. That's why you should click right from the home page to the Shopping for Auto Insurance section. Odds are that you don't live in Illinois, but as in many other Web sites provided by local governments, most of the data is general enough to apply anywhere. You'll find a series of one- to three-paragraph sections on topics entitled Required Auto Insurance Coverages, Auto

Insurance Pricing, Auto Insurance Rating Factors, Ways To Lower Your Auto Insurance Costs, Getting Auto Insurance Price Quotes, and a basic tutorial called If You Can't Find Auto Insurance.

For example, here's a tip from them: "Take the highest deductible you can afford—insurance is meant to protect you from the financial consequences of major losses. . . . By raising your deductibles, you may be able to significantly lower the price for physical damage coverage, but you will pay more out of pocket each time you have a claim."

INDEPENDENT INSURANCE AGENTS OF AMERICA

http://www.iiaa.iix.com/

This group is the trade guild for those agents whose ads you might see on the back cover of your local Yellow Pages. Such agents usually do business with multiple companies, and are thus in the position to shop for the best rates for you. The IIAA has taken this institutional wisdom and put together an interesting Web site, which it calls The Consumer's Independent Guide to Small Business Insurance. It notes that, although large companies are likely to have in-house risk managers, small enterprises can't afford one. The group makes the case well. "While juggling all the jobs that need to get done to make your firm a smooth-running and profitable operation, you may already be asking yourself, 'Who has time to think about insurance?' You do! Keeping risks and losses to a minimum is a cornerstone of business success, especially for small businesses."

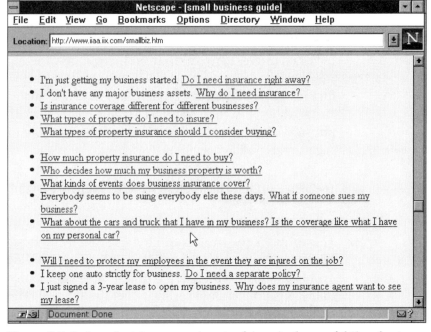

Figure 9-7: *Independent Insurance Agents of America has useful tips about business insurance for entrepreneurs.*

Core site content is a list of more than 20 questions that are perfect for soul-searching by entrepreneurs (see Figure 9-7). Some of the queries include: "I'm just getting my business started. Do I need insurance right away?"; "What types of property do I need to insure?"; and "Is insurance coverage different for different businesses?" It is, and IIAA has a rational reason why. "Because businesses vary, it is impossible to have standard policy to cover all contingencies," the site notes. "Also, some businesses, regardless of their size, do not fit the profile of a standard business-owners policy. For example, restaurants, wholesalers and garages have special liability needs that are not met in the standard businessowners policy. Your insurance agent can advise you of the best policy (or policies) to protect you and your business."

In the summer of 1996, IIAA added an Agency Directory Search capability to their site. You can search for an affiliated IIAA agent by state, county, area code, or three-digit ZIP code prefix (someone in the San Diego area with a ZIP code of 92109 would type **921** in the search field).

ITT HARTFORD GROUP, INC.

http://www.itthartford.com/
On its home page, ITT Hartford tells us that it has insured both Abraham Lincoln and Robert E. Lee. This company provides the general insurance for Yale University, and bonded the construction for Hoover Dam.

This Web site is topically organized a bit differently than some other major insurance companies' Internet sites. As a percentage of overall content, financial planning for retirement probably receives the greater share, less going to comprehensive details on insurance for insurance's sake.

You start out with a choice of five home page icons: Our Story (a corporate summary), Investment Profile, Products & Services, For Our Customers, and News & Issues. Products & Services is the most useful service by far.

For a look, click on the Products & Services icon, which takes you through a series of submenus that lead to text of increasing detail. The main Products & Services page asks whether you are interested in products for yourself or your family, your business, or your franchise, group, organization, or association.

If you select "yourself or your family," you see six choices, starting with Safeguarding Your Auto and Home. From this page, you can go to a pull-down menu (see Figure 9-8). This menu allows you to view auto and home insurance policies specific to every U.S. state and Canadian province.

Figure 9-8: *ITT Hartford Group's site offers a menu of insurance information for all states and Canadian provinces.*

I selected Georgia, and here's what I learned: If I insure more than one car on an ITT Hartford policy, I can save up to 25 percent on my premiums. When I turn 50, my payment might decline by 10 percent. Antitheft equipment will result in 15 percent savings. Finally, if I give up a life as a solitary scribe and take the vows, I'll get a 5 percent "married person" discount.

Late in 1995, my brother-in-law barely survived a horrible automobile accident. Thankfully, he's fine, but his recuperative period hammered home the necessity of knowing how to shop for a safe car. This topic has its own page on the ITT Hartford site. By implication, discounts offered for specific safety features speak of ITT Hartford's—and the insurance industry's—faith in these devices. For example, antilock brakes can save you up to 5 percent on collision coverage. That's nothing compared with 60 percent economies on vehicles with automatic seat belts and airbags in both front outboard seat positions, or 50 percent for airbags in both seat positions but with nonautomatic seatbelts.

After investing in all this safety equipment (not to mention the car itself), you won't want it stolen. ITT Hartford offers premium discounts as high as 25 percent for some types of antitheft equipment.

ITT Hartford also has an Auto Insurance Analysis page. If the truth be told, the page is less of an analysis than it is a glossary. Even so, you'll find useful information here even if you aren't an ITT Hartford auto policyholder. You can also use this information to compare the fine print in your own policy with theirs.

Uninsured and Underinsured Motorists Coverage, we're told, "pays bodily injury claims if you or your passengers are injured by a negligent uninsured motorist, hit-and-run vehicle or a negligent driver without adequate insurance." Replacement Cost Coverage stipulates that "if you have a total loss on a new vehicle within the first 180 days or 7,500 miles (whichever occurs first) after your purchase, ITT Hartford will replace your car, or pay you the amount needed to replace your car."

If, after touring the site, you want to contact an ITT Hartford agent, a 50-state, 12-province pull-down menu of ITT agents listed by city (see Figure 9-9) is available. Some of the agents even have e-mail listings. You can access these cyberwise agents directly from the ITT Hartford site.

Figure 9-9: *ITT Hartford also lets you search for agents by state, province, and city.*

PRUDENTIAL INSURANCE COMPANY OF AMERICA

http://www.prudential.com/

I'm rather surprised, even a little disappointed, that one of the largest insurance companies in the world doesn't have a more comprehensive Web site. At least five of the seven home page icons—Retirement Planning, Home Ownership, Education Funding, Estate Planning, and Investing (see Figure 9-10)—are more about insurance-related investment instruments than they are about policies. Still, the Prudential site definitely has some redeeming virtues.

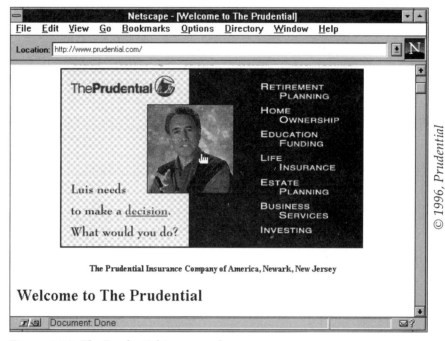

Figure 9-10: *The Prudential Insurance home page.*

The Life Insurance section is comprehensive in its tutorials, especially its detailed differentiation between the various types of life insurance and its discussion of how much life insurance you need. Prudential recommends that you have life insurance equal to five to seven times your annual take-home pay.

A good deal of confusion exists in the marketplace about the parameters of a given policy's "cash surrender value." Most insurance Web sites seem to ignore this topic, so Prudential's description is welcome news. The options included with most policies that can be cash surrendered are to (1) receive the cash value as a lump sum, (2) stop paying the premiums but have the policy continued in force at a progressively lesser amount of coverage, or (3) borrow the cash value from the policy. Repayment of such loans should be done with interest, or else the interest will be deducted from the death benefits paid to your beneficiaries.

Prudential makes a key point clearly: "Keep in mind that with all types of permanent policies, the cash value of a policy is different from the policy face amount." The site goes on to advise that "cash value is the amount available when you surrender a policy before its maturity or your death. The face amount is the money that will be paid at death or at policy maturity."

The Life Insurance page also has a mail-to for more information, and a mini search engine that lets you locate the nearest Prudential representative.

STATE FARM INSURANCE

http://www.statefarm.com/

The information on the State Farm site is divided into four parts: auto, homeowners, life, and health. By going to the Products page from the home page, you can also search for agents near you or send an e-mail for more information. State Farm uses a somewhat unique philosophy to present the data in each section. The four main section's home pages have menus that read like a Frequently Asked Questions list.

On the Auto Insurance page, for example, the eight questions lead off with basic queries such as "What is auto insurance?" and "Why buy auto insurance?". Questions progress in detail until such queries as "Which cars offer the best crash protection?" and "Which bumpers perform best, worst?" are tackled. The questions are hyperlinked to pages that give the answers in detail. Unlike some insurance Web sites, the explanations are not couched in jargon and do not take several pages of text. On the State Farm site, the explanations are in large type and are to the point.

The answer to the question, "Which cars cost the most, least to insure?" gives a brief description of State Farm's standard approach, which, for "safer models," is generally to charge 10 to 45 percent less than the standard collision and comprehensive insurance premiums for an average rate structure within the given price range. Rather than just regurgitate policy for policy's sake, however, State Farm has taken the time to list most models and most makes that fall under either the "cost most to insure" or "cost least to insure" qualifier. As you might guess, the bigger, sturdier cars bring a lower premium.

The questions-and-answers model found in the Auto Insurance Section is altered slightly in the State Farm Homeowner's Insurance page. Content is more tips-oriented, with links such as Inventory Tips, Photo Tips, and a list of Theft-Prone Items.

In case you're interested, some items that State Farm deems "high-risk for theft are antiques, clock radios, computers, guns, jewelry, lawn mowers, stereos, televisions and typewriters." I probably shouldn't make light of this, but in this computer age, what possible value would a typewriter have to a thief—or anyone else, for that matter?

State Farm's Life Insurance page is nothing special. You'll find the standard explanations of term, whole, universal, and 2nd-to-die insurance. Several other insurance company Web sites describe these options a good bit more thoroughly.

The Health Insurance Products section is similarly brief, but does the job with pointed explanations of the difference between disability income policies, hospital-surgical policies, and hospital income plans.

TRAVELERS INSURANCE ONLINE

http://www2.pcy.mci.net/bin/travelers/autohome.cgi
The Travelers site (see Figure 9-11) has just about everything a good insurance-related Web site needs. Travelers Personal Lines Insurance starts out with "personal" messages from real account representatives who work in different insurance areas such as personal lines, auto, and homeowners.

Figure 9-11: *Travelers Insurance home page.*

Each of these representatives introduces him or herself to the Webbed world with a "hi" greeting and a photo. The salutories aren't badly written and do include elementary but mission-critical information about why you need the given type of insurance that the representative sells. Plus, each of the representatives has both an e-mail link (see Figure 9-12) and a gateway to "mini-courses" pages with more detail.

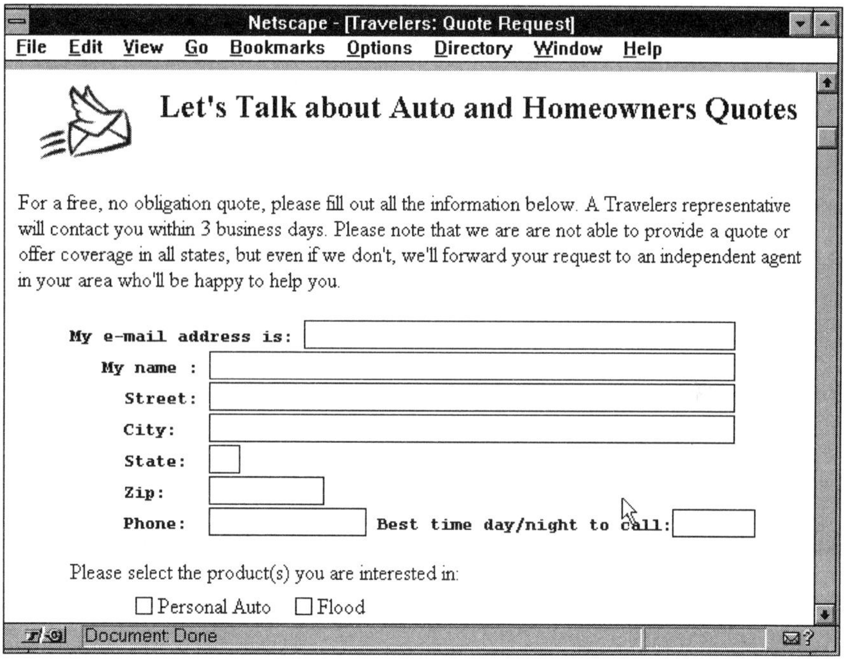

Figure 9-12: *Using the Travelers e-mail link to contact an agent.*

The Personal Lines product rep's page has several mini-courses on insurance subjects such as auto, home, flood, excess liability, boat, yacht, and even antique toys collection insurance. It also has a link to the American Home Business Association Web site.

For homeowners insurance, the subject tree is vast, touching on such topics as dwelling, loss of use, covered perils, deductibles, personal liability, and property damage. *Covered perils* include damage from windstorms, impact from downed aircraft, riots, glass breakage, or volcanic eruption. Some policies also stipulate damage from frozen pipes and snow-crushed roofs, but few if any homeowners policies protect against earthquakes, flood damage, and mud slides.

The Travelers site also has an Estimator and a personal property worksheet. The Estimator gauges the square footage of your rooms, and then projects whether you have enough insurance in force to replace or rebuild your home. The Personal Property Inventory page (see Figure 9-13) links to a worksheet that assists you in taking a room-by-room survey of your valuables.

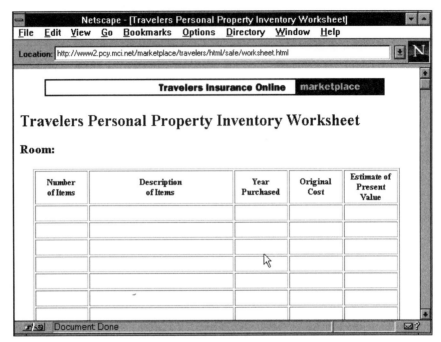

Figure 9-13: *The Travelers Web site offers a handy Personal Property Inventory worksheet.*

MOVING ON

After you've generated insurance policies for yourself and your material possessions, you're ready to look at ways to increase your assets. Investment-related Web sites of quality are the main subject of the next chapter.

Investments

Investment-related material lends itself well to Web sites. The Web is an effective platform for storing statistical data and research reports. The instantaneous nature of the Web permits information such as stock prices and company news to be quickly updated. In-site search utilities allow companies to migrate much of this data to their Web sites, where users can search for the data by keyword. And the Web's graphical capabilities are natural doorways for companies to build sites with illustrated icons that can guide both new and befuddled users to a rich variety of offerings.

Finally, a third reason that investment sites are among the Web's most popular parking places exists: secured electronic commerce. Investment—whether in stocks, bonds, commodities, CDs, or whatever—has to do with the exchange or transfer of money. Products such as the Netscape Secured Commerce Server are bringing a sense of critical immediacy to these types of sites that the mere presence of static information couldn't. This chapter starts by covering what makes a good investment site, and then highlights some of the better sites on the Web.

WHAT MAKES A GOOD INVESTMENT SITE?

I define a good investment site in three ways:

- *Information*   The site must have a strong informational element. Whether you are talking about the historical price of a stock, projected earnings ratio, maturity of a bond, or rate on a CD, the site must impart a lot of mission-critical information, and with luck this information will be stored in an easy-to-obtain fashion.

- *Transaction*   Whenever possible, the site should provide you with a secure transactional ability to buy, sell, or check on your portfolio online. In the same vein, it should provide verification so that you can get a written authentication for your transaction.

- *Navigation*   The home page should clearly state the subject hierarchy. If you are going to a site to find information that relates to your financial health or prosperity, you won't want to spend hours searching for the sections of data you need.

INVESTMENT SITES

Although this list is by no means complete, it does cover some of the sites that satisfy the requirements of a good investment site.

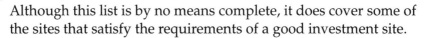

BANXQUOTE

http://www.banx.com/
In the Monday Business section of your newspaper, you can likely find a list of banks in your area and the rates they pay on savings certificates of deposit and money market accounts. Some newspapers even run a list of the top national payers. Frequently, this information is gathered from research organized by BanxQuote, the most complete storehouse of bank rate information on the Web.

BanxQuote's four most useful information fields are its two High Yield Savings CDs Nationwide pages (see Figure 10-1) and its two High Yield Bank Money Markets Nationwide pages. Within each classification, you can find pages for small and large minimum deposits.

All four pages generally list the top 10 rates being paid that week. The page is laid out in table form, naming the institution, city, state, minimum deposit, interest rate, method of compounding (usually daily, quarterly, or monthly) and Annual Percentage Yield, or APY. Under the name of each financial institution, you'll find a link—not to a Web site but to a page that lists the postal address and phone number of the bank or savings and loan.

Netscape - [BanxQuote – 1 Year Savings CDs]

File Edit View Go Bookmarks Options Directory Window Help

Location: http://www.banx.com/banx/savhi/bq-1y-cd.htm

1 Year Savings CDs

Institution	City	ST	Min. Deposit	Rate	Cmp.	APY
M&T Bank NA	Oakfield	NY	$2,500	5.69	D=	5.85
Treasury Bank	Washington	DC	$5,000	5.72	Q=	5.84
First Deposit	Tilton	NH	$10,000	5.68	D=	5.84
Southern Pacific T&L	Los Angeles	CA	$5,000	5.65	D=	5.81
Sterling Bank	Newport Beach	CA	$500	5.61	M=	5.76
Key Bank USA	Albany	NY	$5,000	5.60	D=	5.76
Safra National	New York	NY	$10,000	5.60	D=	5.76
Berkeley Federal	Ft. Lee	NJ	$20,000	5.60	M=	5.75
NBD	Detroit	MI	$500	5.60	M=	5.75
MBNA America	Newark	DE	$5,000	5.55	D=	5.71

Document Done

Figure 10-1: *BanxQuote's Chart of Leading Bank CDs is updated weekly.*

Cannon Trading Co., Inc.

http://www.cannontrading.com/

I've listed this site not because you can do a lot of things on it but because it typifies a philosophy that a Web site is best used for a description of services. For those investment sites that adhere to such modest goals, Cannon sketches out its agenda more clearly than most.

"We specialize in trading U.S. treasury bonds, stock indices, foreign currencies, precious metals, crude oil, agricultures and other products on the futures and commodities exchanges," Cannon notes. Services offered include order execution, instant access to your account information, a weekly fax-delivered newsletter, and a 24-hour trading desk for large traders. The site provides an electronic mail link allowing you to ask questions or get more information (see Figure 10-2).

Hallowed forever in the halls of mercantilism, the words of John D. Rockefeller are used to entice contact: "If you want to become really wealthy, you must have your money work for you. The amount you get paid for your personal efforts is relatively small compared with the amount you can earn by having your money make money."

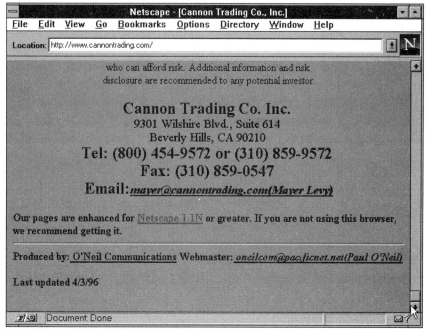

Figure 10-2: *Cannon Trading's site provides an e-mail link for more info.*

CHARLES SCHWAB

http://www.schwab.com/
Schwab the man and Schwab the company are alive, kicking, vibrant entities. So is the Schwab Online Web site. The six home page toolbar icons (see Figure 10-3) include What's New, Investor Tools, Software Center, Accounts & Services, Mutual Funds, and an electronic mail Contacting Schwab alternative. (Mutual funds are covered in more detail in Chapter 12.)

Figure 10-3: *The Charles Schwab Web site home page.*

A good place to start is the Brokerage Accounts page. To get here, click on the Brokerage Accounts link on the Accounts & Services page. The main Highlights page in this area is conveniently laid out, with an e-mail link for (snail-mail) brochures provided not just at the end of the document but under a one-sentence description of each service. This works because it doesn't tie up your browser pulling down page after page of stuff that you don't care about as you wait until the mail-to finally appears.

You can find out more about Investment Service Offerings, including Account Transfer, a No-Fee StockBuilder Plan, a MoneyLink Transfer Service, an Automatic Investment Plan, and an Assurance Trading Service. You may be more familiar with some of these services than others. For the uninitiated, here's a brief review:

■ Account Transfer lets you authorize the periodic transfer of funds from another financial institution, such as a bank, to your Schwab account.

■ The No-Fee Stockbuilder Plan (see Figure 10-4) automatically reinvests dividends from more than 4,000 stocks into additional shares of that stock. Schwab provides this service at no extra charge.

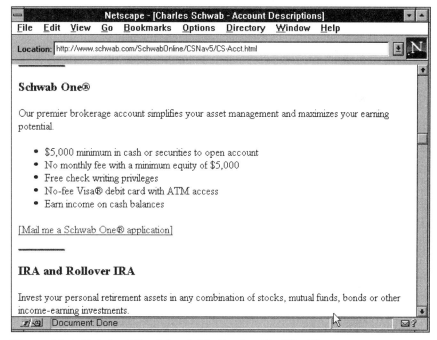

Figure 10-4: *Details of the Schwab No-Fee Stockbuilder Plan.*

■ The MoneyLink Transfer Service is probably the one with which you are best acquainted. This arrangement permits the transfer of cash from your paycheck to your Schwab account on a prescheduled basis.

■ Automatic Investment is a free service that lets you make regular, systematic investment in any of several Schwab funds. Schwab has provided an electronic mail order enrollment form here (see Figure 10-5).

■ The Assurance Trading Service is a good bit more complicated. Contrary to its usual habit of brevity, Schwab devotes several screenloads to the intricate whats, whys, and wherefores of this feature. Schwab does this because the topic really is complicated. In simple terms, Schwab says that "we've developed technology that links multiple computer systems to systematically scan for a better price than the current national bid/ask price (market price) on NASDAQ stocks. In a matter of seconds, you'll know if your NASDAQ stock trade can be executed at a better price than the current national best bid/ask price." As defined by the Schwab site, "NASDAQ is a network of market making phones linked by a central computer and phones. The NASDAQ (National Association of Securities Dealers Automated Quote system) allows multiple market makers for the same stock to compete for customers' trades. The best bid and offer of all competing NASDAQ market makers is known as the 'national best bid and ask.'" (Note that NASDAQ has its own Web site, described later in this chapter.)

In addition, the Schwab Brokerage Accounts page has mail-back applications for several plans, including the basic Schwab Account, Schwab One, and the Keogh Account. The basic Schwab Account requires $1,000 minimum in cash or securities to let you buy and sell stock and other "income-earning instruments." Schwab One lets you do all these things, but asks for $5,000 up front for additional services such as free check-writing privileges, income on cash balances, and a no-fee Visa debit card. Keogh Accounts let self-employed persons or owners of small businesses set up a self-administered profit-sharing or pension plan.

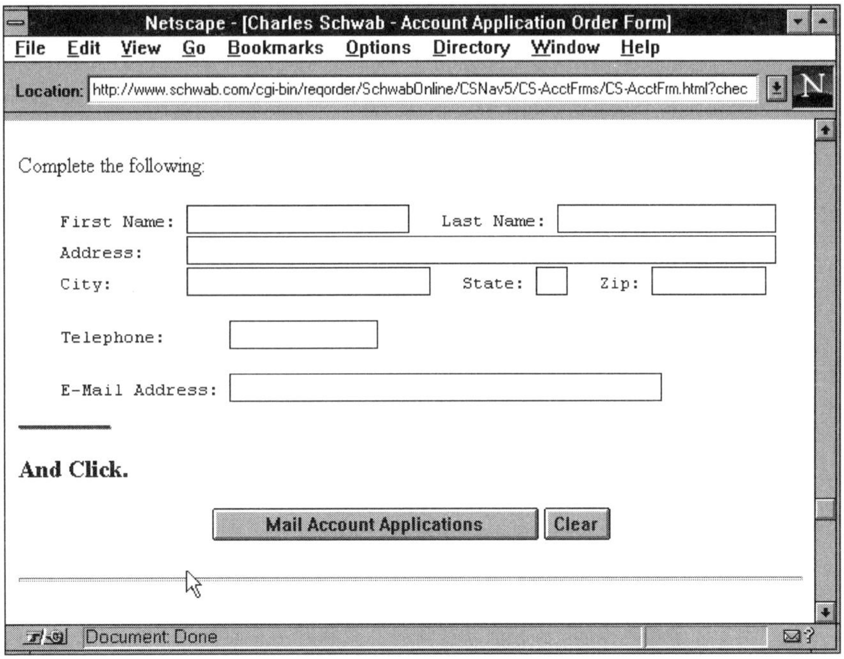

Figure 10-5: *Using the Schwab e-mail link to request information.*

COMPUTEL SECURITIES

http://www.rapidtrade.com/
A division of San Francisco–based Thomas F. White & Co., Inc., CompuTel Securities provides its enrolled members with a store-house of Internet-available information that is unsurpassed anywhere else. You'll be able to do a limited amount of actual trading online, and you can set up your account via a handy icon. After you receive your password, the world of data is yours.

The real virtue of this site is not online trading but rather all the data that is available. Here are some highlights:

■ Real-time interactive stock price quotes, not the 15-minute-delayed quotes that most of the proprietary online services give you.

■ A report on insider trading. When senior officials at pub-licly held companies pursue this option, that's often a clue that something, such as a merger or key expansion, may be up.

- Economic forecasts. The growth in the Gross National Product, employment trend lines, and inflation rates affect not only the economy in general but also specific industries and key companies.

- An e-mail portfolio. Sent at the end of each business day to your electronic mailbox, this portfolio tells you how your stocks did that day. A summary of the day's investment-related news is also included.

- Updates on the latest Internet financial resources. With the growth of the Web, some services doubtless will debut after this book reaches the shelves. This option gives you updates on such new sites.

JACK CARL FUTURES

http://www.jackcarl.com/

The Jack Carl site, a division of Index Futures Group, Inc., offers three trading account plans as well as what is arguably the most complete assemblage of free-to-all information about commodities available anywhere on the Web. You can't execute online trades or even sign up for an account directly from the Web site, but you can e-mail for more data. I include this site anyway because so much information is available for free here.

Accessible from the Online Futures Services page, Jack Carl provides six basic classifications of commodity-related data, including the following:

- *Price Quotes*   Access to a list of daily prices on more than 30 types of commodities.

- *Commodity Calendar*   A monthly updated schedule (see Figure 10-6) of government reports, conferences, and contract expirations. As any commodities trader will tell you, these prescheduled watershed events often foretell sea change shifts in commodity prices and trading patterns. Someone may say something at a conference that will cause gold, silver, or pork belly prices to go way down or way up. Newly released employment statistics in a major nation may have a similar impact.

Figure 10-6: *Jack Carl Futures's Commodity Calendar can foretell events of interest to commodities markets.*

■ *Contract Specs*   Defined by Jack Carl as "contract information for markets in all principal U.S. (commodity) exchanges."

■ *Marketline*   Includes transcripts from Jack Carl's MarketLine Daily Market Update Service. Information in this uncommonly thorough newsletter is organized by commodity classification, including Financials (Treasury bonds, the dollar, gold, copper); Agricultural (cattle, wheat, pork, soybeans); and, as news becomes relevant, other trading areas such as sugar, coffee, cotton, and natural gas.

■ *Margin Requirements*   Requirements for the U.S. commodities market list.

■ *Web Links*   Jack Carl has provided links to most commodity exchanges and to a variety of other futures-related Internet sites.

Jack Carl's three account plans—the Discount Account, the One-On-One Broker Assistance Plan, and the Managed Account Plan—are also briefly described here.

E*TRADE

http://www.etrade.com/

E*Trade was one of the first services on the Web to provide reasonably turnkey electronic trading. When you visit this home page, you are offered a link to "Open An E*Trade Account." You may do this one of two ways: by downloading the application or by writing for an opening package.

You can download an application and transfer form, print it, sign it, and then send it in with the information you need, including a minimum deposit of $1,000 for cash accounts or $2,000 for margin accounts. Or, if you are really anxious to get started, you can wire the money to an address specified on the Web site.

After you are approved, you receive a password, which you can then use to access your account. A secured stock order form (see Figure 10-7) asks for your account number, type of transaction (buy, sell, sell short, buy to cover), number of shares that you wish to trade, stock symbol for the company involved, and then your trading password.

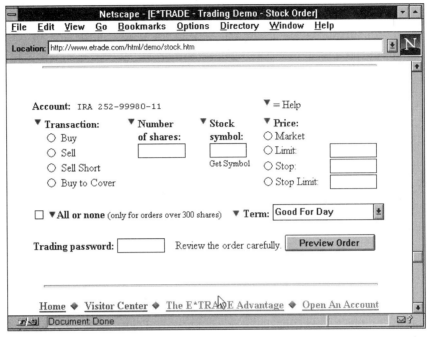

Figure 10-7: *E*Trade's online transaction form.*

After your trade, you receive an electronically mailed confirmation of your transaction. Your trading profile is then updated. You can access this profile from the Portfolio Summary page.

FIDELITY INVESTMENTS ONLINE INVESTOR CENTER

http://www.fid-inv.com/

As one of the world's truly major players in financial markets, Fidelity could be expected to have one of the most exhaustive Web sites anywhere. If that is what you're guessing, you couldn't be more right. The challenge in discussing a Web site such as Fidelity's is not deciding what to describe but rather what to leave out. After all, this site has nearly 1,000 pages! Luckily, you can use the search engine to sift through this information.

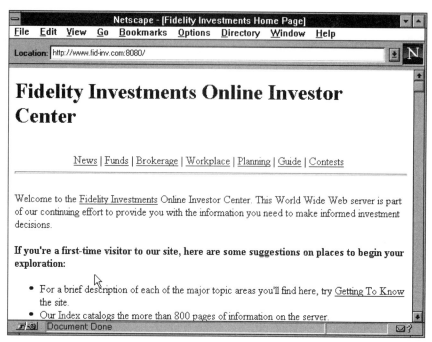

Figure 10-8: *The Fidelity Investments home page.*

To start, try the Online Investor Center home page (see Figure 10-8). From this page, select Brokerage. You see a list of Brokerage Services, with links to more than 15 subject areas, 5 of which are the FidelityPlus Brokerage Account, Fidelity's Ultra Service Account, the Spartan Brokerage Account, The BondDesk, and Standard & Poor's Stock Screens.

The FidelityPlus Brokerage Account section has a rather lengthy but comprehensible description field. This field is about 20 percent salespersonship and about 80 percent hard data. Here you can find out some basic information: you need a minimum of $5,000 to open such an account; your cash balances pay interest under a variety of alternatives; you can write up to 20 checks a year on your account; and, best yet, all your account activity is summarized in one handy monthly statement. With your account, you can trade in a host of investment alternatives, including stocks, bonds, options, U.S. government securities, investment trusts, zero-coupon bonds, CDs, and precious metals.

Fidelity's Ultra Service Account (see Figure 10-9) lets you do all those things, but befitting its steeper cost of admission, it offers some extra amenities, including unlimited free check writing with 100 free checks to start and a Visa Gold debit card that you can use at almost any automatic teller machine in the world. At press time for this book, Ultra enrollees could execute trades through one of three ways: standard; Brokerage Trading and Account Services via Fidelity's On-line Xpress Software; or Fidelity's TouchTone Trader. The latter option gives you a 10 percent discount on trading fees.

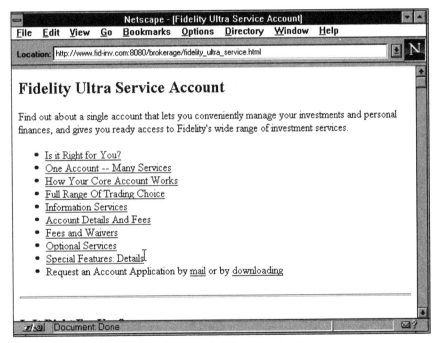

Figure 10-9: *A description of Fidelity's Ultra Service Account.*

Fidelity's Spartan Brokerage Account is aimed at high-volume investors who like to initiate their own trades rather than pay for a broker's input. That, incidentally, is how large brokerages pay for all those highly salaried stock analysts who intimately track a dozen or more corporations and put out detailed reports after every quarterly earnings period on every company they track.

Spartan structures its commissions as low as 2 cents a share, compared to an industry standard of as high as 5 cents a share. If you trade thousands of shares a day, that can add up quickly. Trading via your PC will save you an additional 10 percent in commissions. You'll pay up front for the price break; you have to pay $20,000 in cash or marketable securities. But for this you get a no-fee account with 40 trades a year, a substantial break on margin balance borrowing rates, and account protection as high as $50 million.

All Fidelity customers get a copy of Standard & Poor's *Investor's Monthly Newsletter*, which includes market outlook and analysis. In addition, as a Fidelity client, you can also order customized reports from S&P for a fee 40 percent lower than the over-the-transom subscription price.

Basic information about Fidelity's bond services also is available on the Web site's BondDesk Page.

Fidelity's Investment Center is available not only on the Web but also on several of the online services. These are described in Chapter 19, "The Online Services."

MARKETEDGE

http://www.marketedge.com/join.htm
Who said, "Information is power"? A wise person, indeed, and someone who would have derived a good bit of enlightenment from MarketEdge. This site is provided by Thomson Financial Services, a division of international newspaper and trade magazine publishing giant The Thomson Corporation. You register by printing out a form provided on the Web site (see Figure 10-10). Go there, and use the Print button on your Navigator toolbar. After the form is printed out and you fill in your credit card number and other necessary data, fax it back to Thomson at the number indicated on the site.

```
┌──────────────────────────────────────────────────────────────┐
│ ─            Netscape - [Join MarketEdge]              ▼ ▲     │
│ File  Edit  View  Go  Bookmarks  Options  Directory  Window  Help │
│ ┌──────────────────────────────────────────────────────────┐  │
│ Location: http://lucero.cda.com/tf_white/whitjoin.htm      │▮│ N │
│ └──────────────────────────────────────────────────────────┘  │
│                                                          ▲     │
│  Registration Form                                             │
│                                                                │
│  Last Name: ┌──────────┐  First ┌────────┐  MI ┌───┐          │
│  Preferred I.D.:    ┌────────────┐                            │
│    (case sensitive, one string without spaces)                │
│  Preferred password: ┌────────────┐                           │
│    (case sensitive, one string without spaces)                │
│  Password (again):  ┌────────────┐                            │
│  Telephone:      ┌───────────────────┐                        │
│  WDS e-mail address: ┌───────────────┐                        │
│  Street address 1: ┌─────────────────┐                        │
│  Street address 2: ┌─────────────────┐                        │
│  City: ┌─────────────┐  State: standard abbrev. (2 initials) ┌───┐ │
│  Zip: ┌──────────┐                                            │
│  Country: ◯ USA  ◯ Other ┌─────────────────────┐            ▼ │
│ ┌──────────────────────────────────────────────────────────┐ │
│ 🔳 Document Done                                        ✉? │
└──────────────────────────────────────────────────────────────┘
```

Figure 10-10: *MarketEdge's fax-back registration form is available online.*

After you receive approval and a password, you can log on and get unlimited stock quotes as well as a monthly diet of company and industry reports and historic price charts data. If you exceed more than 25 company reports a month, you are charged $2 for each subsequent request. That's a good bit less than some of the information services assess for each inquiry (such as InvesText and Standard & Poor's, which are found on the commercially available online networks).

MARKET GUIDE

http://www.marketguide.com/
Market Guide (Figure 10-11) differs from MarketEdge in that much of its content is prepared in-house. Market Guide boasts of having "one of the most timely and comprehensive financial databases in the marketplace," and the boast is quite right. Taken with a broad view, Market Guide's offerings fit into three classifications: information, professional investor services, and individual investor services.

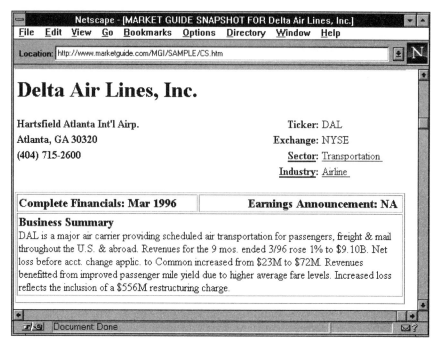

Figure 10-11: *Market Guide's Snapshot stock reports are a popular feature on its site.*

In the information area, Market Guide offers earnings and stock performance data for more than 8,000 publicly traded U.S. and foreign companies. Not only are historical financial performance numbers specified within this site, but this information is visually charted to allow for more detailed analysis and insight than would be possible with a mere table of numbers.

Because investors like to compare the performance of their stocks with competitors in similar or symbiant industries, Market Guide has also organized its repository of reports into 102 industry groups, which are further divided into 12 sector groups. Market Guide's Professional Investor Services, which are further described via hyperlinks, include a 10-page Broker/Trader Report on individual companies. These have all kinds of juicy stuff, including information on product lines, insider ownership, income and cash flow statements, and details on institutional ownership.

This company is also in the software business. Its Market Guide for Windows lets you tap into the database to let you "perform cross-company comparisons, flexible screening and customized reporting utilizing over 500 data items, plus the ability to create and save your own screening variables." Ratio-comparison, earnings estimate, and custom screening services constitute other amenities within Market Guide's list of Professional Investor Services.

Individual Investor Services are only slightly more limited. Membership gives you access to company profiles and one-page snapshots of thousands of corporations (see Figure 10-11). You can also order Market Guide's Select OTC Stock Edition, a quarterly publication that analyzes, in each issue, more than 800 "promising" companies that are traded not on a busy stock exchange floor, but over the counter.

NASDAQ

http://www.nasdaq.com/
When you visit rich-content, obviously well-thought-out offerings such as the new NASDAQ site, you can tell that a lot of preparation went into the presentation. NASDAQ was the last of the exchanges to come to the Web. The birth of this site in the spring of 1996 means that the three leading stock exchanges in North America each now has a Web site. In addition to their firewalls, each of these sites has some redeeming attributes as well as some potential areas for enhancement. But in richness of content, NASDAQ's site is by far the best, earning a detailed look here.

Although the NASDAQ site is the newest, it is the most complete. Clearly worded home page toolbars (see Figure 10-12) are important to any Web site, and NASDAQ has one of the best. A quick look at the bar reveals just how content rich this site is. Index Activity, Company Look-Up, and Glossary are the most useful icons for your purposes.

Index Activity gives you the day's combined prices for a number of exchange-member subcategories, including Banks, Telecommunications, Finance, Insurance, and Computer. Clicking any of these icons takes you to a rundown of the latest prices for every member of the given group. Click on the company symbol for the current stock price. If the firm has a Web site, and most NASDAQ members do, you should find a link as well.

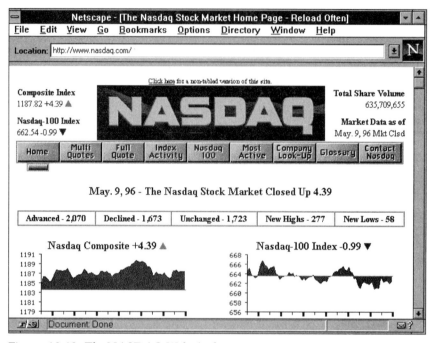

Figure 10-12: *The NASDAQ Web site home page.*

On the NASDAQ Company Look-Up Page, you can search by company name or stock symbol for the price of any NASDAQ stock, subject to a 15-minute delay. Although the other two exchanges post closing prices about two hours after the end of the trading day, NASDAQ is the only one to post quotes in anything resembling real time.

The real gem on NASDAQ, though, is the quite complete NASDAQ Glossary. "Short selling," as an example, is defined as "the selling of a security that the seller does not own, or any sale that is completed by the delivery of a security borrowed by the seller. Short sellers assume the risk that they will be able to buy the stock at a more favorable price than the price at which they sold short."

NATIONAL DISCOUNT BROKERS

http://www.pawws.secapl.com/
Commonly known as PAWWS, the National Discount Brokers site was one of the first places on the Web to integrate stock information, online trading capability, and investment services. To its credit, PAWWS has a simple home page (see Figure 10-13), free of the rich but slow-to-transfer promotional icons that clog up other investment sites. The site uses only three basic commands: Log-In/Enter System, New User Registration, and an e-mail link called Contact PAWWS.

Figure 10-13: *The PAWWS home page.*

When you access the system, the first screen you see is What Products and Services are Available? The screen shows a description of trading choices, products, and types of accounts.

Investors can trade with PAWWS in three ways. You can use NDB Online, which was targeted for availability by the summer of 1996 and is touted as a secured service that enables real-time trading. Users who register online are also able to take advantage of PowerBroker, PAWWS's touch-tone quotes and trading system, the second method for trading. And finally, for those unfamiliar with or untrusting of cyberspace commerce, you can trade directly with a PAWWS broker.

Note that PAWWS provides various products and services. For regulatory reasons, NDB Online accepts only stock orders, whereas only stock and option transactions can be handled via touch-tone service.

If you want to access PAWWS's complete list of services, the site's Products page notes that trading in stocks, options, mutual funds, and corporate, treasury, and municipal bonds is offered via its representatives, as well as unit investment trusts, zero coupon bonds, and certificates of deposit.

Four main types of accounts are available to PAWWS members. These are cash accounts (which require a minimum of $5,000 in cash of securities for online trading), margin accounts, an options account, or an Individual Retirement Account.

To this, add a comprehensive selection of Other Services. You can read a description of some of these through a handy link from the Other Services page. These include the ProCash Plus asset management account, the Rapid Research Line for analyst reports, an electronic notification of your executed trades, and EasyPay, which, via a phone call to PAWWS's toll-free number, permits you to transfer money from your checking account to your PAWWS account 24 hours a day, 7 days a week.

OLDE Discount Corporation

http://www.oldediscount.com/
OLDE provides many of the stock services carried on other sites.
Where it particularly shines is in two other areas: its Bonds and
Design Your Own Investment Portfolio pages.

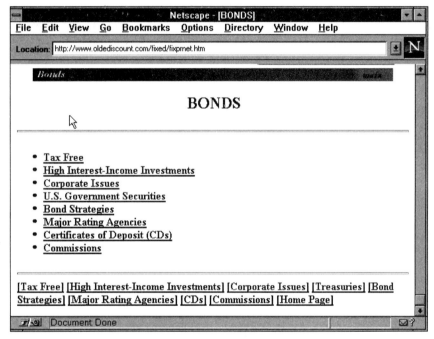

Figure 10-14: *OLDE Discount Brokerage's site is rich with information about bonds.*

You can reach the Bonds section (see Figure 10-14) from the
home page. When you're there, you can jump to links on eight
bond-related topics, including Tax Free, High Interest-Income
Investments, and U.S. Government Securities. You'll find a to-the-
point explanation of tax-free municipal bonds that is instructive to
almost any interested investor. OLDE tells us that "Municipal
bonds are issued by states, cities, counties, school districts, housing authorities, hospitals, and other municipal agencies. Proceeds
from these securities are used to fund local governments, build
roads, bridges, sewer systems, schools, and other projects."

Municipal tax-frees work the following way: "As an example, assume an investor in a 40 percent tax bracket purchases a tax-exempt bond with a yield of 6%, the equivalent taxable yield would be 10%. In this example," OLDE notes, "the investor would need to earn a return of 10% from a taxable security to have the same after-tax return as from the 6% municipal tax-free bond."

The Design Your Investment Portfolio page is laid out in a grid that factors in your current age, income, cost of living, the year you hope to retire, and the percentage of your current income on which you want to be able to retire. One key principle that many people overlook: the younger you are, the more risks you can (but not necessarily should) take because, at least in theory, you'll have more years at peak earning power to recoup the losses from any bad investments.

Because the page doesn't go out of its way to shill for stock as a way to plan for retirement, OLDE's site gets several merit points in my book. If, after perusing the content, you want to locate an office near you, you can use a pull-down menu to search.

Zacks Investment Research

http://aw.zacks.com/
This would be a good place to detail substantial differences between passively delivered stockrooms of market data and actively delivered caches of same. That is, some information is stored and waiting for you to retrieve it, whereas other online libraries are equipped with triggers that will notify you (usually by e-mail) when a noteworthy, preidentified development occurs. The latter is the approach taken by Zacks Investment Research's Analyst Watch on the Internet (see Figure 10-15). The service comprises three basic elements: Portfolio Alerts, Company Reports, and Custom Equity Screening.

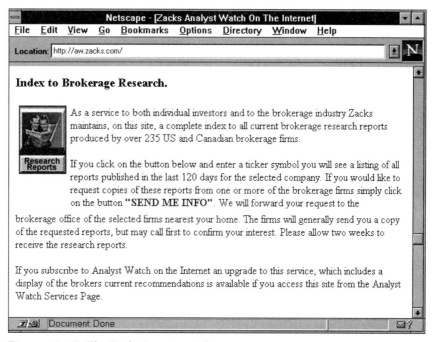

Figure 10-15: *The Zacks Investment home page.*

Portfolio alerts flash you an e-mail whenever certain key events portend an effect on stocks in your portfolio. These alerts can be triggered by occurrences such as changes in analysts' earnings-per-share estimates or buy/hold/sell recommendations, declarations of dividends, major new product announcements, or key news events within the industry in which the given company does business.

Zacks Company Reports generally are eight-page documents that summarize analyst papers and company financial performance. Currently, Zacks provides this information on more than 5,000 companies.

Custom Equity Screening allows you to constantly monitor a set of companies using any combination of 81 investment criteria that you specify, such as herky-jerky price movements and newly released earnings-per-share reports that vary significantly from analyst estimates.

The home page also includes a link that you can use to apply for an account.

MOVING ON

Keeping your financial house in order isn't only a matter of knowing where to invest your money. Driving an automobile appropriate for your station in life, upgrading your resume for an executive search firm, buying ergonomically correct furniture for your office—all these necessities of your business life will be discussed in the next chapter.

Malls, Jobs & Services

Close your eyes for a moment and visualize your favorite shopping mall. This is a place where you can buy a suit, dine on fine French cuisine, visit a travel agency or a bank, purchase furniture for your office, or browse through a bookstore. These are all activities that you can do online as well. Unlike in the "real world," where turning left into a mall parking lot will take you four light changes before it's your turn, you won't have to deal with rude drivers and traffic jams.

Online malls are just like real malls. Not in all, but in most cases, they are sites where a collection of merchandisers or service-providers hang their storefronts. Sometimes, these malls act as marquees that will direct you to the individual Web sites involved.

In other instances, online malls handle the full range of content and transactional matters for their virtual tenants—making the given mall a cross between a super-Web site and a directory. The site acts as a hosting service. If the name of the host site is in the first part of the URL (such as the hypothetical http:// cyberbytemall.com/hemitrav/), you can tell that each store's activities are conducted through the host server. Some even have keyword-search capabilities. You could, for example, type the word **travel** in a search box to find and link to travel services.

Just as in a real mall, you can buy almost anything online. A comprehensive list of items for sale is best left for another place and time. This chapter focuses on sites that let you buy items with a direct connection to your investments, career, your finances, or your daily life as a businessperson.

A+ ON-LINE RESUMES

http://ol-resume.com/
Each week, thousands of new personal home pages arrive on the Web. Whenever I have occasion to read one, I am reminded of a prediction I heard while covering an interactive marketing conference back in 1994: "The Web will be the vanity press of the 1990s."

A good percentage of these home pages contain career resumes. Some are written by recent college graduates, others by downsized middle managers trying to market long-honed skills in this new electronic ether. These pages often come with a scanned-in photo of the subject. Although I have empathy, I am sorry to tell you that your efforts will probably be wasted if you do the same. No matter how many cool multimedia applications you've built in, prospective employers are not going to find your site unless they actually look for it. Even if they did have the notion, that would mean trolling through several branches of an index such as Yahoo, or typing several keyword terms on a search engine such as Lycos. Even then, you have no guarantee that they'll find your home page.

As an alternative, consider companies such as A+ On-line Resumes. This is a service that converts your resume from hard copy to the Web's HTML (HyperText Markup Language) and posts it on a directory that very much resembles an online positions-wanted mall.

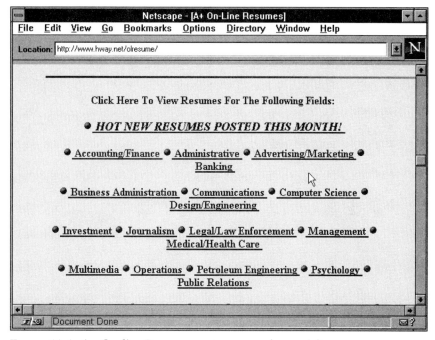

Figure 11-1: *A+ On-line Resumes posts resumes by specialty.*

You prepare your own resume and send it to Hilton Head Island, South Carolina–based A+ either by electronic mail or on diskette via snail mail. Upon receipt, A+ reviews your resume and then converts it to HTML (the underlined copy you see on Web sites). Working with you, A+ makes a recommendation as to on which of its career field Web pages your newly coded resume should be placed.

A+ has nearly 25 job fields (see Figure 11-1), including Administrative/Banking, Journalism (bless their hearts), Management, Petroleum Engineering, Quality Control, and Sales. The site also maintains more than a dozen state-specific pages, where most of the resumes coming from the given state are housed.

Here's how it works: A company looking for a Texas-based petroleum engineer would go to the A+ site. The searcher would click the appropriate icon and up would come several resumes, including yours. You've already put a phone number and an e-mail link in your resume.

Through links from other sites as well as periodic advertising and public relations campaigns, A+ actively promotes the sites to the hiring community. The prices they charge are exceedingly modest—less than the cost of two stamps a day.

ALL-INTERNET SHOPPING DIRECTORY

http://www.webcom.com/~tbrown
This super-site is like a hybrid between an online shopping mall and an Internet directory. Its index is divided into more than 30 topics, including Sporting Goods, Computer Hardware, Garden & Lawn, Pets, and Furnishings & Decor. From the home page, you click on any topic and are transported to a subindex. These subindexes are a great value-added attraction. They start out with detailed but concise descriptions of sites that have paid a surcharge to All-Internet for the privilege of being listed in the Sponsor section of each index. These are followed by alphabetized, linked listings of hundreds of sites per section (see Figure 11-2). Each of these sites is introduced by a one-sentence review.

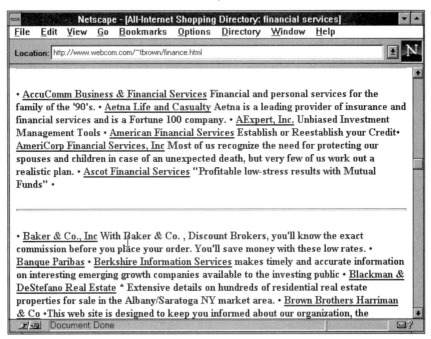

Figure 11-2: *All-Internet Shopping Directory has an alphabetized directory and short reviews of hundreds of online malls.*

Looking at All-Internet's Financial Services directory, you'll see that the first page shows a list of sponsored companies. Because the copy was provided by the sponsor, the information is always upbeat. The following excerpt is therefore included not so much for the comments on the linked site as for an illustration of the kind of information that All-Internet's sponsored site descriptions contain:

> Martin Capital Management is a Registered Investment Advisor providing professional financial and investment advisory services to individuals and businesses as well as corporations and trusts. Publicly available information is provided on "No Load Stocks." A list of all current "No Load Stock" companies, Form ADV and brochure are all available by request.

Martin Capital is linked. If you want, you can go there directly. The rest of the directory lists relevant sites and provides access to each. This part of the mall is loaded with descriptions of and links to insurance companies, brokers, banks, financial planners, and tax advisers. Here are two examples:

- "Debt Counselors of America is an IRS approved NON-PROFIT organization that assists families and individuals with debt, credit, money, and financial questions, problems or difficulties."

- "Dreyfus. By exploring the Dreyfus Online Information Center you can get a clearer sense of the direction to take to match your investment dollars to your investment objectives."

AMERICA II JOB SEEKER SERVICES & CAREER CORNER

http://www.americaiidirect.com/
This site offers the same resume conversion and posting services (see Figure 11-3) as A+ On-line. This site also lets you edit and delete your current listing, a useful feature. Say that your resume

has been up for a month. Today, you've received an award from your professional association and you would like to add it to your resume. Going to the home page shows you a menu of the site's services, including the resume-editing capability. If you've just landed a position or simply want to take yourself out of the market, you'll find a resume-deleting capability as well.

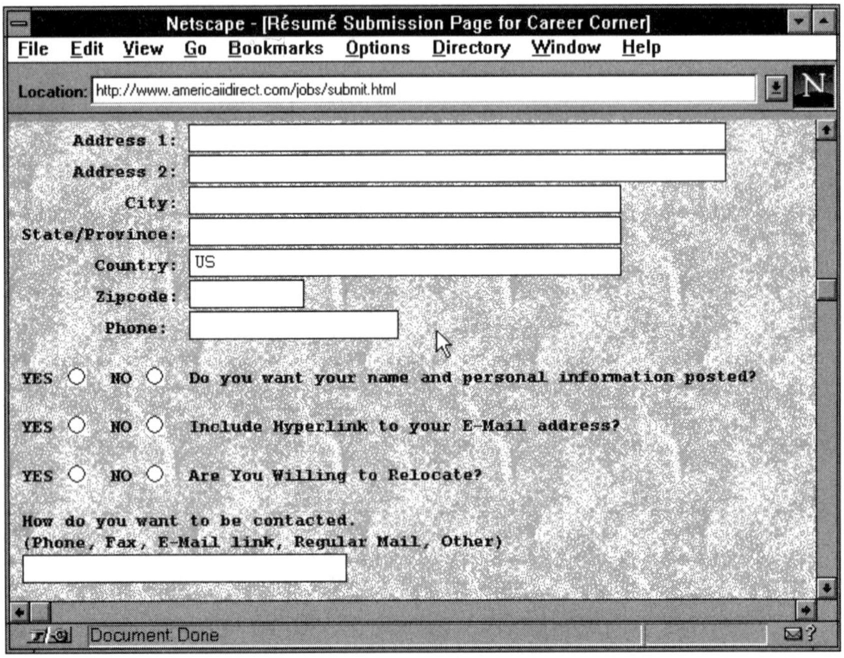

Figure 11-3: *Career Corner's resume submission form.*

A job search organized by topic is the other useful part of this site. More than 20 fields are indexed, including Accounting/Bookkeeping, Aviation, Computer Programming, Hotel/Motel, Retail, and an umbrella category for Sales/Marketing/Advertising.

The site also has a "secure transactions" capability that will mask part of your identity if you don't want it to be public. If you don't want your current employer to know that you are looking elsewhere, you should consider this approach. If prospective employers like what they read on your partially concealed resume, a procedure is in place for them to get enough information to contact you directly. Once they initiate contact, they'll know who you are.

AUTO CONNECTION

http://www.automart.com/
You may be wondering what a review of an automobile wholesaler's Web site is doing in a book on investing and personal finance. Actually, the idea behind it isn't much of a stretch. These kinds of sites often contain leasing information. Taking on a lease or loan for a car is one of the more important financial transactions that you'll make.

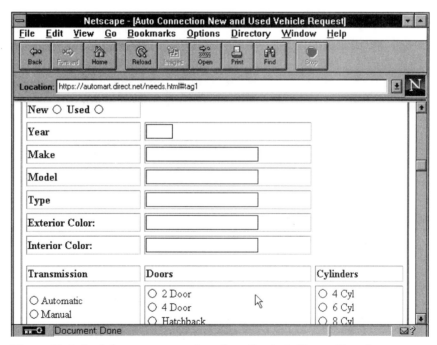

Figure 11-4: *Look for a new or used car from the Auto Connection site.*

Auto Connection's site (see Figure 11-4) is one of the better-organized virtual dealerships on the Web. The home page routes you to a Monthly Specials page containing a menu of specific makes and models. This is your clicking-off point.

My next car may well be a Toyota, so that's where I went on this site. The Toyota section of the Specials page lists three current-year models: a Toyota Corolla, Toyota Camry 4 Cylinder, and Toyota Camry 6 Cylinder. The information for each of these models, in turn, contains three information fields. Select For Price shows the approximate current cost of the vehicle model. The self-explanatory EMAIL FOR DETAILS lets you send a note to Auto Connection with a request for information about the leasing or financing plans available for the particular model. You don't actually purchase the car from Auto Connection; its role is more of a financing source clearinghouse.

On the site, you fill out a Vehicle Request Form e-mail application specifying a particular make and model and send it directly to Auto Connection. If you specify this service, Auto Connection will match your specific request to a list of cars available at dealerships in your area. Auto Connection's database currently has more than 20,000 such listings. You would then purchase the car from your local dealer, going through your bank or other standard automobile loan financing sources to enable the transaction.

The third choice, Click to View Vehicle, is by far the most fun. Web-accessed virtual-reality rides in cars for sale are in the near future, but photos of car models do just fine for the present.

CAREERMOSAIC'S JOB LINKS

http://www.careermosaic.com/
Online resume posting is just one of several features of CareerMosaic (see Figure 11-5). CareerMosaic also maintains the Usenet jobs.offered newsgroup, and mirrors the group's content on the Web site. You can search or scroll through the individual postings until you locate a listing in which you're interested.

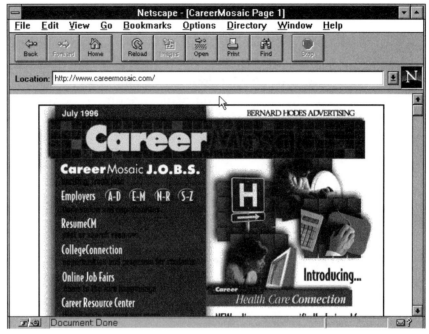

Figure 11-5: *CareerMosaic is a one-stop shop for job information.*

The CareerMosaic J.O.B.S. database lists thousands of jobs offered by several hundred employers. You can also use the Career Resource Center, which contains tips on job hunting and resume writing, as well as links to professional associations. Such entities are vital resources for you to cultivate if you're looking to enter or move up in your chosen profession.

Networking is important. It just might be that an association hotlinked through CareerMosaic has a chapter in your city. Why not go to the association's Web site, call or e-mail member services, and then inquire about a chapter in your metro area? Maybe a meeting is scheduled for tomorrow night! Show up and offer to participate in a given activity.

The other neat feature of CareerMosaic is the direct links to the home or Employment Opportunities pages on hundreds of company Web sites. Going to such sites can be a valuable experience. Personnel directors everywhere agree that applicants who don't know much about the corporation to which they are applying for employment have a major strike against them. You already know that, but who has the time to (a) send out resumes to hundreds of companies who may or may not be hiring, and (b) spend all of Saturday in the library doing research on the companies that you hope will consider your application. By going to CareerMosaic, you can see which companies are hiring. Because they will all have Web sites that contain a good bit of data about company products and financials, you'll be able to scout out your job chances and familiarize yourself with the firm at the same time.

COVEY LEADERSHIP CENTER

http://www3.pcy.mci.net/marketplace/covey
This is one of several dozen Web sites hosted by marketplaceMCI, the Internet mall provided by the international telecommunications giant. Many of the sites they carry offer clothing and gifts, and aren't relevant to our purposes. Covey Leadership (see Figure 11-6) is one of the exceptions.

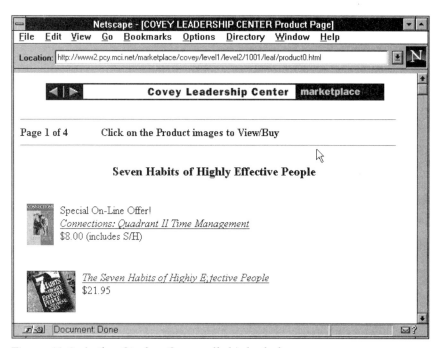

Figure 11-6: *Author Stephen Covey sells his books here.*

The Center is named for best-selling author Stephen Covey, author of *The Seven Habits of Highly Effective People*. The approach here is that of an electronic storefront for ordering several of Covey's works. From the site, you can get the *Seven Habits* book, the *Seven Habits Audio Learning System*, the *Living the Seven Habits Audio Learning System*, and another, lesser-known Covey work, *Connections: Quadrant II Time Management*.

I generally have a problem with sites that simply tell you how important a given book or tape is to your future without giving you at least a taste of what the work for sale covers. Should an exception to this blanket indictment be made for the Covey Leadership Center site? Well, perhaps. Covey's signature work is so well known that it probably wouldn't have been the best business strategy to give away too much info on the site itself. The book presumably sells itself.

Covey and colleagues also do a series of workshops called First Things First, Principle-Centered Leadership, and Seven Habits. Times, dates, and cities of future workshops are available on the site, as is a registration form.

 ## DEALERONLINE

http://www.dealeronline.com/
Because I've mentioned Auto Connection, I also want to specify the feature-rich DealerOnline site. The state-of-the-art tech site features RealAudio broadcasts of automotive news, with frame-rich pages full of cool Java applets. The Webmasters maintain that the high-horsepower site is best viewed with Netscape Navigator 2.01 or above.

Actually, Auto Connection and DealerOnline perform different but complementary functions. Auto Connection's strength is in its financial information, whereas DealerOnline works because of its technology: its ability to search for automobiles by make and model (see Figure 11-7), and its links.

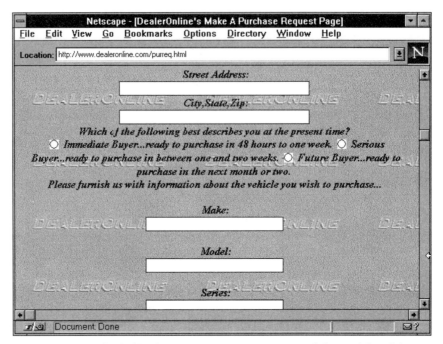

Figure 11-7: *DealerOnline lets you target your auto search by model and degree of urgency.*

The links here make DealerOnline a worthy pit stop. You'll find a click-connection to *Car & Driver* magazine's Daily Insider news report. The most valuable hookups, though, are the direct routes to car dealerships' Web pages and to dozens of automobile model Web sites.

The car dealer links are more utilitarian. They can update Web pages far more quickly than a newspaper ad. Plus, an automobile dealer that hooks up with an enterprise such as DealerOnline can broaden its market area from north suburban Chicago or Littleton, Colorado, to encompass much of the wired world.

INDUSTRY.NET

http://www.industry.net/

Broadening horizons is a key feature of Industry.Net. I find pinning a single label on this offering hard to do. Essentially, though, it is a clearinghouse of information and product-marketing opportunities for its member network of more than 200,000 subscribers in 36,000 corporations. Industry.Net is best described as a business-to-business shopping mall.

You have to register to get the best stuff. Fortunately, you'll derive much of value from it after the gates are opened. As Industry.Net notes on its Corporate Backgrounder page, membership brings buying members "free access to extensive product information, timely news, professional organizations and interactive discussions."

You have to join to get most of this information from the Web site. Sounds like it might be worth it. For the entrepreneur running a small company, the most valuable services are Business Centers, an Online Marketplace (see Figure 11-8), and Industry.Net Target Marketing Services.

Figure 11-8: *Industry.Net takes "net"working to a new level.*

The Business Centers, the company says, "provide participating companies customizable marketing programs to present their products and services to the rapidly expanding base of buying members." Several well-known companies maintain Business Centers on Industry.Net, including Hewlett-Packard, Sun Microsystems, Reliance Electric, Allen-Bradley, Honeywell, GE, and Westinghouse.

You'll find somewhat self-congratulatory but useful information about the Online Marketplace on the Backgrounder page. Industry.Net calls this page the hub of its system. The page provides a wealth of information, including catalogs, corporate profiles, product/service descriptions, drawings and specifications, photos, brochures, demo software, application notes, daily news, career opportunities, and online discussion areas for business and industry professionals to communicate with their peers worldwide, Industry.Net says. "The Online Marketplace incorporates audio and will soon support full-motion video as well. Since information is developed in electronic form, it can be updated instantly, eliminating the cost or delays associated with revising and redistributing printed material."

Jointly based in Cambridge, Massachusetts, and Pittsburgh, Pennsylvania, privately held Industry.Net's Target Marketing Services perform selected buyer-purchaser matching. Available both online and in hard-copy form, *Industry.Net* magazine is published in 16 regional editions. Web site building and management for several professional trade associations is yet another resourceful undertaking in Industry.Net's ever-growing suite of services.

MARKETPLACE 2000 BUSINESS OPPORTUNITIES

http://www.market2000.com/
Assorted services and products are for sale here, but the locus of this site is the Business Opportunities section (Figure 11-9). MarketPlace's mall status comes as a result of its links to the home pages of companies active in business ventures.

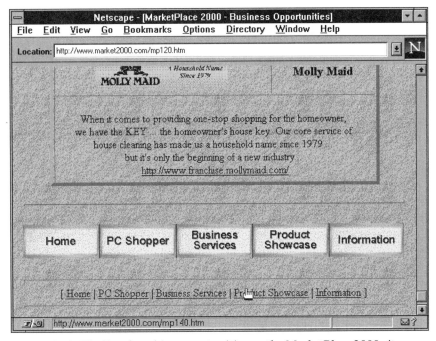

Figure 11-9: *Finding franchise opportunities on the MarketPlace 2000 site.*

If you're looking at buying a franchise, MarketPlace 2000 is worth your time. You'll find links to the home pages of franchisers in fast food, photo shop, specialty drapery cleaning, and home-cleaning industries. New links are added frequently.

After you've arrived at franchiser Web sites, you are liable to see a good bit of self-strutting promotion, but also some good introductory data as to which geographic markets might be available at the time, as well as rate structures for franchise royalty fees. Some sites linked through MarketPlace have their own mail-to capabilities, enabling you to request a preliminary franchise application or send an e-mail directly to the director of franchising.

More is available at MarketPlace 2000 as well. I haven't found any sites that perform prequalifying services, but some of the miscellaneous linked sites look interesting. For instance, one site is maintained by a company that makes loans to beneficiaries of probates or trusts. From time to time, assorted "business for sale" links are also on the Business Opportunity page. When I visited not long ago, the Web site of someone selling an automobile racing track was just a click away.

OFFICEMAX

http://www.officemax.com/

More than 30 million Americans maintain some sort of office in their home. Demographers even have a name for this fast-growing business sector: SOHO (small office, home office). No matter what type of activity you are doing in your office, an office needs a chair, and you can buy it on the Web.

OfficeMax, a large chain of office supply superstores, maintains a site where you'll be able to find what you need. Through its home page icons (see Figure 11-10), you can click to product images of office supplies, computers, fax machines, phones, calculators, and office furniture.

Figure 11-10: *Have a home office? OfficeMax's store on the Web may have the computer or furniture you need.*

When you click on a given listing, a picture comes across the screen, along with instructions for how to order the item. I found leather chairs on sale at $199.99 and $249.99, and a "Wallace Manager's Chair" available for $169.99. The inventory has probably changed since then, but the secure-transaction ordering process hasn't.

TRAVELWEB

http://www.travelweb.com/
The ability for you to sit at your terminal and book a flight or hotel room has been around since even before the Web, but the Web's emergence as a graphical medium has spawned several sites that can help you get the information you need before you make your reservation. Especially for hotel bookings, images are important. Hotels are a visual medium. It can only help to see a photo of the golf course at the hotel where you'll be staying. TravelWeb is such a service. Its powerful search features (see Figure 11-11) let you launch local or regional inquiries for available rooms in more than a dozen major chains as well as scores of independent properties.

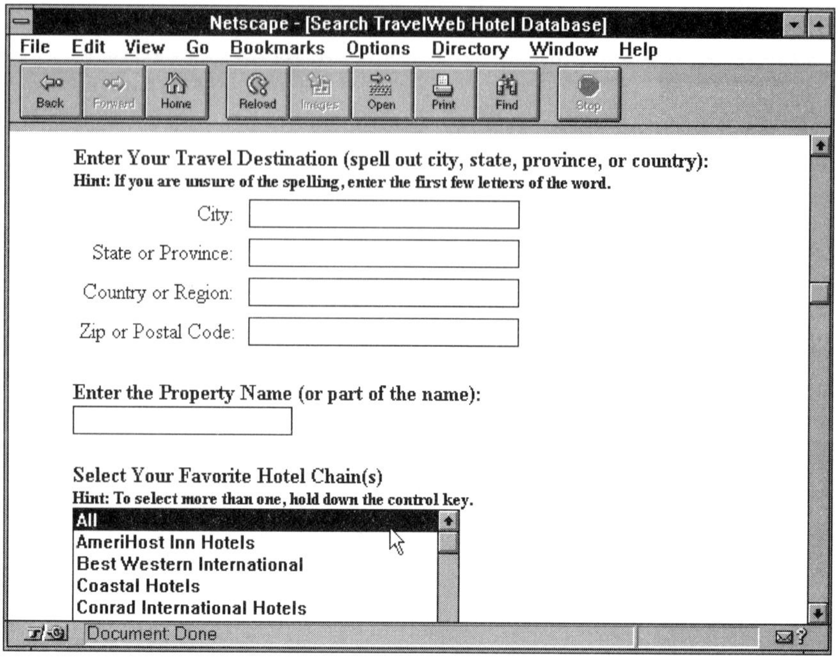

Figure 11-11: *Planning for a future business trip by using TravelWeb.*

Do you own a small chemical company? Is there a convention within your target market scheduled for the Phoenix area? Are you looking for a hotel with a "breakout" room where you can show an interactive video presentation to several would-be customers or stock analysts? A room suitable for such a presentation can help you close key sales and inject even more vigor into your business.

If you are one of the millions of corporate or entrepreneurial road warriors, you might be glad to know that you can probably find suitable accommodations on TravelWeb, see a photo of the property, and then book it directly from your computer.

MOVING ON

I hope that some of the tools and tutorials described here can improve your financial position. If they do, you will need to make some investment decisions. The promise of high returns attracts many people to the mutual funds market, which is what I cover next.

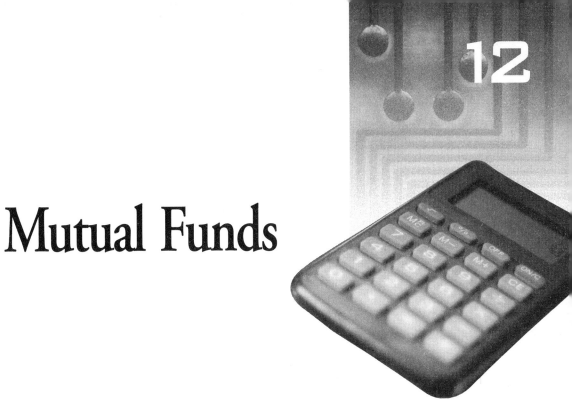

Mutual Funds

For much of the 1990s, rates that banks paid on certificates of deposit remained relatively stagnant. With the exception of a few short-lived, marketing-driven specials, the ceiling seemed to be about 6.50 percent. If you invested $10,000 in a 6-percent, compounded-daily, 5-year CD back in 1992, you stand to gain only about $3,500 when the note matures in 1997.

When the corrosive effects of taxes and inflation are figured into the mix, the gain is even less than that. Plus, you will have tied up $10,000 of money that you could have used to invest in growing your own business or making improvements to your home that would substantially increase its worth.

Or, as tens of millions of Americans have found out in this decade, you could have done far better by investing this money in a mutual fund.

Playing the mutual fund card is not a good strategy for everyone. Because investments in these funds almost always are not insured, you could theoretically lose everything you put in. Ten thousand or even five thousand dollars is a lot of money to most of us. The risk-averse may view any investment not insured by the federal government as tantamount to gambling.

You can point to annualized double-digit fund return tables in the business section of the paper, but some people just won't allow themselves to be convinced that a personal finance strategy involving at least some element of risk versus reward might be sound. This chapter isn't written for them, but rather for those of you who are interested in interest—and want to see what some of the leading mutual funds companies are doing with their Web sites.

WHAT MAKES A GOOD MUTUAL FUND WEB SITE?

Several basic business models come into play here. Some sites are the work of companies that specialize in mutuals. Others are sections of sites maintained by firms with an even broader suite of investment-related services; and a small but growing number of URLs, drawn from both the specialists and the generalists, allow for online portfolio checking or even secured online trading.

Regardless of the category or type of service provided, the best sites do the following:

- Clearly state on their home page what functions they allow.
- Have detailed online explanations of their different funds' philosophies rather than force you to contact them via e-mail to get this data.
- Furnish historical data about the performance of individual funds as well as some general information about the company.
- List the portfolios of their funds—that is, the companies in which their individual funds have significant holdings.
- Provide an on-site glossary or other cogent explanation of how mutual funds work.

Millions of people new to this investment medium regard these sites as a good source for basic training and initial fund shopping. The level of expertise will vary. Some fund sites naturally assume that everyone will understand the jargon. The result is either a clubby or convoluted presentation that precludes those sites from being listed here.

The sites chosen, on the other hand, satisfy at least some of these standards. If a high-earning fund captures your attention, keep in mind that this chapter is evaluating these URLs for presentation and content, not for the financial performance of the individual funds. Such an emphasis is best left for other people and other conversations.

LOOK FOR SOME VALUE-ADDED TIPS

Even if you are not interested in a particular fund and would prefer to buy stocks directly, you can learn a lot about how portfolio managers regard specific stocks by visiting several mutual fund pages.

Many fund sites describe the investment objectives or concentrations of particular funds. They also list fund portfolios. This way, if you visit a fund's site that has descriptions of several technology funds, you might be able to look at the portfolio of, say, a rapid growth income fund. If you see two or three technology stocks with especially strong representation in the portfolio, you can assume that the fund managers view those particular issues in sync with the goals of that fund.

That way, you're getting valuable investment advice for free! The funds, however, would much rather handle your investments for you.

MUTUAL FUND SITES

With a few notable exceptions, this chapter does not list sites for which mutual funds are only a small part of the greater whole. Many of these sites are mentioned in Chapter 10, "Investments." Instead, this section lists some mutual fund specialist sites worth a visit.

DYNAMIC MUTUAL FUNDS

http://www.dynamic.ca/
If you are looking for a site that explains the basics, click here first. More than 4,000 words explain just what mutual funds are, how they should be evaluated, and what type of funds investment strategy may be right for you.

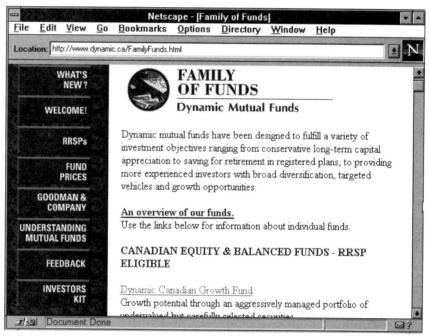

Figure 12-1: *The Dynamic Mutual Funds Family of Funds page.*

"A mutual fund is a pool of money that represents the savings of many people who share the same investment objective," you read on Dynamic's Understanding Mutual Funds page, accessible via a toolbar found on the site's Family of Funds page (see Figure 12-1). "The money is invested on their behalf by an accredited investment manager or team of managers. The mutual fund holds a portfolio of investments that may include interest-bearing securities (such as bonds, mortgages or Treasury bills) and common, preferred, or convertible shares of individual companies depending on the objectives of the fund and the manager's investment strategy."

The next two paragraphs are designed to explain how funds may differ from each other, but that all of these funds afford more flexibility and value to the investor than they would derive if they tackled the financial markets with only one type of investment in their portfolio.

"Mutual funds have been designed to meet different investment objectives such as preserving capital, generating income, achieving growth and maintaining liquidity (ready access to capital)," the text continues. "In some cases, income tax considerations may make one mutual fund more attractive than another."

When the language on a Web site steers toward pointing at variables, you've reached a major fork in the road. At this point, some sites lapse into jargon that only veteran investors would understand. Others, such as Dynamic's, take the time to tell you why diversification will actually make your life simpler.

"Mutual funds were developed to simplify investing," Dynamic says clearly. "By making one investment in a single mutual fund you get many benefits that would be difficult to obtain on your own. A mutual fund gives you diversification that only a large investment portfolio can provide. This can be diversification by type of asset, by industry, by company or even by different countries. You also benefit from the investment experience and market expertise of professional investment managers. Most importantly, you have the advantage of investment liquidity because, with a mutual fund, you can cash in your units by redeeming them from the fund management company at any time."

The language on Dynamic takes a measured tone, remarkably free of the sales and marketing hustle that you might expect would follow. You won't find the usual garish invitation to jump in the investment pool.

If your browser supports tables, you'll want to click next to several pages that describe the philosophy and recent performance of the 20 or so funds that Dynamic offers. As a Canadian company, Dynamic's fund menu is heavy with play north of the border, but about half of its funds invest in or allow investments from international sources.

The site shows three consecutive sets of tables called Canadian Equity and Balanced Funds, Income and Dividend Funds, and International Funds–Foreign Content. Each fund's tabular listing contains vital statistics such as eligibility, minimum purchase amount, management fees, fee schedules, and the fund inception date.

ALGER FUND

http://networth.galt.com/www/home/mutual/alger/alger.htm
The information presented here is not extremely deep but it gets the job done. Explanations of investment philosophy, research methodologies, and portfolio management are handled in just a few paragraphs. A read through the "Alger Investment Approach" passage (see Figure 12-2) shows how adroitly Alger summarizes its mission:

"Over the years, we have been guided by the philosophy that the most profitable investment opportunities are found in companies experiencing a period of rapid change," Alger says. "We believe these dynamic companies fall into one of two categories: High Unit Volume Growth and Positive Life Cycle Change." The latter is defined as "companies experiencing major change which is expected to produce advantageous results. These changes may be as varied as new management, products or technologies; restructuring or reorganization; or merger and acquisition."

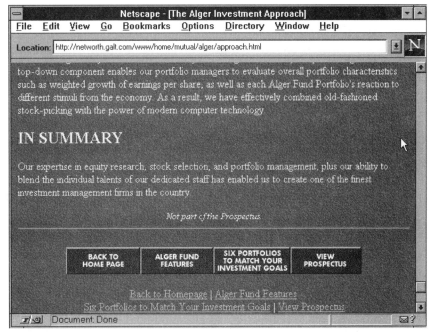

Figure 12-2: *The Alger Investment Approach page.*

Alger describes each fund in a short snapshot that includes the fund's specific objective, a snapshot of its top five company holdings and individual industry groups, and a performance review detailing how the fund has done in the past year, the past five years, and since it was introduced.

The shining asset here is not the conciseness but rather the clarity with which the rationale for each fund is explained. Alger feels, for example, that growing companies with market capitalizations of $1 billion or more "generally have broader product lines, markets, financial resources and depth of management than smaller, newer companies. Growth companies," Alger notes, "are likely to enjoy increased earnings which, over time, translates into increased share prices."

BENHAM FUNDS

**http://networth.galt.com/www/home/mutual/benham/
benham.html**
Benham Investment Group's Benham Funds site assumes some
knowledge level in its visitors. This site doesn't have many basics,
nor does it provide a lot of data. The purpose here is one of generalized introduction, with a "click here" mail-to offered for more
details.

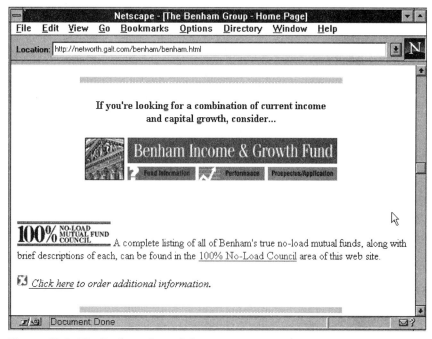

Figure 12-3: *The Benham Group's home page.*

Within its limited parameters, this site gives you the facts about
each fund you'll need to get started (see Figure 12-3). Take a look
at the Benham Income & Growth Fund content to see how this is
handled.

The first paragraph notes that returns on common stocks have historically far exceeded inflation rates, making them good vehicles. Next comes four topics linked to quantifying explanations. These topics and their accompanying text touch on such issues as the following:

- *Strong Returns That Have Outpaced the Market*   A brief quote of one- and five-year averages for the fund.

- *Dividend Growth That Has Exceeded Inflation*   A chart going back to 1946 is provided that shows how, in the last 50 years, dividends paid by stocks of companies on the Standard & Poor 500 chart have grown faster than inflation. This point is illustrated by separate lines for inflation rate and for dividends.

- *Long-Term Growth Potential With Common Stocks*   A chart shows how a dollar invested in the U.S. stock market back in 1925 (before the Depression) would have increased to $1,051.27 in market value 70 years later. This would be an average annual return of 10.49 percent. By predating the start of the growth curve to before the Great Depression, this particular example seems to be a preemptive strike against fears that stock markets are susceptible to sudden downturns.

- *Professional Management of the Fund's Portfolio*   Here, the evaluation methods of Benham's researchers are covered. They look at the 1,500 largest publicly traded U.S. companies and assess each for fundamental value, earnings growth, and dividend yield. Then, the mathematical process of portfolio optimization is used to choose the "optimal combination of stocks to help the Fund achieve its objectives."

Because such methods are proprietary, it's understandable why they aren't explained here. Each fund is accompanied by a bit of amplification on a linked page, where investment objective, assets, and minimal investment amount required are listed. You'll also find a link to the Web site of the Twentieth Century Family of Mutual Funds, of which the Benham Group is a part.

CHARLES SCHWAB & CO.

http://www.schwab.com/

As you learned in Chapter 10, "Investments," Schwab is a diversified financial services corporation of which mutual fund offerings
is just one part. It's such a major player, however, that a separate
section is also appropriate for this chapter.

On Schwab's home page, you can click on a link to a listing of
Schwab Funds. When you're on the listings page, you can jump to
a separate section describing each fund. If you invest in any of
these funds, you'll be able to access your account online (see
Figure 12-4).

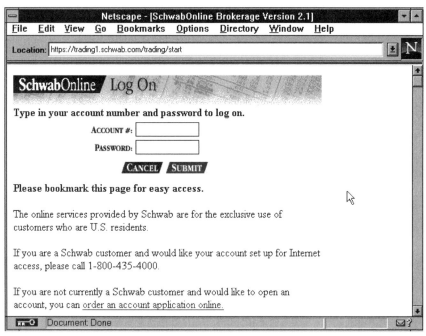

Figure 12-4: *If you're a member of Schwab Online, you can log on to access
your account over the Internet.*

A word of elaboration here: as on most other mutual funds sites, the prospectus is not posted. Most of these sites have a "For Further Information" link from which you can order a prospectus. Other sites, such as Schwab's, let you read a prospectus after you've registered online. This perfectly acceptable method might create the not entirely inaccurate impression of threadbareness, but you'll usually find enough data to get you started.

The presentation on the Schwab 1000 Fund page is typical of what you can expect on the Schwab site as well as on some others. Here's how this section is constructed:

■ *Fund Description*   A paragraph describing the general investment goals of the fund.

■ *Index Description*   A paragraph noting certain criteria that a publicly traded company must meet to be considered a candidate for inclusion.

■ *Minimums*   The amounts necessary for an investor to open an account and to participate in succeeding trades.

■ *Distributions*   The month when dividends are paid.

A Summary of Fund Benefits section is next. Topics broached here include:

■ *Market Performance*   A comparison on how the fund has performed over the past 15 years against competing funds and other investment avenues.

■ *Broad Equity Diversification*   A sentence on how the fund's participation in a range of industries makes the fund less risky than those funds with a concentration on individual companies or only a few market segments.

■ *Low Costs*   Notes that certain fees either are not assessed or are lower than industry averages.

■ *Low Portfolio Turnover*   A paragraph that establishes a relationship between lack of churn (buying and selling funds on a very frequent basis) and low trading costs.

Other sections include Tax Efficiency, Operating Expenses ratios, and the obligatory Fund Performance stats.

The worthiness of the Schwab site can best be experienced by reading the Tax Efficiency section. Tax liabilities are a concern for all investors, but explaining the specific tax ramifications of each fund without going into excruciating detail is exceedingly difficult. On its Schwab 1000 Fund page, the subject is explained clearly:

> When the Fund's portfolio managers must buy and sell securities in the portfolio, they use a disciplined investment approach designed to minimize taxable distributions to shareholders which should help to reduce overall tax liability. Any "unrealized gains" accumulate in the portfolio, helping to build the value of your shares. The fund's low portfolio turnover helps to minimize your capital gains tax liability by limiting the distribution of capital gains. Any unrealized gains accumulate in the fund, helping to build the value of your shares. This tax-smart strategy helps defer taxes on capital gains until you sell your shares.

Dreyfus Online Information Center

http://www.dreyfus.com/
Information about the Dreyfus Mutual Funds is accessed by starting at the Dreyfus Home Page (see Figure 12-5). You then click on the Dreyfus Online Information Center page and then the Dreyfus Family of Funds.

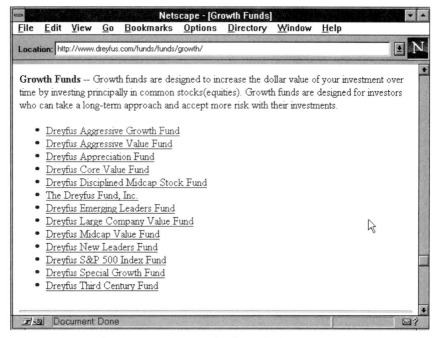

Figure 12-5: *Find out about these Dreyfus funds by hitting any link on this page.*

Many mutual fund investors make their decisions based on the "time horizon" within which they hope to realize a return on their investment and may need access to cash from these returns. Dreyfus regards these horizons within one of three modes. These are as follows: short-term, within two years; intermediate-term, two to five years; and long-term, five years or more.

Each of the Dreyfus Funds is earmarked for one of the three horizons. The Funds have their own Information pages. If the truth be told, these pages are a little light on specifics. I would have hoped for less of a gap between the amount of information on these pages and the exhaustive details in the prospectus. No matter. If you know that going in, this site gives you the essentials you need to get started.

The Dreyfus Core Value Fund shows this minimum content approach. "The Fund," Dreyfus says, "seeks long-term growth of capital with current income as a secondary goal, through investments primarily in common stocks. It invests principally in common stocks and securities convertible into common stocks of well-established U.S. companies. The Fund may invest up to 20% of its portfolio in foreign issues."

Expected information about net assets, dividend policies, management fees, and average annual return follows next. You also find some useful data about Dreyfus Fund privileges. For most funds, these include telephone transfer, automatic withdrawal plans, payroll savings, and direct deposit. Even if you aren't interested in Dreyfus, reading the privileges list will give you a good benchmark for comparing the services of the fund that you are considering.

The information deficit on the specific fund pages is not indicative of the rest of the Dreyfus site. The site provides a useful 10-point advisory on your investment philosophy, as well as a weekly column on investment trends written by Dreyfus's Richard Hoey.

FIDELITY INVESTMENTS

http://www.fidelity.com/
You would expect the largest mutual funds company to have a comprehensive Web site, and it does—more than 1,000 pages worth. It would be really easy for such a trove of content to become unnavigable by sheer weight alone. Fidelity avoids this with two musts that *all* content-heavy sites should have.

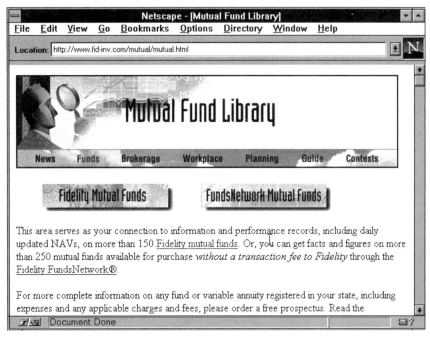

Figure 12-6: *Fidelity Investments's Mutual Fund Library.*

The ability to search by keyword is absolutely critical. The best of these programs let you comb for either a keyword or a concept and then rank a list of "hits." You should be able to click from the hypertexed hit citation right to the actual text. Fidelity has provided this option on its home page. The site also comes with an A-to-Z Index of topics, which is also hyperlinked.

Fidelity is one for daily updating. It maintains a Net Asset Value area where the day's NAV is posted for most funds shortly after the markets close.

The Fidelity server has several main areas. All these touch on mutual fund investing. Here's a quick rundown:

■ *News* Contains notification of new funds or services, an articles library, and a schedule of upcoming seminars given across the country by Fidelity representatives.

- ■ *Mutual Fund Library* (See Figure 12-6.) The central archive for information about Fidelity's funds. Most of the funds discussed in this section list performance history and management philosophy. Unlike some other sites, you can get some prospectuses via direct download from here.

- ■ *Investment & Retirement Planning* Strong on educational materials and tutorials about how to create a portfolio for a range of aims.

- ■ *Brokerage Services* Surveys Fidelity brokerage accounts and bond offerings.

- ■ *Workplace Savings* This is not specifically related to mutual funds, but it does furnish advice about retirement planning through savings plans at work. There are investment articles and downloadable worksheets here.

- ■ *Investor's Guide to Fidelity* As its name implies, this is a guide to communicating with the company along with an overview of its services.

- ■ *Contests and Games* Sports an ever-changing lineup of interactive games oriented toward mastery of investment principles and knowledge.

Most Fidelity Funds have exhaustive profile sections. For example, take a look at the Fidelity Balanced Fund pages. This Fund is noted on Fidelity's Funds Network Mutual Fund Category Descriptions page as one "whose primary objective is to conserve principal by maintaining, at all times, a balanced portfolio of both stocks and bonds. Typically, the stock/bond ratio ranges around 60%/40%."

The first specific FBF page details objective, strategy, and risk. The risk explanation is far more complete than on most sites, providing a reality-check element useful to all investors. This page cautions, for example, that "the value of the fund's domestic and foreign investments will vary from day to day in response to many factors. Stock values fluctuate in response to the activities of individual companies, and general market and economic conditions. The value of bonds fluctuates based on changes in interest rates and in the credit quality of the issuer. You may have a gain or loss when you sell your shares. Investments in foreign securities, especially those in emerging markets, involve risks in addition to those of U.S. investments, including increased political and economic risk, as well as exposure to currency fluctuations. The securities of small, less well-known companies may be more volatile than those of larger companies."

If only other mutual fund sites had that candor. Of course, candor alone does not equal a prudent investment. Take the matter of performance. If your browser supports tables, you can read charts about funds that touch on financial performance criteria, historical total, and dividends return as well as the latest Lipper Ranking. (Lipper Analytical Services, Inc., ranks mutual funds based on total return.) Most Fidelity fund sections also have breakdowns of what companies comprise the largest portion of the given fund's holdings.

The future for this site looks exciting. Fidelity is firmly committed to full-scale mutual fund and brokerage services on its Web site. As it rolls out these new features, you can be sure that it will let the world know. Keep checking the site (http://www.fidelity.com) for the latest developments. Because Fidelity is by far the largest mutual fund company, it's a foregone conclusion that the financial news sites named in Chapter 18 of this book will treat any expansion of Fidelity's already impressive services suite as the major story it will be.

GABELLI FUNDS

http://www.gabelli.com/
The Gabelli Mutual Funds site includes short summations of more than a dozen funds, and gives you the ability to download a prospectus and fund quarterly reports from the site (see Figure 12-7). The prospectuses are in the Adobe Acrobat format, which requires you to have an Adobe Acrobat reader installed as a plug-in on your browser. I prefer downloading content that is in straight text or the Web's HTML format, and am generally put off by the extra hoops that an Acrobat download requires. Yet, if you have money to invest, the few minutes it takes to download and then deploy Acrobat should be a small sacrifice.

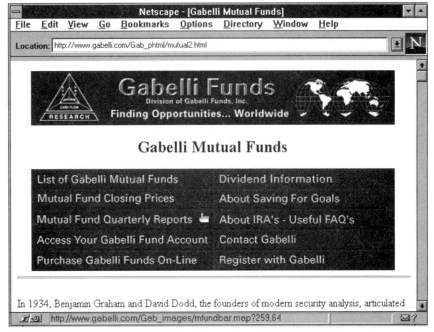

Figure 12-7: *Order a quarterly report by clicking the icon on the Gabelli Mutual Funds home page.*

Gabelli funds are classified as either "conservative growth," "aggressive growth," "global/international," "growth & income," or just "income" funds. From the brief descriptive passages on each, you can click to a more detailed overview.

Under the Conservative Growth Funds category, for example, try the Gabelli Growth Fund. Accessing the page, you can read a boilerplate "Objective paragraph." The description is instructive if not too specific:

The Gabelli Growth Fund is a no-load, open-end, diversified, management investment company whose investment objective is to seek capital appreciation by investing in securities which are perceived by its management to have favorable, yet undervalued, prospects for earnings growth. Current income is a secondary investment objective.

Next come some useful facts listing the Fund's Total Net Assets, the number of companies in the portfolio, the top five industry sectors represented, the companies in the index, and historical performance data.

If you see something you like, you need to register. After your registration is processed, you can download a prospectus from the site. After you read the document, you can download an account application to invest in the fund.

KEMPER MONEY FUNDS

http://www.kemper.com/
London-based Kemper has an especially informative opening page that details the investment strategies of two Kemper companies: Zurich Kemper Investments, Inc., and Dreman Value Advisors, Inc. Each is described in a richly detailed paragraph; Webmasters at other mutual fund sites might want to adopt these paragraphs as role models.

In "On the growth side," you can read that Zurich Kemper Investments, Inc., emphasizes "growth at the right price."

"Using a disciplined team approach, Kemper analysts use fundamental research to identify quality growth companies whose stocks are selling at reasonable prices and whose earnings are growing faster than the market average. Characteristics of these companies include strong management, industry leadership, a high return on equity, a low dividend/high reinvestment rate and recession resistance. Stocks must pass an intensive screening process based on relative price/earnings ratios, relative profitability, present values and momentum characteristics."

Dreman, on the other hand, openly roots for the underdog by focusing "on companies that are out of favor with investors because the market underestimates their value or overlooks their potential. Stocks become undervalued as a result of overreaction by investors to unfavorable news about a company, industry or the stock market in general. Or, they can become undervalued as a result of a market decline, poor economic conditions, tax-loss selling or actual or anticipated unfavorable developments affecting the company. Because the company is out of favor, its stock trades at a price/earning ratio (P/E) that is lower than its potential might suggest. P/Es of value stocks are generally lower than the overall market and lower than growth stock P/Es."

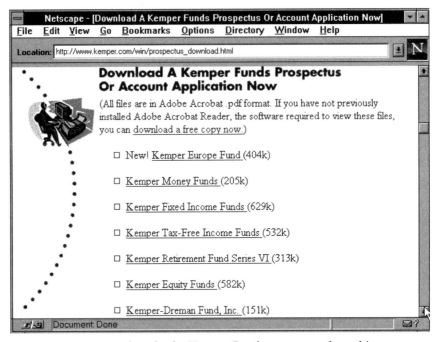

Figure 12-8: *You can download a Kemper Funds prospectus from this page.*

This is yet another site that makes you download Adobe Acrobat. To its credit, you can download and then read the prospectus (see Figure 12-8) without registering. At 648K, the Kemper International Fund and Kemper Global Income Fund is the largest download. In contrast, Kemper-Dreman will take up only 151K of your disk space. That's in addition to the 445K that a downloaded account application will occupy on your hard drive.

Should you be torn about what fund to seriously pursue, Kemper also lets you compare any Kemper Fund against one of several overall market indexes. The results come in a graph covering the last 10 years with additional quarterly breakouts for the most recent year.

VANGUARD MUTUAL FUNDS

http://www.vanguard.com/
Vanguard's more than 80 funds each get a four-section treatment.
Elements touched on include:

- Objective, including investment goals and performance.

- Performance statistics for the previous year, 5 years, and 10 years.

- Contact information for each fund manager. Every mutual fund Web site should have this information, but only about half of them do.

- A reality-check risk assessment of each fund. This is roughly equivalent to the disclaimer that you read before you go into surgery.

Figure 12-9: *Read about a Vanguard Mutual Fund by clicking from here.*

As you've seen elsewhere, a conclusive investment objective statement is absolutely necessary on any investment-related Web site. The Vanguard Explorer Fund page, which you can reach from the home page (see Figure 12-9), isn't as comprehensive as some on other sites, but it more than fulfills the minimum requirement for being informative.

Under Investment Objective and Philosophy, you are told that the $3,000 minimum investment fund "seeks long-term growth of capital by investing primarily in common stocks of small and emerging growth companies.

"The Fund's investment approach acknowledges the fundamental risks involved with owning the securities of small, growing companies," Vanguard continues. "Through a comanager structure, wide diversification, and low turnover, the Fund offsets some of the risk inherent to investing in this market sector. Vanguard Explorer Fund's philosophy is to provide a conservatively managed vehicle investing in high-risk securities."

Although the Objective section is a bit short on specifics, a paragraph on Fees is especially revealing. I know investors in mutual funds who have been blindsided by unexpected fees. They didn't bother to find everything out about the fees before they signed up. To its considerable credit, Vanguard states the fee regimen in language more conclusive than I've ever read on any Web site.

"A $10 annual fee," Vanguard plainly says, "will be automatically deducted from accounts falling below a minimum level. This fee deduction will occur mid-year, and is designed to offset the disproportionately high costs of servicing accounts with low balances. The fee will apply to Uniform Gifts/Transfers to Minors accounts with balances falling below $500. For all other fund accounts, the fee will apply to balances falling below $2,500. The fee will be waived for investors whose aggregate Vanguard Fund assets total $50,000 or more."

If you are thinking about another mutual fund, you might want to compare this fee arrangement with the one that would affect you. Like any relationship—business or otherwise—the more information you have going in, the better.

MOVING ON

Mutual funds aren't for every investor. If you're a stock jockey who likes to go it alone, a variety of software programs are available to help you. You'll find software that tracks not only your investments but the rest of your finances—and your time—as well. Web sites exist from which you can download or order these programs. You can find information on some of the best in the next chapter.

Software

Going to a computer store and buying software, or buying such products via mail order, isn't always practical for people pressed for time. Now you have another option: you can go to Web sites and download the software directly from a remote server to your computer.

Evaluating software sites and judging the software they contain aren't necessarily two sides of the same coin, however. Some very well-conceived software packages are out there that don't really put a lot of information up on their sites. Text often doesn't get any more complicated than a "hi, here's who we are" message that seriously undervalues the potential of the Web to communicate information.

On the other hand, a Web site that is rich with superlatives about a product doesn't mean that the software is relevant and easy to use. It pains me to admit it, but writing glowing copy is easier than writing well-coordinated software code. No site is going to admit that its software is clunky, so downloader beware.

DOWNLOADING & UPDATING SOFTWARE

Software sites that contain programs for your computer involve not only site navigation but also downloading and installation, so you need to understand these topics before you read the individual site overviews.

Software distribution is undergoing a paradigm shift. Hundreds of companies are making their software available via direct download. If you're looking for a program that performs a particular function, you need do no more than log on, direct your browser to one of the major search engine sites, and then launch a keyword search for programs that perform particular functions. An example of this is going to Yahoo (http://www.yahoo.com) and keying in the terms **accounting** and **software**.

Yahoo then points you to a list of sites whose content descriptions match one or both of these terms. When you click on the hyperlink, you go to the site where you can see whether there is download capability. If the site's home page icons are relevant to the site's functionality (sadly, this isn't always true), you should see a sign saying something like "Click Here To Download." If you don't see such a marker, maybe the site has a Frequently Asked Questions list that can tell you whether downloads are possible.

Keep in mind that downloading is not the same thing as installation. It's only part of the process. Many software programs come in a "zipped" or "compressed" form that will activate the functions only when a particular .EXE sequence is followed. You may therefore have to capture the program to a temporary directory and then click twice on the main filename to bring the installation program to life. Look for a readme file with directions.

Two types of tools that may help you keep the software that you buy current will find increasing use on the Web. A number of companies make utility programs that notify you when the content on a given Web site is updated. The installed program works with your Web browser to comb sites for which you've already told it to look. The program may perform this function daily, weekly, or monthly. Then, if it recognizes new content that isn't in your browser's cached (stored) version of the given site, it contacts you via e-mail and gives you notice of the new information, or else downloads the changed page to your browser's mail server. The next time that you are online, you can pull down the new data and your cache will be rewritten automatically.

These programs are flexible enough to respond to keyword parameters. If you want to be notified only when a new note on the site mentions a bug that's been fixed, a product patch that's been added, a tech note that's been posted to the FAQ page, or a new edition that has been announced, you can specify those search terms. You'll be notified only if the update-hunting utility recognizes words such as *bug*, *patch*, *update*, and so on.

The second type of off-the-Web-site software update is even more interesting. You'll be able to actually buy a subscription to a given software product in much the same way that you sign up for a year's delivery of a business or computer magazine. Netscape and several other companies pioneered the process. You can buy a year's subscription to a site. You'll be notified of any updates, which you can then download when you have the chance.

Such pricing plans will undoubtedly drill down through the Web until a broad range of software—including personal finance products—can be bought and updated in this manner. Software developers actually like it, because the immediacy of online distribution will help them funnel fixes and enhancements to the user base much quicker. Formerly, a company would hoard the fixes until it had enough to justify a new edition of the core product. This new way automates the process and saves you a whole bunch of hassles.

WHAT MAKES A GOOD PERSONAL FINANCE SOFTWARE SITE?

It is still fairly early in the automated site-to-software information transfer and update game. It may be close to decade's end before such features become commonplace, so sites lacking these enhancements should not be penalized.

There's still a demanding balance between site content and software functionality that all software sites, including investment-related software pages, need to keep in mind. Here are some standards for quality and relevancy:

- The site must contain a reasonably thorough explanation of how the software works.

- If programs can be downloaded from the site, specifics pertaining to the type of operating system and how much disk space it needs to function should be provided.

- Screen shots of the actual program in use are always helpful.

- Links to pages with more details are also beneficial. These can be on the site or in archived, off-site resources—or both.

- A Frequently Asked Questions page or other Help menu is vital. The first portion of the FAQ should tell you a bit about the company, the product, and what the product does. The rest of the FAQ needs to clearly walk the reader through the installation and application process.

- A phone number should be provided in case you need to talk to a human.

- Stay away from software sites overloaded with marketing generalities and short on specifics about how the product works and what it does.

Keep in mind the stakes here. When you order or download a personal finance software package from a Web site, you are, sight unseen, declaring your faith in a product that will help you sustain or improve your financial status.

 ## Software Sites

When it comes to these kinds of sites, it takes a lot to satisfy me. Several have passed my test with flying colors. Others have enough redeeming qualities to merit a site visit even though the content may be a bit unfocused. This section tells you about some of the sites and programs.

CHARTPRO

http://www.fastlane.net/homepages/wallst/c-pro.html
The term *Japanese Candle charts* sounds like something you'd find
in some health food store or latter-day herbs-and-incense shop.
Fibonacci fans—an opera singer's devotees or some high-end
Italian-made ceiling fan, right?

Wrong. These are two of the stock-performance predictor
models included in ChartPro, Ret-Tech Software's charting and
technical analysis tool for stocks. You can order the program by
phone. To display the number, click the "Contact us" invitation
strategically placed on the ChartPro home page (see Figure 13-1).

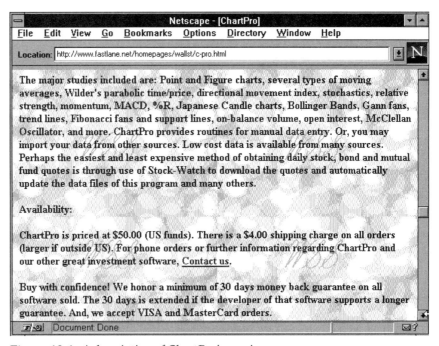

Figure 13-1: *A description of ChartPro's services.*

Some veteran professional stock-pickers swear by these programs; others say that, although these programs are highly sophisticated, they should never overrule your intuitive experience.
Based on what I've seen, I would vote for the latter perspective.

As a Web site, ChartPro fulfills at least one of my criteria admirably. It does a superb, no-frills job of telling the prospective purchaser what the program does and what type of power it needs. Here's the kind of clear definition that you wish every software site's home page contained:

> ChartPro is a superior beginning charting and technical analysis tool. It was written by a trader for traders. It will create high resolution daily or weekly bar charts in the standard High/Low/Close format with Volume charted along the lower portion of the screen. It is designed to chart stocks, funds, futures, etc. The program requires an IBM or compatible machine with color EGA or VGA graphics. No form of CGA or monochrome graphics will run it. It runs off a simple menu system and includes the availability of about 30 different technical studies.

Reading further, you can tell that ChartPro assumes a certain sophistication on the part of its users. That's understandable, but some of the message is at cross purposes here. The marketing tag at the top of the home page reads: "ChartPro—A Beginner's Dream." Yet, the third paragraph is a strange combination of arcane jargon certainly unknown to the beginner, and more language about how easy the program is to use. I've been to thousands of Web sites, but I've never seen more jargon packed into one sentence:

> The major studies included are: Point and Figure charts, several types of moving averages, Wilder's parabolic time/ price, directional movement index, stochastics, relative strength, momentum, MACD, %R, Japanese Candle charts, Bollinger Bands, Gann fans, trend lines, Fibonacci fans and support lines, on-balance volume, open interest, McClellan Oscillator, and more.

An onsite glossary or FAQ would help, don't you think?

THE COLLECTOR SYSTEM

http://www.colubs.com/

At any given time, some of my accounts are past due. If you're running a small business, you may have similar accounts. You have to manage the distasteful business of collection gingerly. Also, bill collecting detracts from your primary missions of servicing current accounts and pursuing new ones. To handle this aspect of your business, you can check out software that performs delinquent account management for you.

One such product with a superior Web site is the Collector System, made by Columbia Ultimate Business Systems of Vancouver, Washington. Collector defines itself as a "comprehensive, fully-integrated, flexible collection software with features including: collection management, pre-collect and forwarding, debtor and client update, trust accounting, on-line credit reporting and skip tracing, auto packeting, payment plans, and a complete legal package."

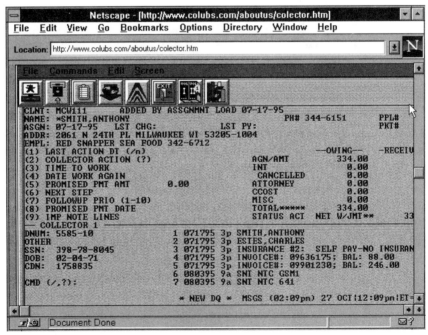

Figure 13-2: *A sample screen as shown on the Collector System site.*

You don't have to be a professional collector to use the service, just a businessperson, professional, or even a small retailer with many accounts. By cogent explanations and use of sample screen shots (see Figure 13-2), the site clearly spells out what Collector does and how it works.

After a three-paragraph introduction, the "Revenue Recovery" section explores how, by using some functions, the (human) collector can do his or her job better. You'll find a series of nifty one-sentence descriptions of capabilities such as tracking promises to pay and scheduling callbacks if the payment isn't received, and an automated generation of payment-due notices based on payment plans that the debtor makes with the collector.

These sound like useful functions. With Collector, the office manager at your dental practice could generate a customizable reminder letter on the 10th of the month to a past due account scheduled for payment on the 15th.

Some lesser software Web sites simply stop at functionality description. The Collector System actually walks you through a series of one- or two-paragraph descriptions of the Collector, Account Inquiry, and Packet (grouping) Display Screens.

"The Collector screen is the primary tool used by collectors for cardless collections," say the instructions. "Using this screen, the collector may request correspondence, record contracts, schedule followups, and perform many other functions." A screen shot of the Collector Screen comes next. Every process-related Web site needs at least one!

FINANCIAL FREEDOM BILLING MANAGER

Downloadable as shareware from **http://www.winmag.com/ library/1995/0395/3worrex.htm**
I've chosen to include this accounts receivable and billing system as a representative of the shareware programs available on the Web. Shareware is usually a free or very inexpensive software program or utility that can be as powerful as some $150 programs you buy in boxes at computer stores. Sometimes, the people who have written these programs believe that software innovations should be shared with the world, and aren't motivated by profit.

There are several thousand shareware programs available on the Web. You can find some through search engine hunts, or find them archived in groups of hundreds on shareware repository sites such as shareware.com (http://www.shareware.com).

Financial Freedom Billing Manager is available from several Web sites, including Windows Internet magazine (http://www.winmag.com/).

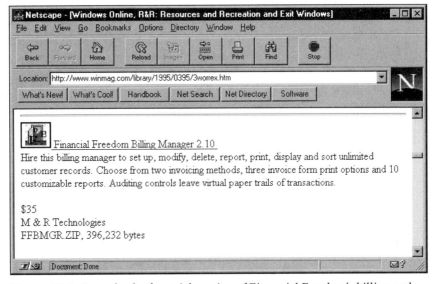

Figure 13-3: *Download a free trial version of Financial Freedom's billing and accounting software from here.*

The program, according to Financial Freedom, "supports multiple companies, unlimited customers, three configurable invoice printing formats, report sorting and sub-total options for over 10 different reports, works with fax software, supports partial payments, user-defined product, invoice and customer codes, complete tax configuration, import and export options, sales/inventory reports, credit limits and more!"

Also downloadable from the Web, the 431K Financial Freedom GOLD tool lets you manage an "unlimited (number of) bank accounts, budgeting, check printing, loan analysis and amortization, bill-reminder utility, password protection, automated account reconciliations and strong reporting capabilities with exporting options." You're also told of GOLD's ability to manage record-keeping for your checking, savings, CD, and money market accounts.

Financial Freedom GOLD needs Windows 3.1 or higher to work, but it can be configured for any printer. You're told this on the site itself. By telling you, Financial Freedom makes a statement about ease of use at the same time that it prevents certain basic customer service calls. Help Desks absolutely hate dealing with the "what operating system will this run on" questions.

HOTEL CAROUSEL

http://www.hotel-carousel.com/
Hotel Carousel is an interactive, virtual financial-training workshop that you can use—okay, "play"—right on your PC. It is set up with a number of interactive "scenes," called "training excursions" by the site writers for manufacturer Good Business Training, Inc. (see Figure 13-4). Each of the five "excursions" are concisely described on the site:

- *Excursion 1*   Visit acts and scenes in sequence or at random:

    - *Act 1*   Basic Accounting Concepts (seven scenes)

    - *Act 2*   Financial Statements—Analysis, Management, and Control (seven scenes)

    - *Act 3*   Internal Control (one scene)

    - *Act 4*   Budgeting and Decision Making (five scenes)

    - *Act 5*   Credit and Bank Reconciliations (two scenes)

- *Excursion 2*   Go to the movies for a scene-by-scene recap of key points. Select a learning point and instantly jump to it.

- *Excursion 3*   Take a self-test with immediate feedback to your responses.

■ *Excursion 4*   Evaluate overall progress with scored multiple-choice testing. A PRE TEST precedes your visit to Hotel Carousel. A POST TEST follows your visit. Results from both can be analyzed. Finally, you can measure and prove the effectiveness of a training program!

■ *Excursion 5*   Glossary. Over 130 terms explained in plain English. No jargon!

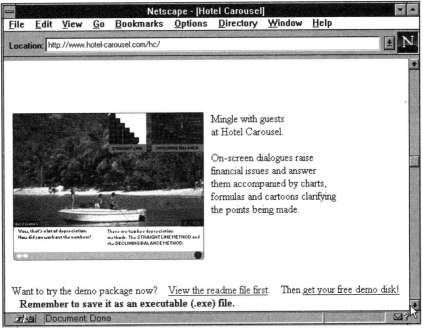

Figure 13-4: *Hotel Carousel's site turns learning about financial management techniques into a fun experience.*

The reason for this light-hearted tone is to illustrate that this site doesn't take itself overly seriously. The topics involved are as serious as a frown from a tax auditor, but the site tone manages to sell the quixotic mixture of boring, important topics and whoopee! product ambience with deft balance.

You'll also find a README.TXT file linked to the site. As you may know, a readme is a set of plain-text instructions contained as separate files within a software program. You are supposed to read them before you install the client. That's why they are in text while all the other files are written in code.

Putting a README.TXT file on a Web site is a superb idea. Downloading it before you pull down the program gives you a good sense of just what the offering is capable of doing. After you download and peruse the readme, you can download a demo disk.

I started this with a lecture about the difference between downloading and installation. The instructions on the Hotel Carousel site bear this point out. This is an executable file that must be saved with an .EXE program. If it isn't, then it won't unzip for you! Carousel lets you know that downloading will take 20 minutes on a slow 14.4 modem, and that unzipping takes up about 5.1MB.

Starting a download on something without knowing how long it will take is frustrating. Ten minutes in, you realize that this is taking forever, but you already have time vested in this process! It's good to know going in whether you have the time to download a software product and the room to store it after it's unzipped. Carousel won't put you on a merry-go-round. They tell you about space and time first.

Despite the playful ambience for which they strive, the people at Good Business Training are well trained themselves. The demo disk expires after a certain number of uses. If the meter is running low, you can order the complete 18MB version right from a link on the Hotel Carousel site.

INVESTOR INSIGHT

http://www1.qfn.com/investorinsight/
You would expect a financial-software powerhouse such as Intuit, Inc., to have a quality investment management offering equal to its pedigree. Investor Insight comes loaded as a Quicken Deluxe for Windows application, or you can download the program (see Figure 13-5) as a separate entity for free from the Web site.

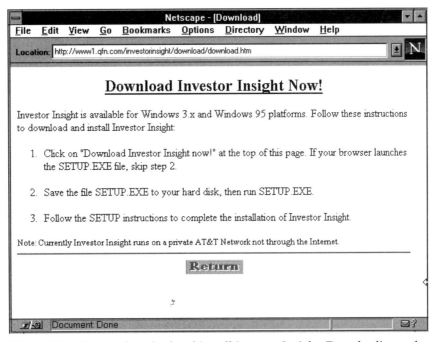

Figure 13-5: *How to download and install Investor Insight. Downloading and installation are not necessarily the same thing.*

The information on the pages is organized in a logical, hierarchical fashion that Webmasters of other sites would do well to emulate. Links from the cover page take you to a sample screen shot, an About Investor Insight page, a description of how that page works, and then, after you are presumably sold on the product, an opportunity to download it.

Although some other softwarecentric Web pages are written by technocrats for fellow geeks, each of the information fields here can be clearly understood, even by a beginner. The writers clearly realize that not every customer will be knowledgeable about computers or investing.

Investor Insight, you read, performs the following functions:

■   "Provides news stories and five years of price quotes for any company and mutual fund listed on the NYSE, Amex, or NASDAQ."

- "Displays charts and reports that show the price performance of each investment, comparisons with other investments, and percentage change over time periods. You can analyze your data in many ways, such as with a personal report that provides an overview of all your investments."
- "Creates custom indexes that let you track trends in a group of stocks or mutual funds, order in-depth company reports, and more."
- "Lets you order in-depth company reports online."

You'll sense a conscious decision having been made here to avoid overloading the site pages with detailed software-use instructions. This has been done partly to avoid intimidating new users, but also because operation is simple. If a Web site says *why* a product is easy to use (as opposed to simply claiming that it is), the argument is more convincing.

One succinct, informative paragraph fulfills the role of describing how Investor Insight works:

"You create a Watch List of stocks and mutual funds that tells Investor Insight what to track," it notes. "The first time you connect to Investor Insight, it downloads five years of historical quotes and 90 days of news for each security on the Watch List. Each subsequent time you connect, Investor Insight automatically brings you up-to-date, downloading only the information you need. You're connected only as long as it takes to capture the information."

Drilling down further, several features are explained. One paragraph is all that's necessary to illustrate what Investor Insight's Watch List, Personal Reports, Price-Volume Charts, QuickZoom (a newsclip-portfolio integration utility), and News Window enable you to do.

THE MONNET FINANCIAL SYSTEM

http://www.monnet.com/
This is a potent office management and bookkeeping system that allows you to manage a variety of accounts receivable and payable functions. You won't be downloading anything from here. This site is for informational purposes only, but it works.

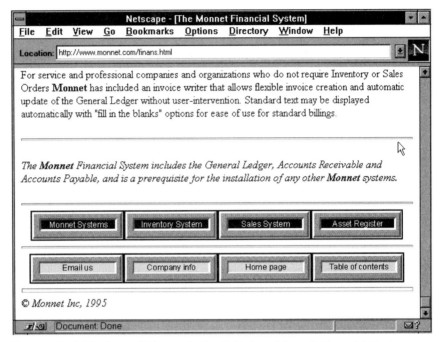

Figure 13-6: *The latest "Monnet": the eight-icon Monnet Financial Systems page.*

The Web pages are organized sequentially. From the home page (Figure 13-6), you can reach sections describing Monnet's Transactional, Banking, and Report-generating capabilities.

When you need to explain a sophisticated program but your URL doesn't include much art, you had darn better write vividly. The challenge here is to put pictures in the reader's mind without engaging in wordy, adjective-laden prose. Monnet assumes that the reader is familiar with bookkeeping terms. The language is on an intermediate level, aimed to describe the functionality rather than the "wow" of the product.

A look at the Displays and Multiple Bank Accounts paragraph descriptors shows how well the site does this dance.

Under "Displays," you read that "General Ledger, Receivables and Payables accounts may be displayed at any time, selectable either from the menu, or, using the 'help key,' from a number of locations within transaction entry programs. All options provide the facility to display individual transaction lines and historical balances; for Receivables and Payables, open items and turnover may also be displayed. When an individual line of a transaction is selected additional information may be displayed including, in the case of customer invoices, a copy of the original invoice as it was printed. Where Sales Orders or Inventory has been installed outstanding Orders are also available for display with the option to see the status of individual lines."

The tone of the Multiple bank accounts explanatory paragraph also reflects Monnet's vision of its Financial System as a tool primarily for pros:

"The banking system incorporated into Monnet allows any number of bank accounts, both in local and in foreign currencies," you read. "Reconciliation facilities, as well as the ability to apply payments directly to customer and supplier accounts, are integral to the banking function. Payments received from customers and payments made to suppliers may be allocated to any combination of accounts, across Accounts Receivable, Accounts Payable and the General Ledger. Full analysis of these allocations may be printed in detail as well as a reconciliation of the bank balance and transactions to the bank statement."

Especially given the name Monnet (a takeoff on the word "money" as well as the artist Monet), the site might have used a screen shot or two, but it's hardly worth quibbling about. Both the product and the site are all business. Monnet pulls off the presentation well, without being too dry or preachy.

SMART BUSINESS PLAN

http://www.smartonline.com/
This site does a fine job of explaining the package's role as a business planning tool. The utility can be set to run off a total of 10 templates. "New" and "existing" business models are included for five categories: retail, wholesale, manufacturing, service, and "custom plans."

The mind's eye is addressed in these next two paragraphs:

"After selecting a section, Smart Business Plan will open the instruction text for that section in the upper half of the window. The user will have the capability (through the use of a radio button) to view an example [see Figure 13-7] text for that section as well."

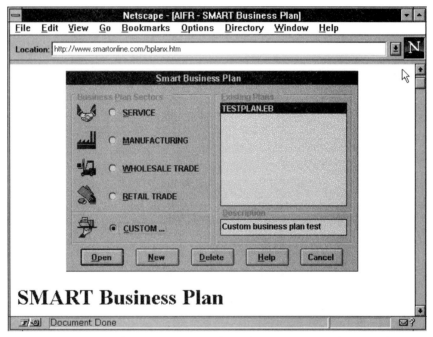

Figure 13-7: *A typical Smart Business Plan software screen, as shown on the site.*

"In the lower half of the window will appear the user's working area. This area is actually Smart Editor. The user has the capability to maximize the lower half of the screen, accessing the full functionality of Smart Editor. The user may also maximize the upper half of the screen, enabling the instructions or examples to come into full view."

Most software sites can use a few links. Too many links may prove distracting, but Smart Business Plan's two links are well considered. Appendix One is a more comprehensive description of the 10 templates referred to in the main information pages. Similarly, the window-customizing abilities of Smart Editor get the full treatment on a linked page.

Clear product definitions and links for more info! An obvious recipe for a worthwhile Web site.

SMART HOME MANAGER

http://www.surado.com/

As any homemaker will tell you, running a home is a full-time job. It has financial management, scheduling, and inventory aspects, just as in a "real" business. Most people try to stay organized, but these nagging record-keeping chores are run by a noncompliant mix of sticky notes, reminders jotted down in day books, spreadsheets, and rubber bands tied around the wrist. There is so much to keep track of. A tool that integrates everything is needed.

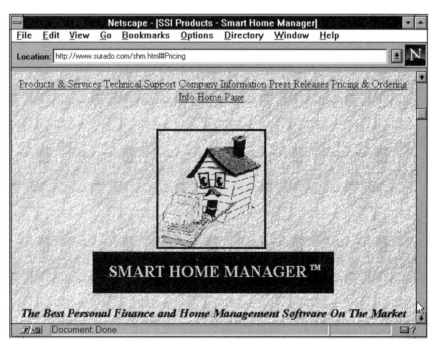

Figure 13-8: *Home is where this screen is: the Smart Home Manager home page.*

Smart Home Manager (Figure 13-8) sounds like such a product. The Web site is basically a brochure for the product, which can process more than 150 reports detailing such functions as income/ expenses tracking, scheduling and budgeting, and check printing.

Modules are also available for duties that are not specifically finance related but involve monetary expenditures. These include tracking home maintenance and repairs, medical records, warranty records, and an inventory system for hobby-related collections. If all this record-keeping wears you out, you can also keep an exercise log in your copy of Smart Home Manager.

The site doesn't have any data on how these apps run, just what they enable you to do. This isn't necessarily a negative, but a matter of choice. No downloads here either: you're simply given an 800-number by which to phone in your order.

Smart Home Manager's site also details what you'll need to run the program. Eating up 18MB of your hard drive, it's a bit of a space hog.

TIME & PROFIT

http://www.bytepro.com/
Your attorney and accountant probably bill by the hour. Perhaps you do, too. Maybe you *are* a lawyer or a CPA. If you are, you'll want to check out the BytePro Web site, which has information on the Time & Profits software package (see Figure 13-9) for time-billing professionals.

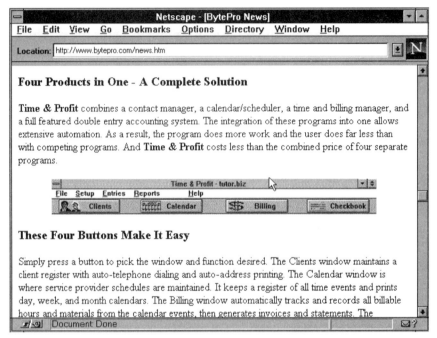

Figure 13-9: *No thick manuals to read: after you obtain the Time & Profit accounting and scheduling package, you can get a tutorial by clicking the cursor here.*

The site is rather bare bones. No screen shots, no sample downloads; it reads a bit like a press release. That's not necessarily bad, because you do get at least some detail about features. These include a contact manager, a calendar/scheduler, a time and billing manager, and a double-entry accounting system.

Time & Profit's core competencies run on four windows. The site describes these windows, not necessarily how they work but what they do:

"Simply press a button to pick the window and function desired," you read. "The Clients window maintains a client register with auto-telephone dialing and auto-address printing. The Calendar window is where service provider schedules are maintained. It keeps a register of all time events and prints day, week, and month calendars. The Billing window automatically tracks and records all billable hours and materials from the calendar events, then generates invoices and statements. The Checkbook window simplifies bill paying with on-screen check, deposit, ATM, transfer, and payroll forms, plus automatic check printing."

The product also enables several customization options, including the creation of special fields for "aged receivables" and "comparisons between differing time segments." These are briefly discussed.

You can phone or fax your order. At copy's end, you'll also find an e-mail link for ordering or correspondence. If only to ensure a line of communication for constructive feedback, every Web site should have a mail-to somewhere.

Moving On

So far, this book has tread somewhat lightly on tax software sites. Because of their highly specialized nature, information about some of the higher quality PC tax-software Web offerings is included in the next chapter, "Taxes."

Taxes

Tax information on the Web acquires an extra degree of relevance every April. Just like good will at holiday time, however, you shouldn't treat tax advice as a discipline for just one month or one season. All the legal tax loopholes in the world won't do you much good if you haven't planned for them in the previous year. You may also have a great deal of tax knowledge, but if money mistakes that you made in the previous year have left you short of money to pay your taxes, you are back at Ground Zero.

Tax planning is intertwined with financial planning. Like watching your weight, it's something you need to be aware of every day of the year.

WHAT MAKES A GOOD TAX SITE?

Many of you do your own taxes; some of you don't. Regardless, you can find some tax-related Web resources that, when taken for what they are worth, might make this less-than-fun subject more palatable.

The best tax sites have at least some of the following features:

■ Clear home page icons. Tax law is voluminous, with hundreds of topics. Site visitors shouldn't have to drill down through six menus to see what they want.

■ A keyword-enabled search engine that will instantly and clearly name all the relevant citations for the terms you request.

■ Tips on deductions for individual and corporate taxpayers.

■ Easy access to federal and state tax forms. These forms can be carried on the site or pointed to via links.

■ Because tax law changes with the judicial and political winds, sites should carry tax-related news or at least point to it.

■ Lots of Frequently Asked Questions lists. Because certain areas of the tax code have very little to do with others, one FAQ with different kinds of information can be distracting.

■ When relevant, information on how to reach a *human* tax preparer. A directory you can search by area is best. Even if they're comprehensive, tax Web sites can only tell someone so much. As taxpayers, as players in the economy, and as human beings, we may have certain tax liability circumstances that are far too specific for a general field of information on a Web site.

Tax Sites

The following sections cover tax sites that meet some of my criteria.

Ernst & Young

http://www.ey.com/
The Web presence of one of the so-called "Big Six" accounting firms, Ernst & Young's site is really big into lists. Three such compilations, each culled from the Ernst & Young Tax Guide, form the core of the site's useful information.

The sectors covered here include Twenty-Five Most Common Tax Preparation Errors, Fifty Overlooked Tax Deductions for Individuals, and Ten Smart Tax Planning Tips.

Because planning, by implication, is proactive, whereas preparation is an exercise reactive to the quality of tax planning that you've already done, I examine the Planning Tips section first.

At least three of the tips touch on investment-related advice:

- *Tip 2* "Make your contributions to an IRA (Individual Retirement Account) or Keogh plan early in the year," E&Y advises. "The combination of making contributions early in the year and compounding will make your money grow faster than if you wait until the last minute."

- *Tip 4* "Consider tax-smart investments for your portfolio. You should focus on the after-tax yield when comparing the returns on different investments."

- *Tip 7* "If you roll over a pension distribution to an IRA account, be sure you do it in a timely fashion. Caution: it may be subject to a 20% withholding tax on lump-sum distributions."

The Fifty Overlooked Tax Deductions page definitely is the most useful part of the E&Y site. That's because this URL not only helps you find deductions as you are doing your return but can also aid in your tax planning by identifying deductions that you can take now and deduct at 1040 time.

On this page, each of these recommendations is followed by a reference to the page on the E&Y Tax Guide where an explanation of the deduction begins. This means that the site, with its wealth of free material, is a promotional vehicle for E&Y's Tax Guide—and, by extension, its army of CPAs. The business model of free Web content as a spear carrier for more extensive paid professional services is perfectly appropriate.

Here are a few of the more interesting, overlooked deductions cited by Ernst & Young (numbered here as they are on the site):

3. "Amortization of premium on taxable bonds."

7. "Business gifts of $25 or less per recipient."

16. "Depreciation of home computers." Most people buy a

new computer every two years, which means that their old one depreciated fast.

22. "Fees for a safe-deposit box to hold investments," such as stock certificates.

28. "IRA trustee's administrative fees billed separately."

50. "Worthless stock or securities." May such a fate never befall you.

Just because something is a deduction, however, doesn't mean that you should rearrange your life to be able to take advantage of it. Deduction 2, for alcoholism and drug abuse treatment, or Deduction 24, for "gambling losses to the extent of gambling gains," may be allowable write-offs, but getting to that stage can ruin your life.

I did get a kick out of Deduction 49. "Wigs essential to mental health." Hmm, does that imply that the IRS thinks bald people are psychotic? I always thought it was what's inside your head that counts, not what's on top!

After you've noted your safe-deposit box fees, figured out your bond premium, and been fitted for a toupee, it's time to do your taxes. Slightly more than half of American taxpayers do their own. All will find the Twenty-Five Most Common Tax Preparation Errors section of E&Y invaluable (see Figure 14-1).

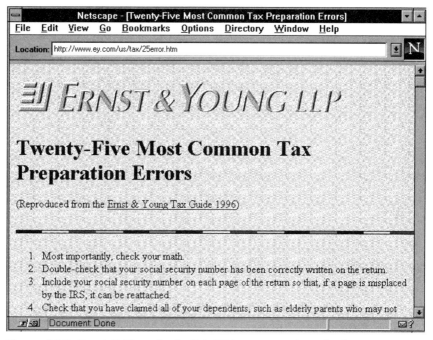

Figure 14-1: *Ernst & Young's site lists 25 tax preparation mistakes.*

Errors 7 and 23 are of the most interest to investors.

"Recheck your basis in the shares you sold this year, particularly shares of a mutual fund," Error 7 cautions. "Income and capital gains dividends that were automatically reinvested in the fund over the years increase your basis in the mutual fund and thus reduce a gain or increase a loss that you have to report."

Error 23 functions as a reminder. "Don't miss deadlines: December 31, set up a Keogh plan; April 15, make your IRA contribution; April 15, file your return or request an extension," E&Y says. The next sentence contains a link to the tax calendar on the E&Y site.

HALE & DORR'S FAMILY BUSINESS REPORT

http://www.haledorr.com/
While the tawdrier aspects of family business are best left to the screenwriters, a need and a hunger exist for practical tax advice in this sector. On Hale & Dorr's Family Business site, this accounting

firm has archived several articles about tax planning for family business.

One of the most critical issues for family businesses is the succession issue. An article by Hale & Dorr co-chair Michael Fay, which is available on the site, describes how, within the next decade or so, the generation of family entrepreneurs that founded their businesses in the 1940s and 1950s will mostly pass from the scene, leaving some key issues for their children to deal with.

"For many families," Fay writes, "estate taxes will constitute one of the most important barriers to the successful and efficient transfer of ownership and control of the family firm to the succeeding generation. For estates valued in excess of $3 million, including family business interests which may be highly illiquid, federal and state estate taxes will be assessed at a marginal rate of 55% (or 60% for estates worth between $10 million and $21 million)."

Simply put, this is too much of a burden for many family-owned enterprises to face. "Few, if any, family firms or their owners have resources sufficient to pay such amounts, even in installments over several years," Fay points out, "without significantly encroaching on the capital and threatening the economic viability of the family firm."

Fay then lays out some key points that the owners of a family business and their financial advisors must face together as they look at the thorny succession issue.

Another article, "C Corporation Vs. S Corporation Status in Light of (the) 1993 Federal Tax Revisions," explores whether the owner of subchapter S Corporations—many of them family businesses—would benefit by converting their firms to C Corporations.

The tome, by Kenneth Csaplar of Brown Brothers Harriman & Co., could use a better explanation of what "C" and "S" corporations are. This happens too often with Web content written by experts. They travel in certain circles of professional peerage in which everyone knows the jargon, so they assume that everyone else does, too. Despite Csaplar's apparent assumption that people reading this article would know their Cs from their Ss, his Planning Strategies section is informative in the way it frames the C vs.

S debate. He poses three questions that all businesses considering this choice should answer:

- "Is the corporation a cash cow with an ability to pay dividends consistently or does the company use all its available cash flow for its operations?"

- "Is there potential for an accumulated earnings tax to be assessed on the company?"

- "Will the S Corporation be sold in the near future, and will the sale be an asset sale?"

Csaplar's one- and two-paragraph answers require at least a passing familiarity with tax law, but are not too convoluted for nonfinancial advisors to understand them. His and the other articles in Family Business Report give enough of a grounding so that you can talk to your financial advisor intelligently.

IDEA CAFE

http://www.IdeaCafe.com/
The name of this business-advice Web site sounds like a great moniker for a coffee bar with whirring espresso machines and lightning-fast, T1 Internet connections at every table. Ideas, Internet; Cafe, Coffee—get it?

Idea Cafe's Business Directory has ratings of and links to several helpful tax sites, but the best value-added click stop for your time is an article by Murray Alter, a tax practice partner in the Big Six accounting firm of Coopers & Lybrand.

Two sections, "Things to Keep In Mind/Tax Changes" and "Stop! Red Flags That May Get You Audited," are especially helpful. A passage in "Keep In Mind" on depreciation should send ripples of guilt through those of us who, with a clear conscience but a bit of a fudging soul, have cut a few corners. Take, for example, Alter's advice on depreciation of computers for business use. Because you've already bought this book (which may or may not be a deduction for you but earns you deep gratitude from the author), I'm guessing you already have a computer.

If you do, read Alter's advice:

"There are different depreciation methods for different types of equipment," he says. "If you've used up the $17,500 'expensing' deductions you should carefully review the nature of what you've purchased to determine if it can be deducted over 3 years, 5 years, 7 years or longer. The faster you can depreciate something, the more money you can deduct each year. Three years is [a] pretty restricted category. The key thing to note here is that telephone equipment with microchips (and nowadays most come with chips but no dip) are depreciated over five years; without chips it's seven years."

"Chips but no dip?" Who said accountants were a bunch of boring geeks with penholders in their pockets?

Alter goes on to cite depreciation length limits for various investments. Some are items you may have; others you most certainly don't. A three-year limit exists for depreciation of breeding hogs, five years for automobiles and computers, seven years for desks and furniture, and ten years for barges. Woe to all of you with 11-year-old barges. If you try to write them off as a depreciation, see you in Tax Court.

INTERNAL REVENUE SERVICE

http://www.irs.ustreas.gov/prod/forms_pubs
Speaking of the tax man, the Internal Revenue Service actually has one of the most thorough of all Web sites. I've seen you in the public library on April 13, standing in a long line by the copy machine, waiting your turn to photostat several pages from some obscure tax form manual that the librarians didn't even know they carried. Don't like standing in line at the copier? Boot up your browser and get the forms you need from this site.

With untold thousands of pages, the IRS site obviously has too much to comprehensively cover here. You can get virtually all the forms and instructions that you need by following a string of submenus to the correct area and then clicking on the topic with a form or other text that you want to retrieve (see Figure 14-2).

Figure 14-2: *On the IRS site, clicking on any one of these choices gets you the full text of each regulation.*

Because this is a book about finances and investing, I've chosen the section on Sales and Trades of Assets. This part of the site covers issues of tax liability involved with selling stocks, bonds, or certain commodities. FYI, the most relevant tax form for these transactions is 1099-B, Proceeds From Broker and Barter Exchange Transactions.

Structurally, the site does a superb job of defining the concept that it is about to explore and then outlining the various implications of each concept.

Handling proceeds from a stock redemption is one of the salient issues of tax law that gets a thorough treatment.

"Whether a redemption is treated as a sale, trade, dividend, or other distribution depends on the circumstances in each case," sayeth the Taxman. "Both direct and indirect ownership of stock will be considered. The redemption is treated as a sale or trade of stock if:

- "The redemption is not essentially equivalent to a dividend." A link is provided here to another part of the IRS site that discusses dividends. On information-rich Web sites such as this, links immeasurably help comprehension and navigation.

- "There is a substantially disproportionate redemption of stock."

- "There is a complete redemption of all the stock of the corporation owned by the shareholder."

- "The redemption is a distribution in partial liquidation of a corporation."

By including the IRS in this book, I've probably already given you a case of the mind-association willies. Ready for some good news? Look at what the IRS defines as a nontaxable trade of investment or business property. The IRS isn't going to let you off easily. As the site notes in Sales and Trades, each of the following six conditions must be met:

- "The property must be business or investment property. You must hold both the property you trade and the property you receive for business or investment purposes. Neither property may be used for personal purposes, such as your home or family car."

   You may want to visit several other sections of the IRS site that spell out the difference between "business" and "personal" use of your residence or automobile.

- "The property must not be property held for sale. The property you trade and the property you receive must not be property you sell to customers, such as merchandise. It must be property held for investment or property held for productive use in your trade or business."

- "There must be an exchange of like-kind property. The exchange of real estate for real estate and the exchange of personal property for similar personal property are exchanges of like-kind property. The trade of an apartment house for a store building, or a panel truck for a pickup truck, are like-kind exchanges. The exchange of a piece of machinery for a store building is not a like-kind exchange."

If you're an individual, you can certainly get by with a tax software package, but the notion of like-kind property is one of those concepts that make accountants essential for businesses. Plus, if you've just traded for a pickup truck, you should also call your local, aspiring country music lyricist. Many country songs are about pickup trucks, so together, you can write a song about the experience, make a million bucks—and then go to this Web site for further advice!

■ "The property must not be stocks, bonds, notes, . . . certificates of trust or beneficial interest, or other securities or evidence of indebtedness or interest, including partnership interests. However, you can have a nontaxable exchange of corporate stocks." The term "corporate stocks" sports a handy hyperlink to a section on the subject.

■ "The property must meet the identification requirement. The property to be received must be identified by the day that is 45 days after the date of transfer of the property given up in the exchange."

■ "The exchange must meet the completed transaction requirement. The property must be received by the earlier of:

The 180th day after the date on which you transfer the property given up in the transfer, or

The due date, including extensions, for your tax return for the year in which the transfer of the property given up occurs."

Like Capistrano swallows, demanding significant others, and certain editors, the IRS knows from deadlines.

MERCURY CENTER TAX GUIDE

http://www.sjmercury.com/business/tax
Several hundred newspapers have WWW sites. Presentation and quality vary greatly. Some just post up bits and pieces of the daily paper; others mirror the entire content of each day's edition. A scarce few others, realizing that server space is cheaper than

paying for ink, newsprint, and Paul Bunyan's health insurance, put copy on their Web sites that they don't have room to print.

Newspaper Web sites are discussed more thoroughly in Chapter 18, "Extra, Extra: Financial News," but one has so much helpful tax data that I couldn't wait. This is the Mercury Center Tax Guide (see Figure 14-3), which is on the Mercury Center Web site of the *San Jose Mercury-News*.

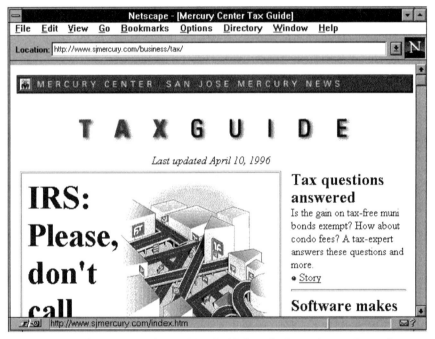

Figure 14-3: *The Mercury Center Tax Guide has the latest in tax tips and tax news.*

I've worked for daily papers, written for journalism trades, and covered the Web. The Mercury Center is, in terms of content, organization, presentation, and tools, without doubt the most comprehensive of all the newspaper Web sites. Some of this owes to the fact that the parent paper is the journal of record for the technology-savvy Silicon Valley area of California. As a matter of fact, the real-world home port for Netscape is in Mountain View, a short drive from the Merc plant in San Jose.

The Tax Guide cover page has links to the IRS Web site, places to get tax shareware (which is discussed in Chapter 20), as well as a steadily updated menu of tax-related, archived stories.

As with any collection of news articles, some have more shelf life than others. Two that have been "up" for some time and are still likely to be as you read this are "Can you take the EZ way out?" and "How to choose a tax preparer."

"Can you take the EZ way out?" is a handy look at the pros and cons of filing your personal taxes with a 1040, or "long" form, compared to a 1040A or 1040 EZ "short" form. The debate is framed in a series of short, frequently one-sentence paragraphs that are easy to understand. You're told, for example, that both "short" forms have the same $50,000 limit on taxable income, but the 1040A lets you file if you're reporting income from dividends, Individual Retirement Accounts, pensions, and annuities.

"File the dreaded 'long form' if you're ineligible to file the 1040EZ or 1040A or want to claim deductions and credits the shorter forms don't track," the Merc advises. "You also must file the 1040 if you earned capital gains, sold your house or are filing a separate return and your spouse itemizes."

Generally, Web sites can benefit from "bet you didn't know that" morsels. To complete the 1995 1040 form, the IRS suggested blocking out 11 hours and 38 minutes of your time. What if you don't have the time? You may wish to access the "How to choose a tax preparer" article.

The uncredited writer asserts that the decision whether to do your own taxes depends on two general factors: how complicated your financial dealings are and whether you have the gumption to compute your own return.

"Whether you need to hire a pro depends on whether your finances are complex or in transition," says the Mercury Center. "But some reasons are more personal. Are you intimidated by tax forms? Do numbers twist you in knots? Will procrastination get you in a fix? If you find yourself nodding at those questions, consider hiring a pro."

MERRILL LYNCH: MINIMIZING YOUR TAXES

http://www.merrill-lynch.ml.com/personal/taxes
Taking the broad view, the thing I like most about the Merrill Lynch site is the way it integrates information about tax law with practical tax and financial-planning advice.

Minimizing Your Taxes has everything a good site should: clear language, lots of links, and clearly organized subsections in a sensible hierarchy. It doesn't call itself a FAQ, but with a question-and-answer format, it is written in the style of a Frequently Asked Questions list. Where appropriate, "tax-planning strategy" advice specific to each question is appended in an ending paragraph of the answer field. Usually, the first sentence of the advice paragraph is italicized and thus stands out with the message of importance.

You'll start on the Table of Contents page, where you will see more than 15 topical links (see Figure 14-4) to sections about such critical investing issues as Capital Gains and Losses, Interest and Dividends, and Tax Investments/Master Limited Partnerships. The cover page has an e-mail link through which you can order a Merrill Lynch Tax Management kit, as well as a route to a search function where you can look for a Merrill Lynch Financial Consultant in your region.

The following describes my brief visit to each of the three sections mentioned in the preceding paragraph.

Capital Gains has 14 questions. One of the most interesting is question 8, "What rules affect the taxation of capital gains and losses on listed stock options?"

"Writing options offers timing advantages for tax purposes because the premium becomes taxable only upon the close of a position by exercise, expiration or a closing transaction," Merrill Lynch says. "The premium income is considered a short-term capital gain if the option expires unexercised."

The tax-planning strategy Merrill Lynch recommends for such a circumstance:

"Trade stock options that expire next year for flexibility in realizing gains and losses," they counsel. "If you trade stock options, you might consider buying or selling put and call options that expire early next year rather than late this year and that do not involve straddles. If you trade options that expire in January, you have the flexibility to close out the position before year end if you have a loss and use that loss to offset income this year. If the position shows a profit, you can keep it open until January and realize the gain in the next year."

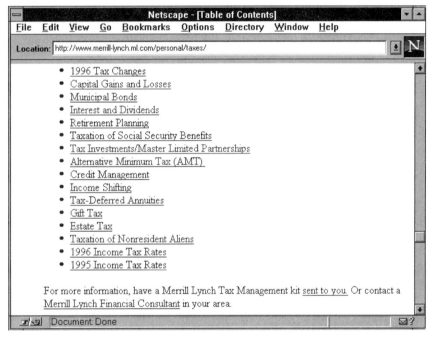

Figure 14-4: *Start at the Merrill Lynch Table of Contents page.*

The Interest and Dividends section has 13 questions, along with Bottom Line tables explaining tax liabilities for taxable bonds, tax-exempt bonds, and dividends.

"Chapter 22," the topic of the first question in this area, asks how interest paid on the purchase of a bond or CD between interest payment dates is taxed. Such seldom-considered but important issues help give the site its heft.

"If a taxable bond or CD is purchased between payment dates, the amount of interest earned on that bond from the last payment date to the date of purchase is added to the purchase price as accrued interest," Merrill Lynch says. "No adjustment to the bond's cost basis is made as a result of this payment."

Sounds too easy. There's a catch, right? You guessed correctly.

"When the next coupon or payment date arrives and the full interest payment is received," you read, "the purchaser should subtract the amount of accrued interest paid in order to arrive at the amount of interest income that is actually taxable for that period. The seller of the bond treats the accrued interest received as taxable income."

The Master Limited Partnership area has seven questions. Arguably the most compelling, Question 51 inquires, "How is the income from a publicly traded partnership (PTP) taxed?" The answer refers to "passive activities." These are not watching pro football when you really should be hanging Sheetrock, but, as you learn in the answer to Question 49, "Any trade or business in which an investor does not materially participate on a regular, continuous and substantial basis is considered a passive activity."

Always wanted to know how PTP income is taxed? On Minimizing Your Taxes, Merrill Lynch tells you how: "A partner's share of the net income of a PTP (both portfolio and business income) will generally not be treated as income from a passive activity. Thus, it cannot be used to offset losses from other passive activities. When a PTP generates both portfolio income and a business loss, the loss cannot be used to offset the portfolio income. It is carried forward to subsequent years to be used against business income of the PTP only."

TAX ANALYSTS

http://www.tax.org/

You shouldn't be surprised that tax law is a living, breathing thing. And you would be well advised to stay current on new developments. Why stay current when you've got all the latest tax software plus a CPA who stays up to speed? The news of the day can interface with tax law in any one of several ways, such as:

- Political campaigns and deals may cause laws to be changed or amended.

- Budget shortfalls may spark tighter IRS collection procedures.

- Judicial rulings may clear up ambiguities, or allow implementation of new taxes that had been held up pending a court challenge.

You can get tax news in one of several ways, but you'll probably have to sift through some nonrelated data. If you care more about tax news than general business developments, you might want to visit and bookmark TaxNotes NewsWire.

TaxNotes, a service of tax news publishing company Tax Analysts, updates its wire every business day at 10 A.M., noon, and 4:30 P.M. eastern time. A typical day's update contains several stories, often analyzing the likely effects of just-rendered court rulings.

Tax Analysts has two other sections worth stopping at. Tax Snapshots, which changes every couple of months, is a statistical table that backgrounds a portion of tax law under scrutiny. In mid-1996, the table noted the number of taxpayers with capital gains, broken down by adjusted gross income. The 1993 figures (the latest available at the time), showed that 2,797,000 taxpayers claiming between $50,000 and $99,999 in adjusted gross income had net income from sales of capital gains assets.

There are also links to specialized discussion group archived postings (see Figure 14-5) in such areas as business tax issues, estate, gift and trust, and partnership taxation. These resemble Usenet newsgroups, but are provided for and administered by Tax Analysts.

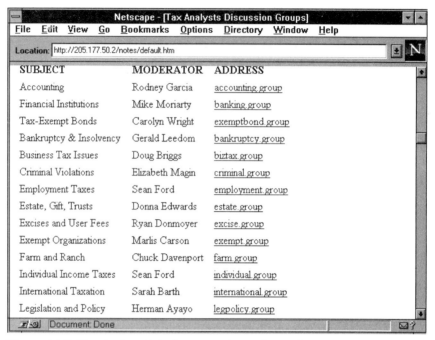

Figure 14-5: *Tax Analysts' site has more than a dozen discussion groups on specialized areas of tax law.*

THE TAX PROPHET

http://www.taxprophet.com/

When taxes are discussed, tax attorneys are not far away. Tax lawyer Robert Sommers has put much of his expertise on his own Web site, which he calls The Tax Prophet. Sommers has structured his site (see Figure 14-6) into six basic areas, including a Firm Profile, "Hot Tax Topics and Frequently Asked Questions," links to publications that have run Sommers's works, an information area on foreign taxes, an "Interactive Tax Applications" role-playing, game-like Q/A, and "Cyber-Surfing," which has links to other tax sites that the Tax Prophet likes.

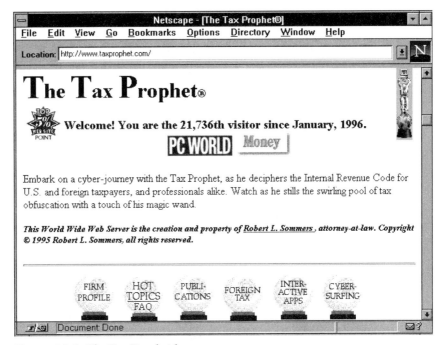

Figure 14-6: *The Tax Prophet home page.*

Some of Sommers's articles have appeared in the *San Francisco Examiner*. One 1996 column, retrievable from a link in the FAQ, covers the taxability of stock sales. One question asks what the taxable gain would be if 20 shares of stock were bought at $50 per share, another 20 shares bought at $100 per share, and, subsequently, 20 shares of each were sold at $110 per share.

In the hands of a lesser sort, even attempting to respond to this question would ask more questions than it answered. Yet, like the good teacher that he is, Sommers explains clearly:

"Gain is the difference between the purchase and sales prices," Sommers writes. "You need to identify which block you sold. For example, if you can identify the stock sold as the second block, your basis is $100 per share, so your taxable gain is $10 per share."

Sommers adds to his explanation with some welcome advice on how to keep the records of the $50 per share and $100 per share stock separate as they are sold. If this can be done, substantial confusion can be prevented.

TURBOTAX

http://www.intuit.com/turbotax

Given that Intuit's TurboTax has been the best-selling tax-preparation software package for several years, one might expect its Web site to be a rich trove of data, text, and news. For comprehensiveness, the TurboTax section of the Intuit site falls a bit short of the mark. The Quicken area, which has been mentioned several other times in this book and is covered in Chapter 20, has more information than you'll find in TurboTax's neighborhood.

Still, TurboTax does have articles that can help you. You can find several sections on how the sale of your home may affect your taxes (see Figure 14-7). Businesspeople and investors especially might want to click to the page titled Postponing Gain From the Sale of a Home.

Figure 14-7: *Intuit's TurboTax site has several articles devoted to real-estate tax planning.*

Perhaps you're reading this book in your home office. Maybe it's not a full-time office, but a place where you can retreat on selected evenings and weekends to write that business proposal, confer with clients, or do research on the Web. Should you need or want to sell your home, what implications—if any—will running a business in your home have for your tax status?

"If you sell property that is used partly for business and partly as your residence," says TurboTax, "the sale is treated as two separate transactions." These "separate transactions" are the sale of a business, and the sale of a personal residence. Selling such a home comes with its usual share of tax code caveats. Rather than simply quote from tax law as some other sites do, TurboTax gives this topic a good overview treatment.

"You must allocate the sales price and the original cost between the personal portion (your residence) and the business portion," TurboTax notes. "Only the gain on the part used as your residence may be postponed. Your investment in your new home must equal or exceed the adjusted sales price of that portion of your old home allocated to your residence in order to defer your gain. If only part of your new property is used as your residence, only the cost allocated to that use is considered reinvested."

If you are thinking of selling your business-hosting home but haven't done so yet, TurboTax says that converting your home office to personal use in the previous tax year before you sell your house may free you up from having to pay taxes on the portion of the residence that you're using for business.

TurboTax's Checklist of Taxable Income is another area that you might want to browse. It's sort of like the polar opposite of Ernst & Young's Overlooked Tax Deductions page. TurboTax gives you a major reality check by noting several musts. You'll have to pay taxes on business profits, capital gains, income on most bonds, joint venture income, and income from profit-sharing plans.

There is justice, though: "embezzlement proceeds, in the year of embezzlement," are taxable. Sounds ridiculous, but such provisions have been enacted so that if prosecutors can't prove embezzlement, at least they can nail you for not paying taxes on ill-gotten gains. Now, how many pens did you "borrow" from the office last year?

MOVING ON

In the last 10 chapters, you have discovered sites or pages that can be easily classified. Some other useful, financial-oriented URLs can't be so easily pigeonholed. The next chapter takes you on a tour of some of them.

Miscellaneous

Some finance-oriented Web sites don't comfortably fit into any of the categories set up so far. Either they overlap categories or have a component about them that few other sites have. This chapter covers some sites that can help you plan your finances, career, and investment strategy, but that are so unique, they can't be pigeonholed.

AMERICAN BUSINESS INFORMATION BUSINESS CREDIT SERVICE

http://www.lookupusa.com/
Been to your computer store lately? If you've managed to visit the CD-ROM section, you may have seen products such as the American Yellow Pages, the 9-Digit Zip Code Directory, the 88 Million Households Phone Book, and the 16 Million Businesses phone directory. These superior offerings allow you to search through the equivalent of several thousand hard-copy phone books with just a few keystrokes.

American Business Information has migrated most of these offerings to its corporate Web site as well. Its site is also a storefront for more specialized features such as its Business Credit Service (see Figure 15-1).

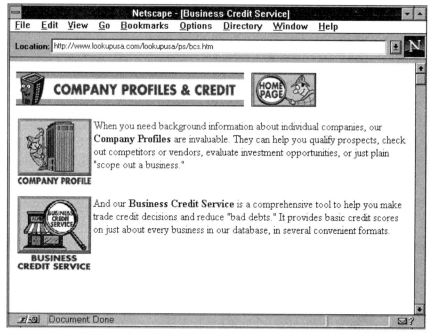

Figure 15-1: *ABI's Business Credit Service page tells you how to sign up for its Business Credit Service.*

Business Credit subscriptions cost $1,295 a year. This sounds like a lot but really isn't when you figure that the service may help you prequalify or reject a sales prospect who could either pay or owe you many more times the subscription cost.

For the price, you get a 12-volume printed directory plus CD-ROM with a credit rating score on more than 10 million businesses. This information is updated with two additional services, Online Access and InfoAccess. Online Access provides more recent information than that on the CD-ROM, whereas InfoAccess charges you $3 for dialing into a special toll-free number, reciting your password, and then ordering a report.

Should you require even more detailed information, both the Online and Info plans allow access to Business Credit Reports from TRW's Business Credit Division's database. These $29 reports detail payment history and whether the company has ever been sued or has declared bankruptcy.

Arguably, it may have been more convenient for ABI to make all of its information available on its Web site via a password, but I guess it considers its boutique services too valuable to give away or support via online advertising. Regardless of the inroads that secured transactions make on our business culture, some Web sites will always exist that adopt a storefront approach. This doesn't lessen the value of the end product. It just makes you work harder for it.

AMERICAN LAW INSTITUTE: UNIFORM COMMERCIAL CODE

http://www.law.cornell.edu/ucc
I've included this site as an example of a library-like directory that contains resources, rather than as an end-destination site in and of itself. For our purposes, the most useful area is the Uniform Commercial Code section.

The Uniform Commercial Code (UCC) is a compendium of state and federal laws that covers just about every type of financial transaction you can think of. At this Web site (see Figure 15-2) you can get a full text of the law on such subjects as Leases, Negotiable Instruments, Bank Deposits and Collection, Funds Transfers, and Investment Securities. You can fully search each of these texts using a keyword.

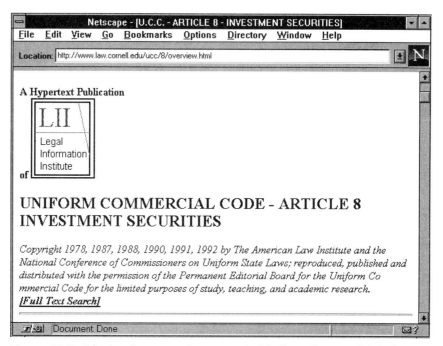

Figure 15-2: *Of prime interest to investors, the Uniform Commercial Code is carried on this site.*

You may think this stuff is written by lawyers for lawyers. You're right, but surprisingly, the language is plain enough for almost anyone with a reasonable amount of financial knowledge to understand. If you're an investor or are a more-than-minor participant in detailed financial transactions, you really should visit this site.

Funds Transfers and Investment Security sections are most relevant to this book, so I've examined how this information is presented.

Article 4A, Funds Transfers, is divided into five general parts.

Part One, Subject Matter and Definitions, defines what payment orders and funds transfers are, along with Federal Reserve Bank regulations concerning these issues.

Part Two, Issue and Acceptance of Payment Order, discusses the circumstances and consequences of a whole host of errors and malfeasance, including erroneous payment orders, misdescription of beneficiary, and the liability and duty of the receiving bank regarding unaccepted payment orders.

Part Three, Execution Of Payment Order by Receiving Bank, touches on the obligations of the bank in executing the payment order, and on issues revolving around the liability for late or improper execution or failure to execute the payment order.

Part Four, Payment, defines such terms as Payment Date and details the obligations of the sending bank to pay the receiving bank.

Part Five, Miscellaneous Provisions, guides banks on issues such as the order in which items, payment orders, and withdrawals may be charged to an account.

Article 8 of the Uniform Commercial Code covers Investment Securities.

Part One, General Matters, contains an index of definitions, as well as a guide to the transferability of securities.

I want to stop there and see what the site's UCC has to say about this:

> Unless otherwise agreed and subject to any applicable law or regulation respecting short sales, a person obligated to transfer securities may transfer any certificated security of the specified issue in bearer form or registered in the name of the transferee, or endorsed to him or in blank, or he may transfer an equivalent uncertificated security to the transferee or a person designated by the transferee.
>
> If the buyer fails to pay the price as it comes due under a contract of sale, the seller may recover the price of: certificated securities accepted by the buyer; uncertificated securities that have been transferred to the buyer or a person designated by the buyer; and other securities if efforts at their resale would be unduly burdensome or if there is no readily available market for their resale.

Part Two of the Investment Securities UCC, Issue-Issuer, is highlighted by discussions on issuer's responsibilities and the "Effect of Unauthorized Signature(s) on Certificated Security or Initial Transaction Statement(s)."

Part Three has 21 sections, including Creditors' Rights and Statute of Frauds. Because anyone can become a victim of securities fraud, check out what the UCC has to say:

A contract for the sale of securities is not enforceable by way of action or defense unless:

(a) there is some writing signed by the party against whom enforcement is sought or by his authorized agent or broker, sufficient to indicate that a contract has been made for sale of a stated quantity of described securities at a defined or stated price;

(b) delivery of a certificated security or transfer instruction has been accepted, or transfer of an uncertificated security has been registered and the transferee has failed to send written objection to the issuer within 10 days after receipt of the initial transaction statement confirming the registration, or payment has been made, but the contract is enforceable under this provision only to the extent of the delivery, registration, or payment;

(c) within a reasonable time a writing in confirmation of the sale or purchase and sufficient against the sender under paragraph (a) has been received by the party against whom enforcement is sought and he has failed to send written objection to its contents within 10 days after its receipt; or

(d) the party against whom enforcement is sought admits in his pleading, testimony, or otherwise in court that a contract was made for the sale of a stated quantity of described securities at a defined or stated price.

Finally, Part Four discusses the issuer's duty with regard to adverse claims, or what happens if certificated securities are lost, destroyed, or stolen.

ART OF SMART AUTOMOBILE LEASING

http://www.mindspring.com/~ahearn/lease/lease.html
Your improved financial standing has now put you in the position
to afford a nicer and newer car. Leasing might be an option for
you. Of all the sites on the Web that describe the financial issues
involved with leasing, the Art of Smart Automobile Leasing (see
Figure 15-3) is by far the best.

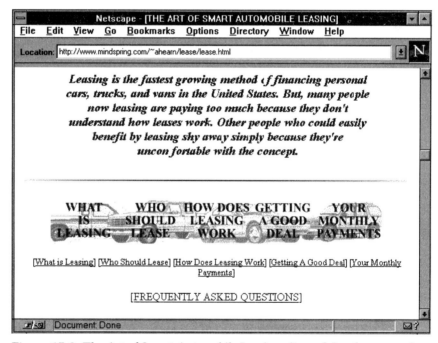

Figure 15-3: *The Art of Smart Automobile Leasing site explains the pros and cons of leasing your next car.*

The writer of this site is Al Hearn, who is described as "an
experienced and educated consumer." That's all he needs to say.
I've financed and leased my share of cars, and I thought I knew
the advantages of each strategy until I read Hearn's insights. This
guy knows his stuff.

Although Hearn lives in Marietta, Georgia, my home town, I haven't met him yet. Further identification is not attempted, but the depth of information is presented in such an objective manner that none is necessary.

Hearn has organized his site around five sections. These include the following:

- What Is Leasing?
- Who Should Lease?
- How Does Leasing Work?
- Getting A Good Deal
- Your Monthly Payments

According to Hearn, leasing might make sense for you if:

- "You like having a new car every two or three years."
- "You want to drive a more expensive car, and have lower monthly payments."
- "You like having the option of not making a down payment."
- "You like having a car that's always in warranty in case something goes wrong."
- "You hate having to sell or trade your old cars, and losing money in the process."
- "You don't like tying up your money in depreciating assets, i.e., cars."

Hearn then presents six equally valid arguments against leasing.

In the "How Does Leasing Work?" section, Al provides a glossary of eight terms anyone considering leasing should know. Residual Factor, for example, is defined correctly as "A percentage, set by leasing companies, used to calculate Residual Value by multiplying times MSRP (Manufacturer's Suggested Retail Price). For example," notes Hearn, "on a specific make and model car, the leasing company might determine the Residual Factor for a 24 month lease to be .65, which means that the Residual Value will be 65% of the car's original MSRP at the end of two years."

With so much helpful information on this superb site, you'd think Hearn was trying to get you to buy something. Yes, you're right, but he charges only $9.95, counting shipping, for a copy of lease-computing payment tables and charts that he's prepared. In a Web world in which some people charge several hundred dollars for information that isn't one-tenth as useful, $9.95 sounds like a cool bargain to me.

If you want to ask him a question, Hearn's site also has a mail-to.

CharterMedia Briefing.com

http://www.briefing.com/
CharterMedia, Inc., a financial research firm, offers something that few if any investment Web sites do: a series of stock and bond market commentaries updated several times a day (see Figure 15-4).

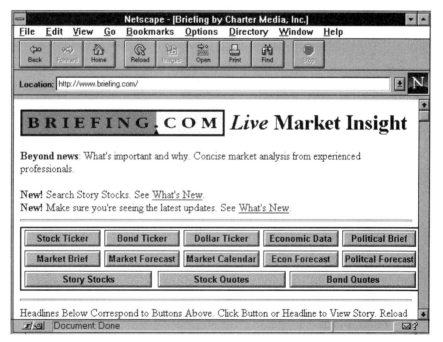

Figure 15-4: *Charter Media's Briefing.com updates its market commentaries several times a day.*

Divided by sectors such as Papers, Drugs, Oils, Financials, and Banks, a rundown of "Strong" and "Weak" New York Stock Exchange and NASDAQ stocks pops up on this site eight times a day, beginning at 9:20 A.M. eastern time. The next two updates are timed for 9:40 A.M. and the opening bell at 10:00 A.M. The last update is provided at 4:15 P.M., 15 minutes after the market closes.

News stories affecting major stocks or industries are abstracted and put online as soon as they are received. Additionally, the Bond Market Ticker is updated five times daily, and the Dollar Market Ticker is freshened three times a day.

To this, add daily Market Forecasts as well as Political and Market Briefs. When events warrant, Economic and Political Forecasts are updated also.

Presentation is in a brief but concise fashion, perfect for busy people. The advantages of coming here are several. You can get more information from a financial service such as Bloomberg, but its dedicated terminals will cost you several thousand dollars. Financial newswires, which are examined in detail in Chapter 19, "The Online Services," will carry much more copy but you'll have to sift through it. Charter's news comes in small, easily digestible morsels—and it's free.

COMMERCENET

http://www.commerce.net
CommerceNet (see Figure 15-5) is one of the major associations that will define the transactional future of Internet commerce. It was started with a $6 million seed grant from the U.S. Government's Technology Reinvestment Project. Today, several hundred electronics, computer, software, financial, and media organizations are members.

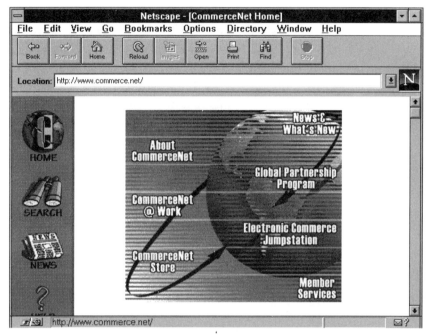

Figure 15-5: *CommerceNet's home page has several icons linking to detailed explanations of several consortium initiatives. Befitting the dynamic growth of electronic commerce, the site may have moved by the time you read this book, but there will be a forwarding address left on this page.*

The CommerceNet site's Frequently Asked Questions list does a superb job of explaining what the organization is and does. Here's a quick overview of the FAQ's major sections:

- General Questions lays out what CommerceNet is and provides a link to the CommerceNet Participants Directory. The Directory, which is alphabetically indexed and keyword searchable, also provides links to each participating company's or group's Web site.

- Participation in CommerceNet tells you how to join. By the way, you don't have to be a multibillion-dollar company to sign up. If you want to join as an information, product, or service provider, follow the registration instructions. After you fill that out, you'll be sent an application.

The best thing, though, is that anyone can use CommerceNet. Most members have "Internet storefronts" on which they tout their relevant services or products. If you're thinking about doing electronic commerce, or just want to learn more about it, you'll want to spend lots of time hopping around these links.

■ Internet Connectivity answers some basic questions about how to get hooked up to the Internet, the minimum modem speed recommended to visit the CommerceNet site (a minimum connection of 28.8K), and what you'll need if you want to be a CommerceNet provider. For this purpose, a browser and Web server software, such as the Netscape Commerce Server, are required.

■ Network Services describes free offerings such as the Internet Consultants directory. This valuable resource is linked from the site and will be of interest to you if you are thinking of putting up a Web site from which you'd like to do electronic commerce. The site also has questions addressing the latest developments on privacy, authentication, and secure payment protocols for electronic commerce over the Internet.

CommerceNet's site also has an interesting Pilots and Projects section that describes the organization's several marketing and technical studies. Two of the most interesting are an "End-to-End Commerce" pilot that will measure the return on investment to small businesses that adapt Internet commerce to sell their services or goods, and a "Business Value of Electronic" pilot that develops measuring yardsticks to help businesses determine whether sales from "electronic catalog" Web sites justify the expenditures involved in setting them up.

Future CommerceNet initiatives will be posted to the site as they are developed. If you're curious about the electronic transactions that new technologies will enable, CommerceNet should be one of your frequent pit stops. Bookmark their site and come back often.

FINANCIAL SERVICES TECHNOLOGY CONSORTIUM

http://www.fstc.org/
Ever wonder who really is making decisions about the future of banking and electronic commerce? No, it isn't the Trilateral Commission, but a group called the Financial Services Technology Consortium (see Figure 15-6). It defines itself as "a consortium of financial services providers, national laboratories, universities, and government agencies who sponsor and participate in non-competitive collaborative research and development on interbank technical projects."

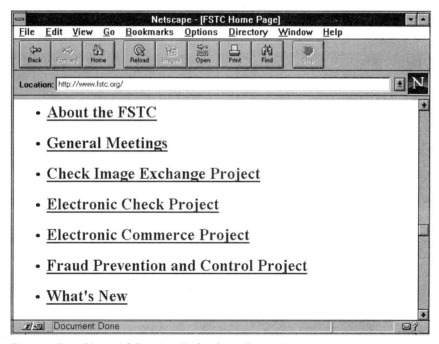

Figure 15-6: *Financial Services Technology Consortium gives you an overview of what bankers think are the important electronic commerce issues.*

Go to the FSTC site and you can read revealing position papers, most of them written by high-ranking bankers. These are some of the key players in determining how business will be transacted online in the near- to mid-term.

One of the goals of electronic commerce is to gain the ability to conduct transactions by means of check image exchanges and electronic checks. Rather than read through incomprehensible technical treatises written by mid-level functionary wonks, FSTC's General Product Information page will tell you what's really going on.

So, what's this about Check Image Exchange?

"The FSTC has a vision to build a national check imaging system based on interoperable, open systems architectures that provide flexible, economical services for the financial industry, the retail services industry, and for the consumer," explains Citibank's Bill Krajewski. "In order to achieve successful implementation of interbank check imaging, standardized check image representations of acceptable quality levels must be exchanged electronically in a secured fashion between financial institutions and clearly demonstrate check truncation as a viable and necessary solution which will benefit the whole industry. That secured electronic exchange is part of the FSTC vision."

Electronic checks, which will be integrated into existing bank check-clearing systems, will before the end of the decade be a standard way to pay for services or merchandise bought over a public network, such as the Internet. The software is secure, but unless the banking community is confident, it will never be widely accepted. John Doggett of the Bank of Boston, project chair of the FSTC's steering committee on electronic checking, is an ardent believer in the technology.

You can read Doggett's most current thoughts on the site. Also valuable is his on-the-mark description of electronic checking's processes and benefits:

"The electronic check consists of an ASCII text block, cryptographically signed by an electronic checkbook, as an electronic mail counterpart to the existing system of paper checks and physical mail," Doggett notes. "The consumer has an electronic checkbook which he or she will insert into a personal computer or screenphone in order to 'write' an electronic check for transmission to a merchant or service provider for payment for goods and services. This form of payment will be of particular value in paying for electronic or network services where no previous relationship exists between buyer and seller."

NETEXCHANGE

http://www.tradeguide.com/
At any one time on the Web, numerous sites are "under construction." Usually, they aren't worth visiting until they are complete. When I last visited NetExchange (see Figure 15-7), it was new and incomplete but the concept was highly promising.

Figure 15-7: *Looking for offshore investment opportunities? NetExchange may have some leads for you.*

"NetExchange," say the site masters, "promotes businesses, professionals and associations involved in international trade, investment and finance. Are you interested in finding products to import or export, increasing sales, consulting, marketing, or starting entrepreneurial ventures? Our site is growing with direct trade leads, brochures and information to assist your business in today's global marketplace."

The first substantive section to go up on NetExchange was the "CaribGuide Index." This is a keyword-searchable guide to conducting Business and Commerce in the Caribbean region, and has links to trade and transportation services and to product manufacturers and distributors. The Index also has listings of Banking and Financial Services, Computers, and Software, as well as a section on Direct Investment opportunities, such as government contracts and bidding procedures, investment information and company profiles, and property available for investment.

If you want to do business in the Caribbean, or anywhere else for that matter, you may want to visit first. That's where CaribGuide's country, travel, and lodging information can help. You can also find details on the art, culture, and sports of most nations for which NetExchange carries listings.

STERN MANAGEMENT CONSULTING

http://www.stern.nyu.edu/
The faculty of your local college probably contains a lot of brainpower. Some professors either teach or do research that will wind up in obscure academic journals or be communicated in symposia that you'll never hear about.

But what if a prestigious university's business school decided to market that brainpower to the local business community? You'd have an entity such as Stern Management Consulting (SMC), an educational and consultation service offered by the Stern School of Business at New York University (see Figure 15-8).

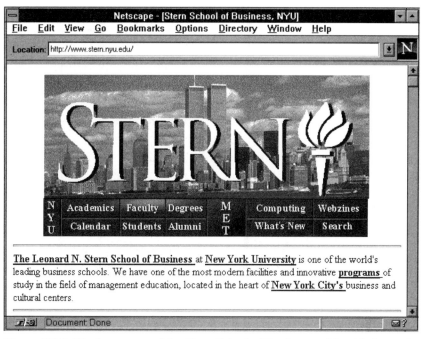

Figure 15-8: *The home page of the Stern School of Business at New York University.*

Stern has its own Web site, on which it posts an online brochure outlining its offerings. You learn that the Consulting initiative is part of the Stern School's MBA specialization in management consulting degree program. Students who already have been trained in management, accounting, marketing, finance, operations, and information systems are made available "to help companies like yours address key business issues."

These teams are led by a Steering Committee of Project Advisors, who are Stern School professors with various areas of expertise. Their input is supplemented by the guidance of an advisory board comprising practicing consultants from prestigious firms such as Andersen Consulting, Booz-Allen & Hamilton, McKinsey & Co., IBM, Bankers Trust, and Citibank. The cause of comprehensiveness would have been helped by some posted case studies, but you'll find enough information here to give you a general idea about what SMC is and does.

The site plainly states that projects undertaken by SMC should be afforded the same respect that a regular management consulting effort should. "To do an effective job for a client, the engagement team may require access to confidential company information," SMC says. "Clients should be willing to make all relevant information available to the students. In turn, all SMC participants agree to treat the information with complete confidentiality."

To ensure maximum value, companies agreeing to work with SMC should appoint a contact person from their own staff. This person or persons should be available on an as-needed basis.

Statistically, it's very likely that your business is not based in the New York area. If that's true, this site can still be of value to you. Perhaps a business school in your region has a similar program in place. Maybe your area has a school that could start such an initiative, but no one has thought of it. You might want to download and print the information from the Stern site and then show it to a business school professor. These are people who are rated, in part, for their ability to integrate their curricula with real-world concerns. If your contact with them eventually leads to a program similar to SMC, credit will be distributed to deserving parties.

You, as the person who presented the idea, will be seen by the business community as one heck of a networker and doer. That will be great for your business.

If you aren't sure how to present the idea, you can e-mail Stern Management Consulting's Managing Director via a mail-to link provided on the site. By the way, sites that have mail-tos to key people—not to some autobot mailbox read only by customer service clerks—get an A+ on my report card.

MOVING ON

In this chapter, you've seen how the diversity of Web sites contributes to the vitality of this medium. Vitality also spurs momentum and conversation. In large part, the Usenet section of the Internet is devoted to conversation. Although they aren't part of the Web, Usenet newsgroups share some common interests and topics. In the next chapter, you take a closer look at some finance-related newsgroups.

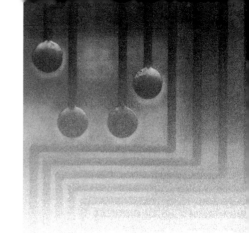

Other Places for Finance Information

Using Usenet

The World Wide Web and Usenet each are sectors of the greater Internet, but that's just about where the similarity ends. When it comes to news and advice about investing, handling your personal finances, or your career, both can be immensely helpful sources of information. Where the difference lies between, say, an investment-oriented Web site and a like-minded newsgroup is in how the information is gathered and presented.

If you honestly think that you have a foolproof way to predict stock prices, you can establish your own Web pages for a few hundred dollars. Usenet newsgroups strike even a better deal. If you're paying your ISP or online service a small, flat, monthly charge for Internet access, you can post your comment to any newsgroup for free. Absolutely without charge.

You may be thinking that in this world in which Web sites are cheap and newsgroup postings are gratis, heeding financial advice given there is something only a sucker would do. Your caution is not entirely ill advised, but is somewhat overstated.

When it comes to matters of commerce, there is, at least, some filtering of Web sites. In their names and URLs, many bear the proud imprint of a well-respected commercial name—a Merrill Lynch, a Charles Schwab, a Wells Fargo Bank. Content on other sites is managed by a trusted, objective institution such as a financial research firm, a major business magazine, or an academic institution. Even novices can instantly detect the quality and credibility gap between a richly detailed, frequently updated, soberly worded major insurance company site and a thrown-together, poorly coded, typo-ridden site put up by some guy on his lunch break.

 ## WHAT IS USENET?

Usenet is the area of the Internet devoted to postings and opinions about anything from the merits of this year's episodes of "Frasier" to the art of picking penny stocks. Although the more than 20,000 newsgroups in existence represent the entire scope of human inquiry, belief, and endeavor, they have a similar structure. Basically, these are a collection of topical messages organized into *threads*, or topic areas.

Without actually going to a newsgroup, the best way to visualize what a thread is would be to imagine yourself at a large cocktail reception at which 50 separate conversations, all about investing, are going on at once. Each conversation has 10 participants. Every time one of the participants makes a statement in response to what was immediately said before, that statement would be another contribution to the thread. If someone in the group wished, however, to change the subject of the conversation (but still keep it relevant to the designated topic of investing), he or she would be starting another thread. Conversationalists would feel free to join that thread or to revisit topics they had talked about 10 minutes ago.

Typically, a *newsreader*, a utility that comes with your browser or dial-up Internet connection, can read postings that were made at any time from the last few seconds to the last few weeks. For each group you visit, you'll see a subject tree with a one-sentence description of each thread. Typing in the number of the thread will display the first message of the thread on your screen.

Some groups are moderated, most often by an unpaid volunteer who probably thought up the idea for the group, submitted it through Usenet's peer-judged certification procedure, and now "manages" the site.

This management is likely to be akin to the relatively lenient policing practiced by municipal gendarmes in university-dominated college towns—control public boorishness, make sure that the victory rally doesn't mushroom into a riot, and so on.

Such a procedure generally involves setting up some ground rules. On newsgroups, these rules are most likely to be found in Frequently Asked Questions lists, or FAQs. A whole subculture of FAQ "maintainers" has arisen on Usenet. FAQs that you find in Usenet are quite dissimilar from the marketing-driven FAQs that you find on lots of ".com" Web sites. Whereas commercial Web FAQs exist in large measure to explain how super the products being sold are, most Usenet FAQs concern themselves, at least in part, with setting ground rules about what the purpose of the newsgroup is and what topics will be appropriate for postings. Some of the better-run Usenet FAQs also explain the subject of the FAQ.

Other newsgroups don't have the luxury of a moderator or FAQ maintainer. With no policing except the peer-pressure wrath of other posters, groups devoted to affairs of commerce can closely resemble a carnival full of fast-buck types shouting their invitations to the onlookers cruising the midway. Get-rich-quick schemes can be posted with near impunity on unsupervised newsgroups, so don't believe everything you read.

I know I've sketched out a most unappealing tableau. You might be wondering, why visit Usenet at all? Alas, there are advantages. The best one is that you are among friends. There may be hustlers lurking about, but at least on financial-related groups, most of the postings are by people like you, looking for information not necessarily from experts but from people who have undergone what you are contemplating.

If a penny stock offer that you've read about sounds too good to be true, is it? Well, all you have to do is ask. You'll probably get multiple responses. Not all of them will agree, but you should be able to glean a consensus.

WHAT MAKES A GOOD FINANCIAL USENET NEWSGROUP?

I am going to apply a different criteria set to newsgroups than I did for Web sites. The Web, of course, is a visual, multimedia medium in which the presence and utility of such elements go a long way toward assessing the worth of a site. With very few exceptions, however, most of the 20,000 or so newsgroups are text-only, and must rise or fall based on their verbal content.

At their best, Usenet newsgroups can fulfill the role of a wise, altruistic counselor or friend. This isn't always the case, so the best way to answer the question is by examining what makes a "bad" newsgroup that isn't worth your time.

If you're looking for financial advice, stay away from news-groups that:

- Have too many "offers" and not enough advice. In their thread titles, many solicitations appear in ALL CAPS, a spelling style generally counter to rules of Netiquette. This means that someone is shouting, putting volume over substance. What's even worse, these same danged offers may well appear on a dozen newsgroups. Such multiple postings are called "spamming" and are unacceptable behavior in most circumstances.

- Contain many threads with these words: "ONLY," "EXCLUSIVE," "NOW," or threads with titles ending in an exclamation mark (!). Because any poster can name his or her thread, this once again shows boorish manners. Nothing wrong with selling something if the group culture allows it, but why shout?

- Contain numerous postings widely different from each other. Newsgroups have a typical growth cycle. They are born from a very specific topical idea, but can change as new visitors unfamiliar with the group's original intent start to post irrelevant messages, or new developments in the chartered subject broaden the field of discussion. When this happens, the frequent result is that a few of the original participants will split the group into parts. A new group, with a clearer mission, is created.

- Doesn't have a FAQ. This isn't absolutely necessary, but a clear sense of mission will go a long way toward ensuring that the dialog remains focused, civil, and ethical.

USENET NEWSGROUPS

Not all the financial-related newsgroups will satisfy every one of my demands, but each bears at least a visit. The following sections take a look at some.

ALT.INVEST.PENNY-STOCKS

This newsgroup (see Figure 16-1) has its share of solicitations, but there are a good number of postings of material previously published elsewhere (a questionable practice that may be challenged by a publisher's litigious attorneys). To this, add a heavy dose of "here's what I think, now what do you think" threads, mixed in with a few cries for help. In short, a typical menu for a financial newsgroup.

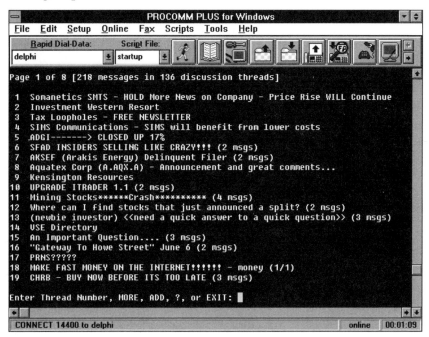

Figure 16-1: *The thread menu for alt.invest.penny-stocks.*

Unlike a Web site, which can follow the same structure for years, a newsgroup changes its entire content every few weeks. That's how long most newsreader utilities will search back, so older postings usually drop off. Specialized search services such as Deja News (http://www.dejanews.com) can resurrect these older postings for you, but unless you know what you are looking for, the current thread menu is the best guide.

Although the individual posts cited will have long since "fallen off" by the time you read this, an overview of them should define the long-term nature of each group.

Some of the typical threads posted on alt.invest.penny-stocks during the immediate two weeks preceding my visit, included the following:

- Does anybody know any good investments?

- AVOID TAXES on Your Investments!

- What's the minimum $ to open an E-broker account?

- What's the cheapest way to trade 1000$ in stock?

- FTEL—FRANKLIN TELECOM–Article from Los Angeles {Daily} News–6/5/96. (A word of advice here: if, in a posting, you quote only isolated sections from a body of copyrighted work, you're probably in the clear because of "fair use" laws. Quoting a work in its entirety will leave you far more vulnerable.)

- FREE Investment Advisory Newsletter. (This post typifies an appropriate use of a newsgroup to sell an informational service.)

- SMTS Recieves FDA Approval, Volume increasing, over 3.5 million traded, Check it out! (Sometimes, the dividing line between invitation and direct solicitation can be a little blurred.)

- DOES ANYBODY HERE KNOW STRATEGIES FOR MAK- ING CONSISTENT PROFITS IN PENNY STOCKS? (The all-cap monster strikes again, but this post sounds more like "Help!!")

- China Pacific—CHNA. (Most investors have opinions, and some are willing to share them. This note is a good example of how this is done on Usenet.)

"If earnings mean anything, than this stock has to go up," Larry Polte wrote. "Right now it is at 1 7/16. Latest 1 quarter earnings–11 cents/per share. Company is predicting record earnings for 1996. Company is also buying back stock because it is so under-valued. Also today, China announced plans to build 1000 hotels. Building that many hotels will take a lot of steel. Don't take my word for it. Do some research and you will be happy you did."

ALT.BUSINESS.MISC

Like many newsgroups with .misc as part of their name, this is truly a voluminous assemblage. When I stopped in, alt.business.misc (see Figure 16-2) had more than 3,200 messages posted in over 2,100 discussion threads.

Because the stated purpose of this group is the presentation of business opportunities, the bazaar-like atmosphere here can be forgiven. Indeed, 14 of the first 19 thread titles were in all caps.

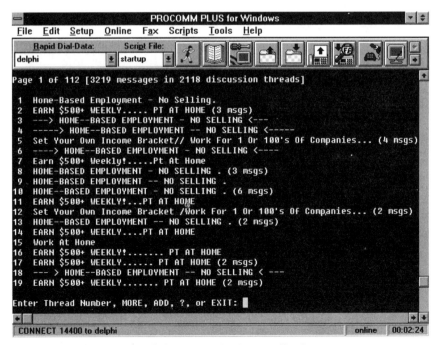

Figure 16-2: *Newsgroup alt.business.misc is an online bazaar.*

These posts primarily are people making business offers instead of people discussing them. Most threads have only a few messages. The thread titles here range from the truly inviting to the garish.

Some of these titles are even a bit entertaining. Here's a good idea of what you'll get if you come here:

- Set Your Own Income Bracket/Work For 1 Or 100's Of Companies.

- Australian Franchise Opportunities.

- For Sale: Shuttle flown chopsticks (Onizuka) Challenger. (Something about eating sushi with utensils that orbited the planet defies description.)

- Canadian Insurance. (Insurance for sale is offered here.)

- CEMETERY SALES COUNSELORS WANTED, EVERYONE'S DIE N TA SEE YA!!!!!

- Unsecured Visa Credit Card Application, Regardless Of Past Credit History, Or If You Have No Credit. (This was an offer for a Visa card issued by a New Jersey bank.)

  "Have you had difficulty obtaining credit because of past credit problems, or because you have no credit history?" asked the post. "You probably think that the only way you can get a VISA card is to get a secured card. Well now you can have an UNSECURED VISA card, even if you have had past credit difficulties!"

  An e-mail address was provided through which to send in an application.

- Commodity report. (Usenet brims with people who want to share their expertise with the world.)

  "I will send you a free report on the top professional commodity trading advisors in the world," wrote Jon Cashwell. "The report shows rate of return, trading methods, preferred markets, drawdown history and information on opening an account. The report is over twenty pages long and includes charts and tables so please include your regular mail address and a phone number."

- Belize Offshore Trust, Taxfree Savings/TaxFree Income. (Displaying a very nimble business strategy, numerous Web sites promote themselves on topically similar newsgroups. This is a good way of finding Web sites of interest to you. Here, the message is simple: "Visit our site for info, click on http://www.erols.com/skizm.")

BIZ.MARKETPLACE.SERVICES.DISCUSSION

Relatively small and compact, this newsgroup (see Figure 16-3) averages only about 150 messages in approximately 100 discussion threads mostly devoted to services for sale. The all-caps phenomenon is much in evidence here, but you can find some interesting offers, Web site cross-referrals, and requests for information.

Here are a few that I found:

- Marketline International boosts stock profits up to 300% or more. (This is a cross-referral to the Marketline International Web site at http://www.gen.com/lp-global/ml.htm.)

- Auto Insurance Rates. ("I'm having a heck of a time trying to get auto insurance-just liability-without paying a lot," someone identifying himself only as 223 Infoshop wrote. "Which companies out there are cheapest & best? Is anything online for comparison?")

- New Website: United States Business Owners Association. (Walter Hodge of the United States Business Owners Association put up this post to plug the group's Web presence. It sounds like quite an idea.)

  The sales phraseology is aggressive but thorough, and the site (http://www.usboa.com/) boasts a trial membership package. It also contains such features as "Unlimited Telephone Consultation, Unlimited Consultation on the Internet, No cost Workshops, No cost Networking, No cost Business and Financial Analysis, No cost Bad Check Collection, No cost Bad Debt Negotiation, Discount Products and

Services, Discount Professional Services, Discount Credit Card Processing, Access to Commercial and Private Capital, Emergency Funding, Prepaid Legal Services, Prepaid Calling Cards, Health Insurance Plans, Discount Advertising, and Discounted Equipment Leasing."

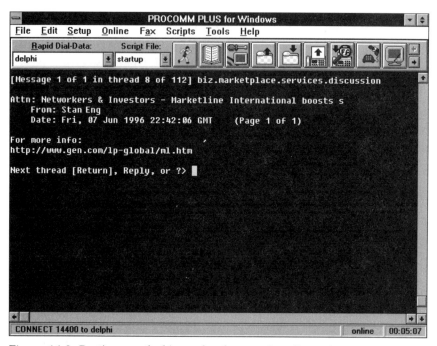

Figure 16-3: *Postings on the biz.marketplace.services.discussion newsgroup frequently tout topically similar Web sites.*

COMP.OS.MS-WINDOWS.APPS.FINANCIAL

This is another specialized newsgroup, devoted to discussions of financial-services software (see Figure 16-4). Many of the threads contain questions about how to use programs such as Quicken or Microsoft Money—and answers from the helpful Good Samaritans of cyberspace.

Contemplating an upgrade from Quicken Version 3.0 to 5.0, Jeff
Charlton posted this note:

"I'm currently running version 3.0 of Quicken and am looking
to upgrade," he wrote. "I have a couple of questions for interested
people to answer. First, is it possible to upgrade to 5.0 fairly
painlessly. Second, and more important, is it worth upgrading.
I've been seeing a lot of negative comments about 5.0 (granted,
people rarely say when they're happy), so I'm wondering if I
should switch to MS Money. I haven't seen that many negative
comments about it (probably because the 3 people that use it don't
read this group :-). Any help is appreciated. Thanks. Jeff."

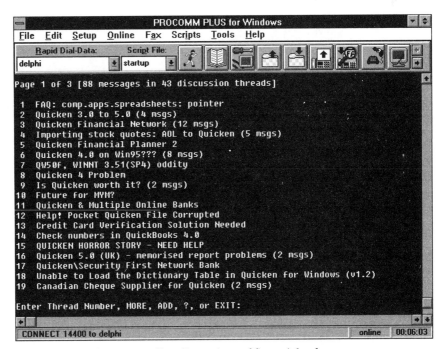

Figure 16-4: *This group offers discussions of financial software.*

I may faint! A newsgroup post that is polite *and* contains no
typos or embarrassing grammatical fluffs. Generally, you can get
people on your side by being nice. It worked with Mike Bryan,
who answered Jeff's question thoroughly.

"In QW3, you could make do with a 4MB 386 system," Mike wrote. "With QW5, you will want at least a 486 with 8MB of memory, and if you're running Win95, you'll probably want 16MB of memory. Depending on the other applications you run, you might want more in either case, but that's highly user-dependent. After you upgrade, make sure you have version 5.0f (in the Help | About display). If you have an earlier version, download the patch for 5.0f from Intuit's web site before using it for anything, including opening your original file (which will start converting it)."

On Usenet, as the old saying goes, you may have friends that you haven't met yet.

ALT.MISC.INVEST

This group is by far the most extensive collection of investment-related insights, opinions, and offer-pointers you'll find on this part of the Internet. The type of counsel you get on alt.misc.invest (see Figure 16-5) differs greatly from that found on Web sites. On the Web, financial advice may come from financial analysts, practitioners, and investment-tracking journalists. Here, on Usenet, the advice is most likely to be given by investors themselves.

Which is better? It's kind of like deciding where to go on vacation. The veteran travel writers may recommend a trip to the Canadian Rockies, but your retired, well-traveled neighbors are urging you to go to the Grand Canyon. If you're like me, you'll take all this input into consideration and make a measured choice that satisfies your goals and conforms to your budget. Usenet advice from peers—when dispensed by people with a grass-roots understanding of a product but not a vested interest in it—is sometimes better than advice from experts.

On alt.misc.invest, a fair percentage of regular posts are what might be called invitational. Here are some typical examples, drawn from a series of visits to this newsgroup:

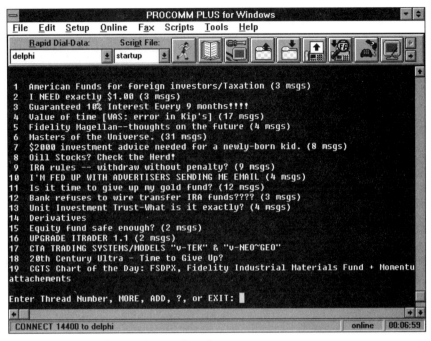

Figure 16-5: *An alt.misc.invest thread menu.*

■ An investment advisor put up a notice claiming that he had prospective investors willing to commit between $300,000 and $90 million for unspecified "projects," and invited readers to respond to his e-mail address for more information.

■ A man posted his daily interpretation of stock pricing trends implied by the most recent Standard & Poor's 500 stock index.

■ An investment counselor offered a prospectus on the tax advantages of offshore banking.

■ A posting touted the free, full-text availability of Applied Derivatives Trading magazine on its Web site, http://www.adtrading.com.

■ Frequent poster Jenna Sera Dobkin, a trader in small cap stocks for more than 25 years, sang the praises of a print publication, *Walker's Manual of Unlisted Stocks.* "It profiles 500 companies that trade over-the-counter," Dobkin wrote. "Most are non-SEC reporting companies, which makes attaining information on the companies extremely difficult because they are not covered in any of the information investment publications or databases."

■   Another visitor asked for recommendations on low-cost methods of trading stocks online. His caveats were specific: common stocks only, OS-2 compatible, Web delivered rather than provided via an online service, and deep-discount broker in lieu of pricier "hand-holding." Within a few days, he got several helpful responses.

Christopher Lott, FAQ maintainer for alt.misc.invest (see Figure 16-6) and several similar newsgroups, should be credited with keeping the tone relevant, civil, and relatively free of hustle.

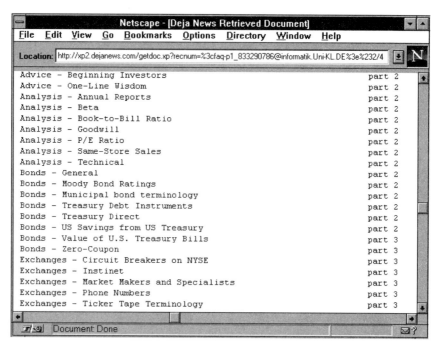

Figure 16-6: *Christopher Lott's definitive FAQ keeps alt.misc.invest relevant and informative.*

MISC.INVEST.FUNDS

One thing about newsgroups is that their titles are often self-explanatory. If you haven't guessed by now, this is a gathering place for discussions about mutual funds. The tone is enthusiastic but relatively restrained when you compare it to other groups that offer products or services for sale.

As opposed to alt.misc.invest, the threads here have multiple responses. That typifies the "advice sought" nature of many of the topic threads. Questions will always produce more individual messages within a thread than will an offer—which can be replied to via e-mail outside regular newsgroup communications.

The usual mixture of investment offers and questions is typified by this collection:

- An investor offered his opinion as to why one Capital Appreciation Fund that performed poorly in a Wall Street Journal ranking was floundering. His opinion drew several responses, some of which disagreed with his outlook.

- Poster Robert Lister indicated that he was thinking about buying a financial sector fund and asked for advice.

  "Over the past 10 years," he wrote, "they seem to have done almost as well as technology sector funds, and this would help to balance my technology sector funds without diluting my returns. Now my question is what has been driving the financial sector funds in the past 10 years? Are these returns expected to continue over the next 10 years, or were they some kind of fluke caused by bank mergers or some other unique circumstances?"

On a typical day, at least one-third of the other posts solicit opinions on the merits or weaknesses of various mutual funds. Fidelity Investments and Vanguard, the two biggest, are frequent subjects.

Thinking about investing in a mutual fund? You'll get some balanced opinions here from people who have placed a good bit of their resources in one or more of them. There's a good balance between the positive and the negative. Whether for ego, altruism, or a combination of both, some folks love to boast about how a given fund or stock did well for them. Toward the other polarity, newsgroups are a great place to vent.

Visualize investment-related newsgroups as the modern equivalent of gentleman's clubs, where investors in smoking jackets
sipped from brandy and traded their investment perspectives.
Now, the gentleman's club is the den, and the pontificators are
sitting at their terminals, sipping Sumatran blend from Starbucks
while their 28.8 bps modems flash their opinions to the world.

MISC.INVEST.FUTURES

I'm a little disappointed. I was expecting lots of talk about commodities such as pork bellies and gold, but what I found on
several visits to misc.invest.futures (see Figure 16-7) were a lot of
cross-postings from other investment newsgroups. This was not
due to any congenital flaws in the group's topical emphasis, but to
a lack of imagination on the part of the posters. It could be that
commodity traders are less Internet-savvy than stock pickers, but
you have to really look hard here for any meat.

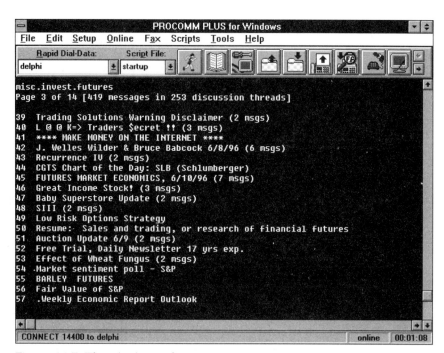

Figure 16-7: *The misc.invest.futures newsgroup.*

If you ask the right questions, though, you'll get some thoughtful answers. In one such exchange, Dennis Chen asked whether it would be wise to buy short on oil futures for, say, three to six months out. He got several well-considered responses, including this one from Shawn Devlin: "I wouldn't say it's WISE to short 3-6 mo, but I sure as hell wouldn't get long there either. OPEC probably won't cut back production, even when prices do fall," he wrote.

MISC.INVEST.STOCKS

Here's another marketplace-type newsgroup (see Figure 16-8) in which, depending on the thread you read, you can get sincere advice or be beaten over the head with ALL-CAPS hustle. Of the more than 2,600 posts in nearly 1,300 threads that were up during the summer of 1996, the thread with the most postings featured some lively debate about one of the major U.S. presidential candidates. Didn't have a lot to do with stocks, but it pointed out the fact that some newsgroups are magnets for irrelevant conversation.

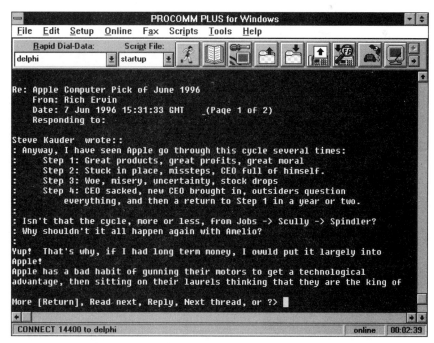

Figure 16-8: *Misc.invest.stocks attracts investors who like to talk about the merits of various publicly traded companies.*

Most of the threads concern the investment worthiness of various stocks. Opinions are like, well, noses: we all have them. On this group, if you have a modem and a newsreader, then you're a financial guru.

This is an overview of the material that you're likely to find on misc.invest.stocks:

- A disgruntled investor claimed that he lost more than $15,000 in potential profits by engaging in online trading with a particular company.

- Several posters debated the long-term financial viability of Apple Computer.

- Two members asked for recommendations on stock shareware.

- A Canadian Discount Brokers FAQ was posted, containing contact data on all discount brokers north of the border who sell stocks, commodities, or mutual funds. This FAQ is a cross-posting from the misc.invest.canada newsgroup—which itself carries many cross-postings from other groups.

- One writer asked for opinions as to whether bank trust departments were afflicted with an ingrained conservative corporate culture that precluded participation in potentially lucrative but high-risk investments.

For the sake of politeness, I've left out several topics—compared to the restrained tone of alt.misc.invest, this place is a shouting match. Then again, so is the floor of the New York Stock Exchange. People can get quite passionate about money, whether it's theirs or not. You'll find quite a lot of disingenuous passion and anger here, but you also find quite a bit that's useful. Should you have a question to ask or a point to make, just open up your own thread and you'll have an audience.

MISC.INVEST.TECHNICAL

A number of scientific, market-predictor software tools are available. Some are used by brokerages whereas others can run on your PC. Misc.invest.technical (see Figure 16-9) is the place where these tools and methodologies are explained and discussed.

Here are some typical posts:

- Technical patterns in random data? (This is a timeless, chicken-versus-egg argument that is often made but will never be answered to everyone's satisfaction.)

- WHEAT and Planetary Cycles. (Sounds kind of New-Agey, but raises some valid points about the effect of medium-term climactic variations on the price of wheat.)

- TeleChart 2000. (Several posts decried allegedly unresponsive customer service on the part of this DOS-based stock predictor program.)

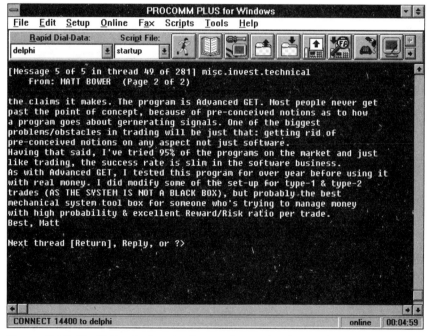

Figure 16-9: *Predictive tools get a thorough examination on the misc.invest.technical newsgroup.*

Occasionally, an investor will write in with new formulas of that person's own making. When such posits are well-constructed, they make good food for thought, as did this offering from Bruce King:

"I don't have correlation coefficients for the indices themselves but I have determined for them for several funds," King wrote. "Using the Vanguard index funds for S&P 500, Wilshire 5000 (Total Market Fund) and Russel 2000 (Small Cap Index Fund), as stand-ins for the indices, one can estimate the correlation coefficients between the indices."

MOVING ON

Back before the Web became popular, most of the qualified research on the Internet was found in text-only Gopher sites. Befitting the heritage of the Internet as a collection of government information or scientific or academic research, most Gopher sites have come from these areas. Not everyone has a Web browser, so the textual construct of Gopherspace fills a niche there as well. Despite being eclipsed by the Web, the number of Gopher servers is still growing. More than a few contain financial-related information. In the next chapter, you will take a look at why Gopher is not yet a Goner.

Gopher Guide

Comparing Gopher and Web sites is a bit like contrasting the output of a late-model electronic typewriter with that of a manuscript composed on a spiffy word processing program such as Microsoft Word or WordPerfect. Lots of great works have been written on typewriters, which could display these documents only in plain text. In a world of Web browsers, 28,800-baud-and-up modems, and personal computers that can execute 300 million calculations per second, Gopher is a bit like that electronic typewriter. Although doing tables and charts in Gopher is still technically possible, Gopher mostly allows only a straight-text representation of words from a site to appear on your screen. It lacks the coding to display visuals—not to mention multimedia features such as Java, Shockwave, and RealAudio. Most important, putting a link from a Gopher site to another is a cumbersome process.

What Gopher sites are, essentially, are blocks of text. Asking a powerful Web browser such as Netscape Navigator 3.0 to show you a Gopher page is like driving your Lamborghini to the corner convenience store. It can do so much more!

Given Gopher's limitations, why is a full chapter devoted to a section of the Internet that many cybernauts consider an anachronism from an earlier epoch? Because, at least for some functions,

Gopher is still useful. This chapter examines why and then gives you some key financial Gopher sites to visit.

When Gopher Makes Sense

Some people don't have computers that can run "visual" Web browsers. Perhaps their machines are running with operating systems too primitive to allow a browser to work up to minimal potential. Some older monitors lack the resolution to display graphical elements on Web pages.

This limitation is not necessarily a handicap. Some sites that contain banks of statistics are perfectly acceptable when they are viewed in Gopher format. In fact, because little if any graphics are there for your computer to load, getting access to Gopher pages normally is quicker than "pulling down" pages on Web sites. Some businesspeople travel around with old laptops powered by Intel 286 chips. These people may have modems that can use text-only, dial-up online services that can, in turn, provide access to the basic text elements of the Internet.

There's a primeval, text-only Internet browser called Lynx that does a great job with electronic mail and other word-only communications elements. It can depict most Web sites, but only the words on them. Where a picture sits on a page, Lynx shows the word <IMAGE>. Multiple <IMAGE> designators on a monitor are distracting and frankly quite ugly. In contrast, straight text, as you would see on a Gopher page, is displayed cleanly. That's why Gopher works better than the Web on text-only browsers.

How a Gopher Site Is Set Up

Gopher sites are structured differently from Web site menus. The site usually has a main Gopher menu (see Figure 17-1). This menu contains information about what is on the site, as well as key resources. Each of these listings will, in turn, have submenus that describe more detailed elements. For example, the main menu of a university Gopher server might have a listing for Libraries. Click on that listing and you'll reach another Gopher menu. This menu might then provide a catalog of the books and magazines available in the library.

Much like with a Web page, you "get around" Gopher sites by clicking on the respective links—except that you won't see pretty graphics and icons to help you along.

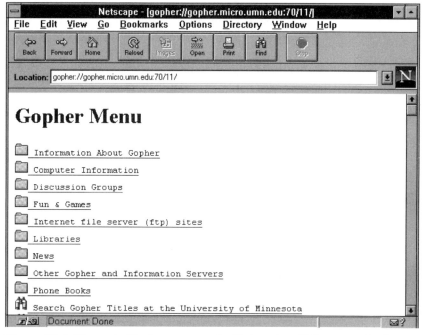

Figure 17-1: *The main Gopher menu at the University of Minnesota Gopher site. Gopher is named for the school mascot.*

WHAT MAKES A GOOD GOPHER SITE?

Gopher sites that maximize the few advantages of this presentation form over Web pages show the most utility. Grading Gopher sites is, then, largely a matter of judging whether the content is appropriate for Gopher.

Here are some characteristics of worthwhile Gopher sites:

- The site should have large clumps of text that don't cry out for illustrations. This might mean long tables of statistics, detailed academic studies, scientific treatises, and library catalogs.

- There should be a top-of-site Gopher menu that exactly describes what is on the following pages.

- The hierarchy should not be too extensive. You shouldn't have to go down through six or seven submenus to find the information you want. Because none of the search engines such as AltaVista and Lycos are equipped to search the full text of Gopherspace (unlike Web pages), ease of navigation is doubly important.

- The subject of each Gopher page must be clearly named. The rudimentary Gopher tools that are available (such as Veronica) can search only page titles (not full text). If a Gopher page issued by a state department of agriculture has a listing for its graded feeder pig commodity prices, a Veronica search using the term "pork" wouldn't find the feature.

- The Gopher URL should be relatively simple. Most Web page addresses are relatively easy to enter. Gopher server addresses can be undecipherable and may have percentage marks (%) in the middle of the domain name. Some accessors type URLs, so it stands to reason that the more complicated the designator, the greater the chance of an error.

- Finally, as in Web sites, contact information is useful. Where, for example, can you write the professor who compiled the economic study that you've just read?

Gopher, then, may be a bit of an antiquated notion, but it isn't obsolete.

GOPHER SITES

Now you'll take a look at some worthwhile, finance-oriented
Gopher sites.

BUREAU OF LABOR STATISTICS CONSUMER PRICE INDEX GOPHER

gopher://ftp.SHSU.edu:70/00/Economics/bls/doc/cu.doc
If you own a business, pricing trends will affect your bottom
line—not only how much you spend on everyday items, but the
cost of capital as well. The Bureau of Labor Statistics Consumer
Price Index Gopher (see Figure 17-2) publishes quarterly updates
that track average expenditures in 91 metropolitan areas of the
United States. Seven price classifications are tracked. Some of
these will be of interest to investors, entrepreneurs, and
businesspeople.

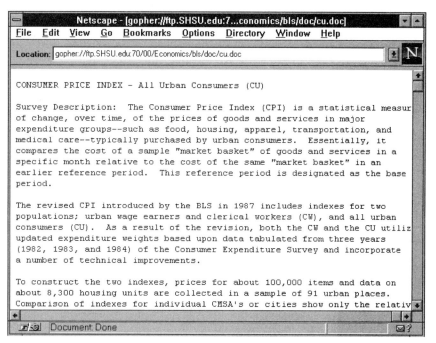

Figure 17-2: *An explanation of the methodology used on the Bureau of Labor
Statistics Consumer Price Index Gopher.*

■ *Entertainment costs*   Take clients and prospects out to dinner regularly? Especially with the deductible part of this expense now being only 50 percent, spikes in these costs may cause you to think twice.

■ *Homeowner and rental costs*   Gauges the pricing trend for mortgages and rental housing. If the cost of rents is rising faster than the national average in a market in which you are thinking of expanding, you may have trouble finding service workers.

■ *Medical care costs*   Rises in the cost of health care will affect the cost of health insurance premiums for your employees, and may have an effect on your bottom line.

■ *Transportation costs*   Do you have a fleet of salespeople canvassing your region? Did you buy or lease three new company cars this year? Are you deliberating whether to fly to that big investment conference in San Francisco? Can you afford the seminar at that five-star Arizona hotel? If gasoline, air fare, and hotel rates are going up in a given region, you may have to cut back a bit on your travel.

THE HOLT REPORT

gopher://wuecon.wustl.edu:671/00/holt/holt.current
Some of us love statistics and turn to the sports pages to check up on the latest batting averages. George Holt loves statistics, too, but devotes his acumen to a daily smorgasbord of charts and tables that detail key performance criteria in financial marketplaces.
  On this site, you'll find the following:

■ A table with more than 30 price indexes from most of the major stock exchanges.

■ Summaries with the number of "advancing," "declining," and "unchanged" issues from the New York Stock Exchange, the American Stock Exchange, and NASDAQ.

■ A currency chart relating the worth of the U.S. dollar to 18 foreign currencies, including the British pound, Deutsche (German) mark, the French franc, and the Japanese yen.

■ The latest gold, silver, and Treasury bill rates.

■ The 10 most-traded issues on the NYSE, ASE, and
NASDAQ, along with volume (number of shares traded),
last closing price, and the change from the previous quote.

■ Stocks with trading volume increases of greater than 50
percent from the previous day's session (see Figure 17-3).

■ Stocks that reached a new all-time high in the previous
day's trading.

■ A section on actively traded stocks with high EPS (Earnings
Per Share).

```
Netscape - [gopher://wuecon.wustl.edu:671/00/holt/holt.current]
File  Edit  View  Go  Bookmarks  Options  Directory  Window  Help

Location: gopher://wuecon.wustl.edu:671/00/holt/holt.current

 Stocks with VOLUME increases of greater than 50% Mon, Jul 15, 1996
                                               VOL% PRICE  PRICE%
 EQUITY NAME          HIGH    LOW    CLOSE   VOLUME CHANGE CHANGE CHANGE SYMB
 3COM               41.375  36.750  37.625   59677  +99% -4.188   -10% COMS
 ABBOTT             44.375  43.375  43.500   20575  +64% -0.750    -2% ABT
 AETNA              62.875  60.125  60.875   28824 +184% -2.000    -3% AET
 AMGEN              55.750  53.625  54.875   35626  +59% +0.500    +1% AMGN
 AMR CORP           83.375  79.125  79.500    9265  +66% -3.500    -4% AMR
 ASARCO             25.875  24.625  24.750    4038  +59% -1.375    -5% AR
 BANK OF BOSTON     51.125  50.500  50.750   11265 +115% -0.125    -0% BKB
 BOISE CASCADE      36.250  32.750  32.875    7821 +120% -3.750   -10% BCC
 BROWNE SHARPE      10.125  10.000  10.000     191 +108% +0.000    +0% BNS
 BURLINGTON RES     46.375  45.250  45.375   10123  +70% -0.375    -1% BR
 CABLETRON SYS      65.500  59.500  60.125   17200 +120% -5.375    -8% CS
 CHRYSLER           56.750  55.250  55.375   30676  +74% -0.875    -2% C
 CISCO SYSTEMS      55.250  50.500  51.875  125599  +92% -3.500    -6% CSCO
 COMPAQ COMPUTER    44.500  41.250  41.500   32156  +73% -1.750    -4% CPQ
 COMPUTER SCI       69.500  67.125  67.750    5007  +68% -1.750    -3% CSC
 DEERE              37.375  34.875  35.875   13426  +76% -1.500    -4% DE
 DELTA AIRLINES     79.000  73.500  75.000   11766  +55% -3.500    -4% DAL
 DISNEY             58.125  54.625  54.750   28367  +80% -2.125    -4% DIS
 DUN & BRADSTREE    59.750  56.500  56.750    7561  +76% -3.250    -5% DNB

Document Done
```

Figure 17-3: *Fast-rising stocks are shown daily on the Holt Report Gopher.*

If you're an investor, two things are certain: you care about
statistics, but you have little time to assimilate them. That's
where Holt comes in. These charts are as handy a plain-text
presentation of financial market performance as available anywhere on the Internet.

INSURANCE INFORMATION INSTITUTE GOPHER

gopher://infx.infor.com:4200/

Your home is one of your major investments. Ensuring, and insuring, the security of your dwelling is vitally important. For some reason, the Insurance Information Institute has chosen to display most of its data in Gopher rather than in Web form.

The most helpful hyperlink is to the "Insurance Information Institute–Consumer Brochures" page. On this submenu, you'll locate around 20 pointers, including Home Security Basics, Insurance for Your House and Personal Possessions, Insuring Your Home Business, and Settling Insurance Claims After a Disaster. I zero in on two others: Twelve Ways to Lower Your Homeowners Insurance Costs (see Figure 17-4) and How to Burglar-Proof Your Business.

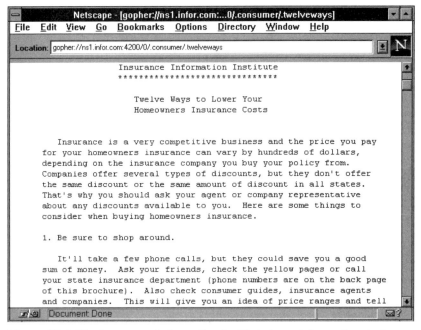

Figure 17-4: *The Insurance Information Institute has advice on how to lower your homeowners insurance costs.*

Pointer 4 on the Twelve Ways page advises you on insurance issues to consider when you buy a home. "Consider how much insuring it will cost," the Institute counsels. "Because a new home's electrical, heating and plumbing systems and overall structure are likely to be in better shape than those of an older house, insurers may offer you a discount of 8 to 15 percent if your house is new."

You also learn that because they are resistant to wind, brick homes are looked on favorably in the eastern United States. Conversely, frame homes, which resist earthquake damage better than brick, are a better insurance proposition in the West. Avoid areas prone to floods and you might save $400 a year on flood insurance.

How to Burglar-Proof Your Business has some tips to secure your property as well as to confuse the robber who has gained entry. Keep in mind that a successful heist not only will increase your insurance costs but possibly lessen the market value of your business. If your retail establishment represents a major invest-ment for you, then you certainly don't want that to happen.

PENNSYLVANIA DEPARTMENT OF AGRICULTURE GOPHER

gopher://psupena.psu.edu:70/
Hundreds of thousands of investors participate in commodities markets, hoping that a purchase of wheat or grain futures today will be rendered profitable by price increases next quarter. These price trends, in turn, will influence how much consumers will pay for a loaf of bread, builders will spend for lumber, and restaurant patrons for steak.

The Pennsylvania Department of Agriculture's Gopher server updates several classes of commodity prices on a daily or a weekly basis. The Index page has six current classifications, including "Livestock Market Menu" (see Figure17-5), "Graded Feeder Pig," "Graded Feeder Cattle Sales," "Grain Market Summary," "Hay Market Summary," and "Woodlands Timber Market Report."

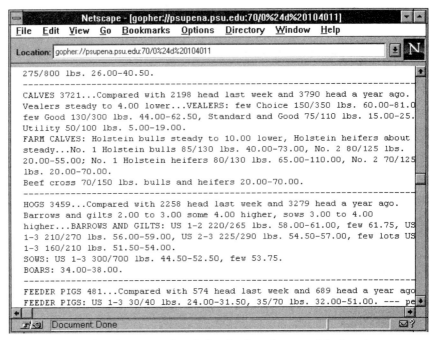

Figure 17-5: *Prices for Pennsylvania-bred calves, hogs, and feeder pigs are listed here weekly.*

Most survey sections pertain only to Pennsylvania-centered activity, but the information is laid out in useful grids. Grain prices, for example, are broken out for four sections of the state. A one-paragraph summary provides a weekly trend overview for each commodity. Barley No. 3 prices might be 10 cents higher than last week. Then, if you go to the section charts and see that Barley No. 3 prices were higher in central than in western Pennsylvania, you might presume that central Pennsylvania barley futures might be a pretty good bet.

Plus, who knows? The barley whose futures you buy today might wind up in a keg of frat house party beer next spring!

ROLE OF LUCK IN STRATEGIC PERFORMANCE

gopher://ursus.jun.alaska.edu:70/00/working_papers/davis1

Oh, academic papers! What possible relationship could they have to the real world? In too many cases, not much. This paper, by Business Administration professors James Davis of the University of Notre Dame and Dwight Lemke of the University of Wisconsin–Oshkosh, is a happy exception. It explores the phenomenon in which "firms make luck attributions for poor (bottom-line) performance and strategy attributions for good performance" (see Figure 17-6).

Sound familiar? How many of us have griped and scapegoated when we didn't get a contract, but noted our superior preparation when we closed a six-figure deal?

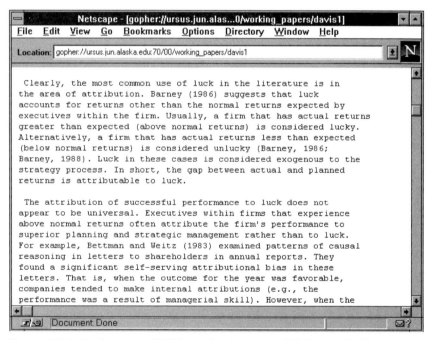

Figure 17-6: *Lucky or good? This academic paper will help you decide.*

The profs take about 35,000 bytes to meticulously explore this issue and then end with 10 key points. Some of these may appear to be obvious, generalized assertions. Others, to put it mildly, fly in the face of conventional wisdom. Each point, however, is painstakingly documented:

1. Strategic planning is important to the success of the firm.
2. A large part of any company's success can be attributed to luck.
3. Industry attributes influence firms' success more than strategic planning.
4. Unsuccessful firms do not engage in strategic planning.
5. The market controls the performance of the firm more than the actions of management.
6. Strategic planning is futile because, in reality, management has no choice at all.
7. The decisions of management are more important in determining strategic performance than luck.
8. Management cannot influence the organization's environment.
9. Global economic conditions are the best predictor of firm performance.
10. The business cycle, the regular ups and downs of the economy, cannot be diminished by actions of management.

SMALL BUSINESS ADMINISTRATION SBA ONLINE GOPHER

gopher://www.sbaonline.sba.gov/
For businesspeople, the most useful sections of this Gopher are seven Small Business Success Series articles. To reach this area, click on the Business Development icon on the Main Gopher page. This will take you to a subindex where you'll find the term, Small Business Success Series. You'll see a table of eight series. Each of

these has its own submenu of 8 to 12 articles on average. The Series volumes are as follows:

- Starting a Business
- Considerations
- Marketing a Business
- Business Survival
- Winning Business
- International Trade & More
- Secrets to Success
- The 21st Century

You'll find "Are You Making a Profit?" (see Figure 17-7) on the Starting a Business submenu. This article is exceptionally useful, going into comprehensive but comprehensible detail about how you can analyze and compare your profits and expenses, and how to calculate your net worth.

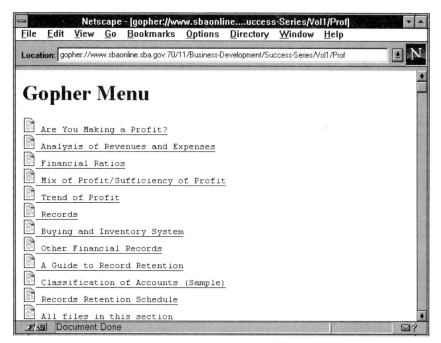

Figure 17-7: *The subject menu for the "Are You Making a Profit?" section of the SBA Gopher site.*

At first glance, some of the advice here may seem like number crunching, but it's number crunching with a purpose. Every businessperson has had to deal with the collection issue, for example. Question 7 bears this in mind, asking whether you know your average collection period. You find this ratio by "dividing accounts receivable by daily credit sales," the SBA says. (Daily credit sales = annual credit sales divided by 360.)

"This ratio tells you the length of time that it takes the firm to get its cash after making a sale on credit. The shorter this period, the quicker the cash inflow is," the SBA advises. Conversely, they note that "a longer than normal period may mean overdue and uncollectable bills. If you extend credit for a specific period (say, 30 days), this ratio should be very close to the same number of days. If it's much longer than the established period, you may need to alter your credit policies. It's wise to develop an aging schedule to gauge the trend of collections and identify slow payers. Slow collections (without adequate financing charges) hurt your profit, because you could be doing something much more useful with your money, such as taking advantage of discounts on your own payables."

The SBA's got it right. Learning how to "do something useful with your money" will, I hope, be one of the major benefits that you'll get from accessing the Internet.

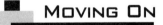

MOVING ON

As informative as the advice-givers on Gopher and Web sites are, the merit of their counsel can be affected by rapidly unfolding developments. The next chapter discusses how to gain access to investment and financial news as it's being reported.

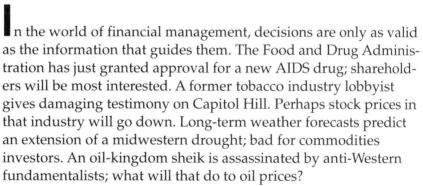

Extra, Extra:
Financial News

In the world of financial management, decisions are only as valid
as the information that guides them. The Food and Drug Administration has just granted approval for a new AIDS drug; shareholders will be most interested. A former tobacco industry lobbyist
gives damaging testimony on Capitol Hill. Perhaps stock prices in
that industry will go down. Long-term weather forecasts predict
an extension of a midwestern drought; bad for commodities
investors. An oil-kingdom sheik is assassinated by anti-Western
fundamentalists; what will that do to oil prices?

Last week's business magazine, or even this morning's newspaper, might be out of date. Fortunately, the Internet and the
proprietary online services brim with news services that keep
you current on industry, financial, and world developments.
Most will also interpret them for you. This chapter looks at
some of these offerings.

HOW THIS CHAPTER IS ORGANIZED

These news-oriented content providers are grouped into three sections:

- "Publications With Original Content" covers newspapers and magazines that prepare their own stories for their sites as well as for print.

- "News Wire Feeds & Sites" spotlights services that provide a nonstop flow of business news stories covering a wide variety of topics. These feeds may be available on Web sites, online services, or via direct subscription.

- "Content Aggregators" discusses sites that gather and integrate material prepared by other providers, such as news wires and financial research organizations, and then furnish this information on their Web sites.

WHAT MAKES A GOOD NEWS SITE?

A news site is, obviously, only as good as the content it contains. Worthy news sites generally have the following attributes:

- They are updated frequently, once a day at least.

- They are easy to navigate. If a keyword search function is not practical, articles are arranged in chronological order.

- Because statistics are the plasma of financial news, a site with lots of numbers is useful. When possible, these numbers should not appear within the text, but be broken down into tables, charts, and graphs.

- Interpretation is critical. Mere reporting without analysis from experts is shallow and won't give you the insight you need to harness all this information.

Now you'll take a look at some financial news sites and services that are definitely worth a visit.

PUBLICATIONS WITH ORIGINAL CONTENT

Relying on their own reporters and columnists, these sources prepare most or all of their coverage.

AMERICAN BANKER

http://www.americanbanker.com/
Banking is at the heart of our economic system. The daily newspaper *American Banker* is the bible of that system. This superb site is divided into five categories: News by Section; a Company Index of bank news classified by individual institution; excerpts of articles from Recent Issues; a Search Archive where you can look for articles from previous weeks or months; and a Market Monitor, a frequently updated repository of banking industry statistics.

Much of the value is in the current news, most of which you won't find anywhere else. Many of these articles (see Figure 18-1) might appear to be of interest only to bankers, but because most of us have relationships with banks, these topics will have direct relevance in our financial lives.

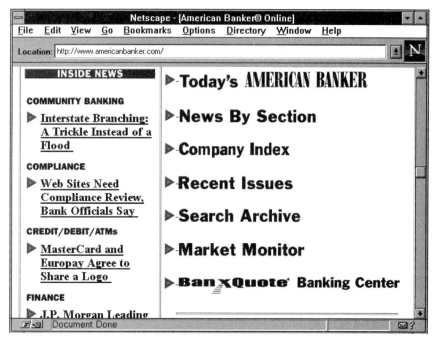

Figure 18-1: *A story menu from the American Banker Online site, which is updated daily.*

Here's a typical daily story menu by section:

- *Regional Banking*   Stories about the financial performance of specific banks.

- *Washington*   Existing, revised, or proposed regulations and how they may affect banks, businesses, and consumers.

- *Community Banking*   When that small bank on Main Street does well, the economy of your town will, too. Read about it here.

- *Credit/Debit/ATMs*   Issues, trends, new products, new initiatives.

- *Finance*   How are bank shares doing on Wall Street? What do pension fund managers and other institutional investors have to say?

- *Investment Products*   If a large bank opens up a new division to sell mutual funds, you'll read about it here.

- *Mortgages* Has one bank bought out the mortgage loan portfolio of another? Are rates trending down or up? If so, why?

- *Regional Banking* Management issues affecting large regional banks. Is an Oregon bank looking at expanding into Idaho? What are some possible takeover targets?

- *Special Supplement* Devoted to less specific, management-centric issues. How did a large metropolitan bank determined to add women to its board find and recruit qualified candidates?

- *Technology* Is what it says. Are there, for instance, new products that quicken the check-proofing process? How did a given bank prepare for, secure, and launch its new Web site?

AMERICAN CITY BUSINESS JOURNALS

http://www.amcity.com/
In the 1990s, the rising cost of newsprint has forced many daily newspapers to cut back on space devoted to news. At the same time, a marketing-driven philosophy that emphasizes personal finance advice over analyses of the business fortunes of local companies has affected business sections as well.

City-specific business journals have admirably rushed into the breach. It is here, not in the dailies, where you'll find the most informative stories about the local, privately held firm that is planning to go public and sell shares; the out-of-state bank expanding into a given market; the cutthroat war between three neighboring, upscale shopping centers that are owned by competing real estate investment trusts.

Several publishing groups have entered the city business journal market, but none on a more widespread basis than Charlotte, North Carolina–based American City Business Journals. Its Web site reflects the breadth and scope of this operation, which in 1995 was acquired by Advance Publications (publishers of the *New Yorker, Vanity Fair, Parade* magazine, and more than 25 daily newspapers).

The complete content of the current week's editions of all 28 American City magazines is available on this publisher's Web site. The home page lists the lead stories culled from each of these various papers, and provides a link from which you can click to read the full text (see Figure18-2).

You can also access each of these 28 issues directly. If, for example, you are thinking of buying shares in a company based in one of these markets, you can click on the city where the firm is located.

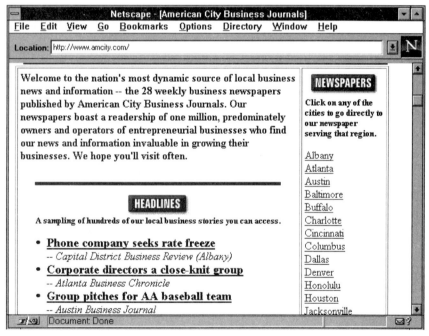

Figure 18-2: *Go to business journals from any of these cities by clicking on one of these links.*

Then, you would do a keyword search for the particular corporate name. If the latest issue has a matching story, you'll be able to read it. Is the company president leaving to start a competing firm? Are stock analysts worried that he'll take long-term customers with him? Because these local business journals have more detailed business reporting than all but the best daily newspaper business sections, you may find out something about the company that you wouldn't have been able to know otherwise. As they say, information is power!

INVESTOR'S BUSINESS DAILY

http://ibd.ensemble.com/
Because it carries more statistics and fewer lifestyle articles than its arch rival, the *Wall Street Journal*, this newspaper likes to claim a status as the only "pure play" in daily financial journalism. The *Wall Street Journal* wouldn't agree to that assertion, of course, but the scope of statistical data here is unsurpassed anywhere on the Web or in print.

IBD offers its content via America Online as well as on its own Web site. The Newspaper icon on the home page gives you a list of the day's stories. Each are linked; click and you get the full text.

For a more definitive classification of content, several other icons call up a list of stories and information:

- *Inside Today*   A rundown of highlights from the current print edition of IBD.

- *Front Page*   A list of front-page news stories.

- *Executive Update*   News and advice for decision makers. A typical story here is how to choose an all-suite hotel if you travel on business, or how to enlist your company in a self-insurance pool of health coverage for your employees.

- *Computers & Tech(nology)*   Coverage of computing trends, as well as marketing and technology initiatives undertaken by individual high-tech companies or groups.

- *The New America*   Profiles of new and emerging companies, most of them publicly traded.

- *The Economy*   Periodic updating of various measuring methods such as the Consumer Price Index.

- *The Markets*   The current or previous day's stock exchange price index, treasury bill rates, and dollar exchange rates for selected foreign currencies.

■ *Vital Signs*   A detailed graphical analysis of a given trend either affecting the economy in general or a major part of same (see Figure 18-3).

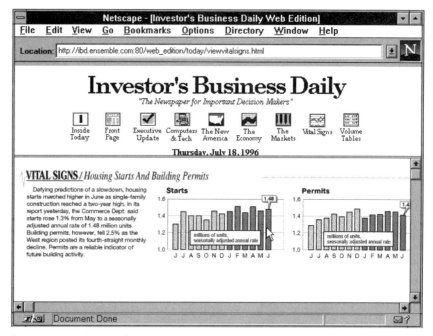

Figure 18-3: *An article on the Investor's Business Daily Vital Signs page.*

■ *Volume Tables*   A list of the day's most heavily traded stocks.

Subscribing to IBD's Web edition is free. After you've completed an easy registration process on the site, you're in. Duly certified subscribers to IBD's Web edition also get the ability to keyword-search back issues of the publication. You can do this on AOL without registering directly with IBD, however.

MONEY MAGAZINE: PATHFINDER

http://pathfinder.com/@@VrPxQAYAQPYo5YCM/money/
Money magazine's Web presence exists as part of the Pathfinder Web site. Pathfinder is the general site for Time, Inc., magazines,

which include *Money, FORTUNE, Sports Illustrated, Entertainment Weekly, People,* and, of course, *Time* itself.

Some of the *Money* content, such as a list of low CD and credit-card rates, is available elsewhere. The Tools section, which is accessed via the home page, nevertheless is a handy gathering of such content. Two more unique areas here are Best Loan Rates, with a linked list of the lowest mortgage rates in more than 100 metropolitan areas, and Quick Quotes, which shows current stock prices after you key in the trading symbol for the issue you want.

By far the most entertaining feature on *Money* is Money Daily. You get there by clicking on the Money Daily link under the Report section on the home page's What's Here toolbar. Usually, one story (see Figure 18-4) is there that microinspects the previous day's stock exchange activity. Most of the statistics are relegated to a graph in a box. The real value here is the depth of content. The article is only about 500 words but is chock full of relevant analyst quotes.

Figure 18-4: *The Money Daily feature article.*

The Money 30, which you can also find here, is the magazine's version of the Dow Jones Indexes. You won't find dead weight here. *Money* says that the companies in this index were selected "to represent dominant companies in fields that will drive the expansion of the U.S. economy during the next century. All companies have a market cap of $5 billion or more, annual sales of $1 billion or more, a strong financial position, above-average market cap growth during the past five years and above-average projected earnings-per-share growth for the next five years."

Some of the companies on this index are cellular phone giant Airtouch Communications; Cisco Systems, which makes routers used in Internet connections; Home Depot, the do-it-yourself hardware retailer; and Sun Microsystems, also another major player in Internet technology.

Motley Fool

http://fool.web.aol.com/
The Motley Fool is many things, not all of them easily categorizable. Best put, it is a comprehensive business news and forum site known for its insight, depth of content, and more-than-occasional irreverence and good humor. The humor does not detract from Motley Fool's authoritativeness. This is truly a difficult balance to achieve, but Motley Fool carries it off brilliantly.

With a series of books, a site on America Online, and a free Web presence as well, Motley Fool is very much a valid enterprise in its own right. Because the Web site allows for the easiest navigation as well as the most efficient way to print out pages, I use Motley Fool's Web presence as a road map.

The home page (see Figure 18-5) has a selection of clickable business news stories, many of which are written by "Fool" editors themselves.

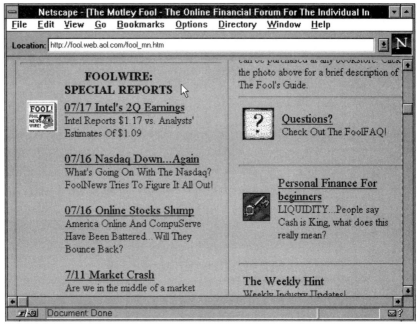

Figure 18-5: *The Motley Fool story menu, which is on the home page.*

One is struck by the integrity here. In the summer of 1996, for example, a story noted the erratic performance of online news service stocks such as CompuServe and America Online. This was unflattering news to partisan boosters of AOL—which, as just noted, carries the Motley Fool in its own content area. You won't see partisan content here, nor a surfeit of "obvious" stories. Most of the front-page articles put a future spin on the events of the day: what effect will a winter cold snap in Florida have on the price of orange juice? Should we discontinue the penny? Is buying stocks without a broker a good idea? That kind of stuff.

Past the home page are six other main sections: Investing Foolishly, Evening News, Stock Research, Hall of Portfolios, Foolish Games, and Fools & Their Money. Most of the uniqueness of the site can be found in the first three sections I've cited.

A typical day might find the Investing Foolishly home page adorned with a list of investment tips and news. The tips, which are usually in the left corner of the page, are hyperlinked to another page deeper in the Investing Foolishly section, where each tip (such as "Consider small-cap growth stocks" or "Give Thought to 'Shorting' Stocks") is explained more fully.

The Evening News gives you all the market stats but furnishes an overview of the day's trading that is both authoritative and conversational. All assertions are rigorously documented with a sea of stats, but with an informality that suggests a conversation with your stockbroker over a beer. It is in this balance that the Motley Fool truly shines.

The Industry Information Center, which can be found in the Stock Research section, has customized stock analysis research reports on more than 15 industries, including Airlines, Biotechnology, Health Care, Oil and Gas, Paper and Forest Products, and Utilities.

MUTUAL FUNDS ONLINE

http://www.mfmag.com/
Mutual Funds Online, the Web site for the monthly Mutual Funds magazine, has several features and tools that will be of interest to you if you own mutual funds. Its 7,000-fund database is one of the largest on the Web.

Services are organized into three areas of availability: options available to all site visitors, services available to (paying) members and (free) registrants, and offerings available to paying members only. Membership costs only a few dollars a month and is worth it.

The most compelling features here are the tables of and links to fund families, fund brokers, and fund services. The site also has a Fund Performance Calculator (see Figure 18-6) that you can reach from the Screens, Reports, Tools page. Want to compare the performance of your fund on November 10 compared to October 20? You access this facility, then type the symbol for the fund and the dates that you want the Calculator to compare.

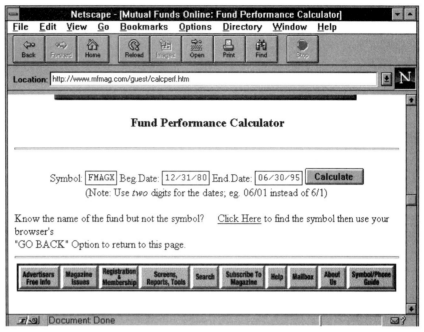

Figure 18-6: *Mutual Funds Online's Fund Performance Calculator.*

Here are the other helpful site features, as Mutual Funds Online describes them:

■ *Symbol & Phone Guide* Ticker symbols and phone numbers on more than 7,000 funds.

■ *Top-Performing Funds of the Day* The #1 fund day-by-day.

■ *Load Performance Calculator* Which share class has the lowest load burden for you?

■ *Closing Quotes* Net asset values on any fund for the last 30 days.

■ *Performance Rankings* Best- and worst-performing funds in the last 4, 13, and 52 weeks.

■ *Fund Profiles* Charts, ratings, and key investment informa-tion on 7,000 funds.

■ *Fund Selection System* Select funds to meet your personal goals and objectives.

At press time, Mutual Funds Online was planning a $4.99-a-month Personal Portfolio page that will let you create your own online portfolio of funds. A tracking system on the site will automatically upload and compute the day's performance of each fund that you specify.

THE NEW YORK TIMES BUSINESS SECTION

http://www.nytimes.com/
Generally regarded as the flagship daily newspaper in the United States, the *New York Times* puts its Business section on the Web seven days a week. The "great gray lady," as veteran newspeople like to call this American institution, has adapted well to the Web.

With exceptions for major breaking news, the *Times*—unlike the *Wall Street Journal* or *USA Today*—does not update its story menu during the day. The main value of the site is the statistics it provides. To reach this section, click on Stock & Indexes, which is on the Market Quotes icon on the right side of the Business section home page. Doing so sends you to the Current Quotes page.

On the Current Quotes page (see Figure 18-7), you'll be able to retrieve the latest stock prices for up to seven issues. You can also set up a portfolio of up to seven stocks. If you do this, the prices of each will be displayed every time you access this feature.

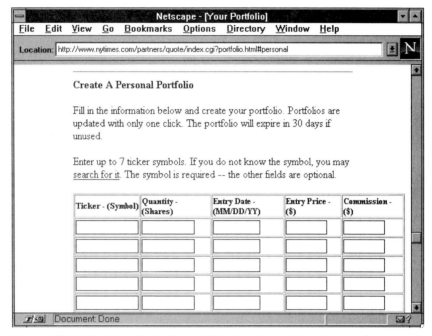

Figure 18-7: *The* New York Times *Web site Current Quotes page lets you set up a stock price information portfolio.*

Current Quotes also offers:

- *Daily Charts*   Dow Jones Industrials, the Standard & Poor's 500 Index, the NASDAQ Composite Index, and the S&P OEX (Options Exchange Index).

- *Indexes*   Major Market Indexes, Dow Jones Industrials, and Foreign Exchange Rates.

- *Stock Markets*   Most Actives, Biggest Gainers, High Alerts, Low Alerts, Biggest Losers, Volume Alerts, 52-Week (stock price) Highs, and 52-Week Lows.

- *Industry Groups (information)*   Price quotes for stocks in several industries, including Internet Stocks, Computers (PCs), Airlines and Aircraft, Biotechnology, Leisure Products, Consumer Electronics, Computers (Workstation), Computers (Networking), and Computer Software.

A similar presentation is available on the Mutual Funds Page, which also can be accessed via the Markets home page icon. Up to seven quotes are also available here, along with three classes of mutual funds data, including:

- *Stock Funds* Aggressive Growth, Growth, Growth and Income, Equity Income, Diversified Emerging Markets, Multi-Asset Global, Short-Term World Income, Europe Stock, Foreign Stock, Pacific Stock, Balanced, and Asset Allocation.

- *Bond Funds* Convertible Bonds, Corporate Bonds—General, High Quality, and High Yield; Government Bonds—General, Treasury, Mortgage, and Adjustable Rate Mortgage; Municipal Bonds—National, Single State, New York, and California; World Bonds; and Multi-Sector Bonds.

- *Specialty Funds* Technology, Communications, Financial, Health, Natural Resources, Precious Metals, Real Estate, and Utilities.

USA TODAY MONEY SECTION

http://www.usatoday.com/money/

The complete text of the *USA Today* Money section is carried on the newspaper's Web site. Befitting the nonstop flow of financial information on business days, the content is continually updated.

The home page has a graph of the Dow Jones Industrial average. The graph is updated every two minutes during the New York Stock Exchange trading hours of 9:30 A.M. to 4:00 P.M. eastern time (see Figure 18-8). This frenetic refreshment is scheduled more frequently than virtually all other sources on the Web. You'd pretty much need a real-time stock ticker of your own to match this pace!

Figure 18-8: *On trading days,* USA Today's *Web-based Money section continuously updates stock prices.*

In the upper-right part of the page, the Markets icon routes you to a one-paragraph summation of most current business stories. At the end of most briefs, you'll see either a Full Story hyperlink that leads you to the full text version of the dispatch, or a link to related resources. For example, a story mentioning rumors of one airline looking to buy another—which, if consummated, could affect air fares between certain markets—might link to an archive of business travel advice stories published previously by *USA Today*.

On business days, the Money section also has an often-updated story about how the day's trading is going so far. These stories combine stock-market trading statistics with stock analyst overviews. If, for example, a favorable earnings report has caused a flurry of morning trading in a particular company's stock, an analyst comment about the situation is usually provided.

Other areas of the *USA Today* Money section site have a daily round-up of mutual funds performances, an archive of the latest economics reports, the text of business columns from that day's print edition, and links to more than 30 relevant Web sites. You'll find links to everything from the Federal Reserve Bank of Cleveland to the site for the Securities and Exchange Commission.

WALL STREET JOURNAL INTERACTIVE EDITION

interactive4.wsj.com/edition/current/summaries/front.htm
The *Wall Street Journal* Interactive Edition requires a subscription for access. Subscribers to WSJ's print edition pay $29 a month for a Web sub; those who don't get the newspaper have to fork over $49 a month. The Interactive Edition is organized similarly to the print version. By no means is all the print content offered here, but what is available allows for a quick read of fast-breaking business and financial news.

The heart of the home page (see Figure 18-9) is the What's News column. This is a series of between 15 and 20 one-paragraph summaries of news stories that have broken from a few minutes to 24 hours ago. A typical diet is a mixture of market averages, company earnings reports, and major corporate announcements likely to affect the price of a stock.

Figure 18-9: *The* Wall Street Journal *Interactive Edition home page.*

The home page also has a Money & Investing icon from which you can link to read the leading story from the eponymously named section of that day's WSJ. For a table of contents to the rest of the site, go to the toolbar on the left side of the home page. You'll see a series of icons that deliver current and back-issue stories about sports, the economy, politics and policy, and tomes about worldwide, Asian, and European business issues.

The site also has a keyword search function by which you can look for citations of given words within that day's offerings. If, for example, you want to see whether the current version of the site has any stories about Dreyfus mutual funds, just type **Dreyfus**, and a list of stories that contain the term will appear on your screen.

News Wire Feeds & Sites

Coverage of breaking news as it happens is the stock-in-trade of the newswires. Here are some of the leading ones.

Associated Press Financial Wire

available on CompuServe
The Associated Press is the largest news service in the world. Virtually all newspapers, television, and radio stations subscribe to it. If you were willing to sign a five-year contract for a few thousand dollars a month, you could, too. You'd receive a continuous flow of hundreds of stories per hour at your computer desktop, as they come across the wire—not the following morning when only a small percentage of these dispatches make it into your morning paper. This is akin to a movie fan getting a copy of virtually every new film before it hits the theaters.

Plainly, this option is not practical. There is a way to get much of this data to your terminal for only pennies a day. Most of the major online services, such as America Online and Prodigy, carry significant portions of the various AP wires. As an investor, the Associated Press Financial Wire will be the most interesting to you.

The presentation of this wire is most complete on Compu-Serve's Executive News Service. You reach this $15-per-month premium service from CompuServe's main News & Weather menu. You'll find this menu on the home page; just click and you'll see a listing of News & Weather features, including ENS.

Between 200 and 300 stories are available every business day (see Figure 18-10). The stories that are posted go back 24 hours and contain pretty much everything happening in the business world during that time period. Has a company released a quarterly earnings statement? Is a leading corporation a candidate for a buyout? Has a regulatory agency issued a ruling that will be harmful to shareholders of an airline, a broadcaster, or a tobacco company? Is a leading business figure planning retirement? If so, who will succeed him or her? What are the most actively traded New York Stock Exchange issues today?

Figure 18-10: *The Associated Press Financial Wire as carried on CompuServe.*

On all the online services, pulling up stories on the AP Financial Wire is easy. Just type the number or check the box corresponding to the stories you want to read.

BLOOMBERG PERSONAL

http://www.bloomberg.com/
You may recognize the name Bloomberg from the Bloomberg terminal that your stockbroker is sure to have. The Bloomberg here refers to Bloomberg L.P., the booming financial news service founded by financial information tycoon Michael Bloomberg.

The Bloomberg terminal used in brokers' offices may cost several thousand dollars a year. For this price, the subscriber gets a full suite of financial and general news whose insightful depth is rarely matched by competing services. The company's philosophy about the distribution of this information is a bit different from competitors such as Dow Jones News Service or Reuters. Rather than put up a huge amount of data on a network such as CompuServe, Bloomberg believes that a more effective strategy is to make people pay for what they get. Michael Bloomberg has said just as much in interviews.

You'll get only a tiny portion of Bloomberg content by visiting this Web site. It's almost as though the Bloomberg Personal site was a storefront for the main service, which is available only through Bloomberg-dedicated terminals and not on the Web site. This sounds limiting, but if all you need are the basics, this is a time-efficient site to visit often.

The home page (see Figure 18-11) contains a one-paragraph Top News Story and links to submenus such as World Markets, Bloomberg News, and Financial Analysis.

Figure 18-11: *The Bloomberg Personal Web site home page.*

World Markets has current stock averages and links to places with information on Treasury bills, foreign exchange rates, and mutual funds. If, for example, you follow the Top U.S. Mutual Funds link, you get a chart of Best Performing Funds with historical performance data for each. Bloomberg News delivers "Major Newspaper Headlines," a collection of one-paragraph summaries of top stories from that day's major newspapers in 14 nations. If you have business interests in France, Germany, or Japan and want to keep abreast of what's going on there, Bloomberg Personal is the best place to do so.

BUSINESS WIRE

http://www.businesswire.com/

Have you ever wondered how journalists find out the time and location of press conferences, or hear about a new brand extension? Two highly competitive news services, Business Wire and PR Newswire, contract with corporations and others with a story to tell.

Say that a publicly traded company has just acquired a new division, or is readying a 2-for-1 stock split. The company e-mails one or both of these services, which will convert the press release into an appropriate graphical format and then send it out "on the wire."

You don't have to be working at the business desk of your metropolitan daily to get access to these stories. All you need is a computer, a modem, and a subscription to an online service or an Internet service provider.

Business Wire posts its full feed on several online services, but its Web site allows for customization of the information that you receive. I focus on five of them: Business Wire e-Mail Select, IndustryTrak, CompetitorTrak, BW Wall Street By Fax, and Wall Street Industry Notes. Each of these sections is accessed through icons on the Business Wire Web site home page (see Figure 18-12).

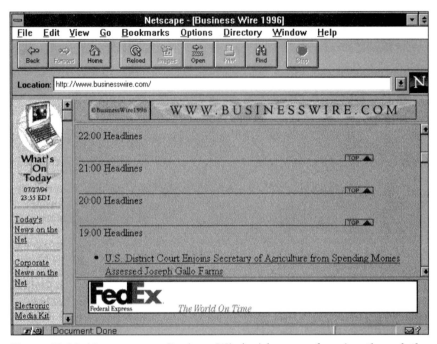

Figure 18-12: *You can access Business Wire's rich menu of services through the home page.*

For less than a dollar a day, e-Mail Select will, true to its name, e-mail you an unlimited menu of stories from the categories that you choose. Categories are grouped by industry. For example, if you hold stock in a biotechnology company, you'll want to add the biotechnology selections to your user profile.

These articles aren't all bunched together but rather are organized by news categories, including earnings, dividends, mergers and acquisitions, product announcements, management changes, advisories, and trade show information.

You'll find value added here as well. e-Mail Select gives you not only all the Business Wire stories that match the topics you choose, but also stories from newspaper content aggregator Intell.X/Data Times and high-tech news-provider Ziff-Davis Interactive.

IndustryTrak is similarly organized but gets stories to you via fax. It gives you one-paragraph abstracts of stories from 24 industries, including banking and financial services, insurance, and real estate. In addition to the wires excerpted for e-Mail Select, IndustryTrak furnishes feeds from Knight-Ridder Tribune Business News and American Banker. If an abstract interests you, then you call an 800 number to order the full text of the article. Subscribers get several full-text stories for free each month, with a small charge for additional content.

CompetitorTrak allows you to specify fax or e-mail for all stories with certain keywords. Such keywords might be the company name of your competitors or key customers. The feed costs $3 per week, per keyword.

BW Wall Street By Fax is a storefront for a complement of fax-on-demand reports. Subscribers call an 800 number to request company reports from sources such as the following:

- *Standard & Poor's*   Company background and historical information on more than 4,400 companies.

- *First Call Consensus Earnings Estimates*   Accesses both annual and quarterly consensus earnings estimates on more than 5,400 companies.

- *Argus Company Reports*   Each report gives the buy, hold, or sell recommendation of Argus's independent research analysts on more than 300 of the most widely held companies.

- *Vickers Insider Trading*   Reports when a company's insiders buy or sell their own stock.

- *Lipper Mutual Fund Reports*   An analysis of up/down market performance, ranking, portfolio holdings, and fund cumulative returns.

Wall Street Industry Notes is a fax-on-demand service that sends industry reports from more than 40 Wall Street analysts to your fax every Monday morning. Participating brokers include Alex. Brown & Sons, Brown Brothers Harriman & Co., First Boston Corporation, Dean Witter Reynolds, Donaldson, Lufkin & Jenrette Securities, Goldman, Sachs, J.P. Morgan Securities, Merrill Lynch, Montgomery Securities, Morgan Stanley & Co., PaineWebber, Prudential Securities, and Salomon Brothers. The 800 number that you call to subscribe is listed on the Business Wire Web site.

DOW JONES NEWS SERVICE

available on CompuServe, Genie, and Prodigy
In terms of sheer volume, the Dow Jones News Service posts more business stories per day than all the other business wires combined. It's not uncommon for a busy financial news day to find between 2,500 and 3,000 stories on the ticker. A premium service that can cost between $5 and $10 an hour, it is normally accessed through the News menu on the online services that carry it.

A selected few stories are also available on the *Wall Street Journal* Interactive Edition Web site. Considering that Dow also owns the *Journal*, that's not surprising. Yet no paper or Web site could possibly have room to incorporate all this stuff.

The level of detail is much richer than you'll get on competing services. If a company is planning to issue a new series of bonds, or a stock analyst lowers her EPS (earnings per share) estimate of a given company from $3.48 to $3.42, or you're curious about the business plans of an obscure corporate spin-off (as well as who might head that new company), Dow is the place to look.

True, there's a lot here. In the next chapter, you learn how some of the online services let you configure a clip file so that stories containing certain keywords are "clipped" for you as they cross Dow Jones and other wires. Dow even lets you do it directly.

PR NEWSWIRE

http://www.prnewswire.com/
The presentation model for PR Newswire's Web site differs substantially from that of its arch rival, Business Wire. The latter (covered previously) offers several customizable newsfeed services that you can configure. Generally, you pay for this privilege. PR Newswire's emphasis is on searchability of its existing database. For this type of service, there's generally no charge.

The PR Newswire Web site home page has three useful categories. News is a posting of current day press releases. These are searchable by industry, company name, stock symbol, or state from which the press release was issued (see Figure 18-13). If you want to see all the day's press releases from General Electric, then you would type the conglomerate's stock symbol (GE) in the search box.

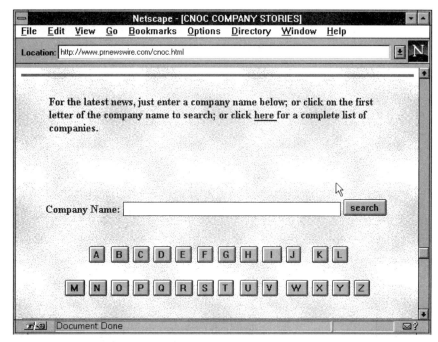

Figure 18-13: *Using the company news search functions on PR Newswire.*

Also in News, you can find Feature News and Industry Focus. Feature News has that how-to story that you're likely to find on page 4 of your business section the next day. This is where, for instance, you might encounter press releases sent to PR Newswire by a publicist for a new book about a new type of automobile leasing plan.

Industry Focus, as you might infer, groups stories in industry categories. Some of these stories might not concern an individual company but would be important to investors in such sectors as Automotive, Entertainment, Healthcare/Biotech, and Technology. Has a public watchdog group come out with its annual safety ratings of minivans? If one brand proved extraordinarily safe, that would obviously be good news for shareholders of the manufacturer's stock. The Industry Focus section of PR Newswire's News category is the place where you can get a jump on such developments.

PR Newswire also has an Online Magazine and a General Information choice. Online Magazine's Money Talks option gives you several business columns per day, whereas the Information section gives facts about PR Newswire and provides an e-mail connection to it.

REUTERS FINANCIAL WIRE/REUTERS BUSINESS ALERT

http://inwp.reuters.com/default.htm

This site has two separate content models with presentations so different that you'd have a hard time believing they were prepared by the same organization. That organization is Reuters, the British-based news service with more than a century of hallowed journalistic service.

The Reuters Financial Wire is a straight-text feed of several hundred business stories per day and is available via dial-up, subscription-based online services such as CompuServe, Delphi, and, to a limited extent, America Online. The CompuServe presentation model, which is arguably the easiest to navigate, simply contains a list with a one-line headline for each story and the time the story was "moved" (distributed by Reuters to its client newspapers and broadcasters). Because most online services don't encode their text with the HTML (HyperText Markup Language) coding that shows up as underlined words on Web pages, you link to the story you want either by marking the appropriate check box or typing the story number that corresponds to the particular article you'd like to read. (You'll read more about online services in the next chapter.)

Reuters Business Alert (see Figure 18-14) doesn't have as complete a resource of just-in-time content as the Wire version, but it lets you target your searches more effectively than the Financial Wire is set up to do. On the home page, news selections from a given country and two selected industries are available.

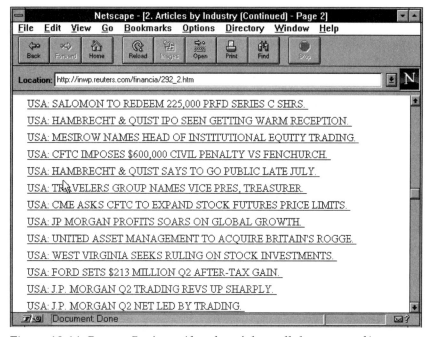

Figure 18-14: *Reuters Business Alert doesn't have all the content of its news feed, but groups articles by selected industry sectors.*

These choices, which change weekly, have their own links to submenu pages that allow you to organize available articles by date, industry, source, topic, or region.

UNITED PRESS INTERNATIONAL

available on CompuServe and Delphi

During the last 25 years, United Press International has declined from being one of the top three or four wire services in the world to being an afterthought. Few newspapers subscribe to it anymore, but its financial coverage is one of its few remaining strong points.

Under the UPI Financial choice, CompuServe's $15 a month Executive News Service (reached through the News & Weather menu icon found on the CompuServe home page) provides a running list of UPI's business stories (see Figure 18-15). There's no search capability; each story is listed in reverse order of the time it was posted. The content mix isn't so strong on business news stories of interest to investors, but it does contain numerous reports on commodity, bond, and stock prices.

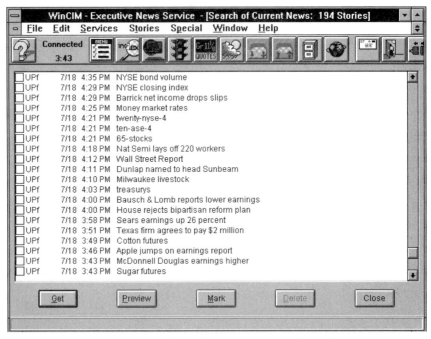

Figure 18-15: *A typical UPI Financial story menu on CompuServe.*

These specialized areas of strength make UPI Financial an occasionally helpful adjunct to other online news sources.

Content Aggregators

As a general rule, these sources originate little content but make news coverage prepared by other organizations such as newspapers and wire services available.

CLARINET

accessed through the Usenet clari-biz. area

ClariNet (see Figure 18-16) gathers hundreds of news stories prepared each day by other content providers and then distributes them over the Internet. Unlike most of its competitors, though, it doesn't use the Web, but uses Usenet instead. To access ClariNet stories, you'll need to configure your Netscape Navigator browser's NewsReader function. The process is described in Chapter 2, "What Is a Browser & How Do I Use It." After you're enabled, go to the newsgroup area called clari-biz.

Here are some of the investment and finance-related story classifications that you can find in clari.biz:

- *clari.biz briefs*   Business newsbriefs
- *clari.biz.earnings*   Businesses' earnings, profits, losses
- *clari.biz.economy*   U.S. economic news
- *clari.biz.economy.world*   News of the world's economies
- *clari.biz.features*   Business feature stories
- *clari.biz.finance*   Interest rates, currencies, government debt
- *clari.biz.industry.banking*   Banks and savings and loans
- *clari.biz.industry.insurance*   The insurance industry
- *clari.biz.industry.real estate*   Housing and real estate
- *clari.biz.industry.retail*   Retail stores and shops
- *clari.biz.industry.services*   Consulting, brokerages, services
- *clari.biz.market.commodities*   Commodity reports
- *clari.biz.market.misc*   Bonds, money market funds, other instruments
- *clari.biz.market.report*   International market reports
- *clari.biz.market.report.asia*   Asian market reports
- *clari.biz.market.report.europe*   European market reports
- *clari.market.report.top*   Overview of the markets

```
┌─────────────────────────────────────────────────────────────────────┐
│  ─        Netscape - [Ordering the ClariNet e.News]         ▼ ▲       │
│  File  Edit  View  Go  Bookmarks  Options  Directory  Window  Help    │
│  ┌─────────────────────────────────────────────────────────┐         │
│  Location: http://www.clari.net/ordering.html               │ ▲  N   │
│  ─────────────────────────────────────────────────────────────────── │
│  Please enter the following information:                          ▲   │
│                                                                       │
│      •  Your name: [                                    ]             │
│      •  Your organization: [                               ]          │
│      •  Your e-mail address: [                              ]         │
│      •  Your phone number: [                      ]                   │
│                                                                       │
│  I would prefer to be contacted by: ○ E-mail ○ Phone                  │
│                                                                       │
│  Sending us the following information will help us in responding to   │
│  you, but if you prefer you can go to the end and have a sales        │
│  representative contact you directly.                                 │
│                                                                       │
│      •  Do you represent                                              │
│         ○ yourself as an individual?                                  │
│         ○ a business or government agency?                            │
│         ○ a school, college, or university?                           │
│         ○ an Internet Access Provider (IAP/ISP/BBS)?             ▼    │
│  ◄                                                              ►      │
│  Document: Done                                               ✉ ?     │
└─────────────────────────────────────────────────────────────────────┘
```

Figure 18-16: *Use this electronic form to order ClariNet via the Web.*

- *clari.biz.market.report.usa*   U.S. market reports
- *clari.biz.market.report.usa.nyse*   New York Stock Exchange reports
- *clari.biz.mergers*   Mergers, acquisitions, spinoffs
- *clari.biz.misc*   Other business news
- *clari.biz.review*   Daily review of business news
- *clari.biz.top*   High-priority business news
- *clari.biz.urgent*   Breaking business news
- *clari.biz.world.trade*   GATT (General Agreement on Tariffs and Trade), free trade, trade disputes

CNNFN

http://www.cnnfn.com/
CNNfn, the new financial cable television channel affiliated with
Cable News Network, has its own Web site with several useful
content offerings. A toolbar at the left corner of the home page (see
Figure 18-17) has several jump-off points, including Hot Stories,
Markets, Your Money, and a reference area called Research It.

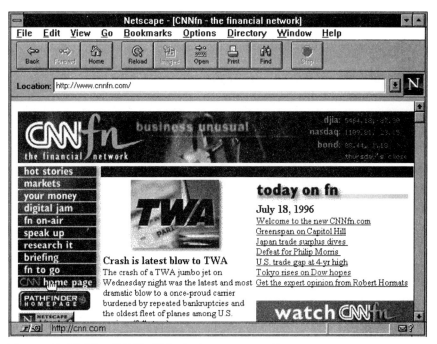

Figure 18-17: *The CNNfn Web site home page toolbar.*

The content in each of these sections is not especially deep, but
can be useful—especially if you're in a hurry and have time for
only a quick briefing.

Hot Stories typically has about a dozen general business articles. Markets carries frequently updated graphs depicting the
latest averages from the New York Stock Exchange, the American
Stock Exchange, and NASDAQ. It also has interest rates, commodity prices, and a menu of stories from Knight-Ridder Tribune

Financial News. Your Money has articles of interest to consumers and investors, whereas the Reference Desk carries a glossary of business terms and links to the Hoover's MasterList corporate directory.

Hoover's publishes several annual guidebooks in which major U.S. corporations, emerging companies, and international company giants are profiled. The information in the annual printed books is good for background. Combined with the updated citations available in cyberspace, Hoover's gives the investor a good grounding in companies in which he or she may be interested. When you combine resources such as Hoover's with the immediacy of televised reporting such as that provided by CNNfn, the informed investor has access to comprehensive knowledge about companies and industries.

FIDELITY INVESTMENTS @82 DEV

http://www.fid-inv.com/82DEV/index.html
When Fidelity Investments, the largest mutual funds company in the world, designated an "at" symbol (@) for part of its new financial news site, it meant the @ to have a double meaning. The symbol refers not only to the cyberspace location of the service but also to the physical location of Fidelity's worldwide headquarters, which is "at" 82 Devonshire Street in Boston.

The site is divided into four subsections, each of which is a worthwhile stop. Fidelity describes these as follows:

- *The Hub* A daily news summary jam-packed with critical and objective information such as data on equity, bond and world markets, currencies, and other economic indices.

- *The F (for Fidelity) Files* (Obviously a takeoff on "The X Files" television show.) "Investing concepts and methods covering a range of investor sophistication. Tell us what you want to see and share your ideas."

- *Focus Today* "Daily special feature stories on topics such as mutual fund investing, industry overviews, 'behind-the-scenes,' planning your future and investing in the electronic age."

■ *02109* (Fidelity's postal zip code, obviously included for a humorous touch.) "Fidelity-central. Fidelity press releases, Fidelity product and service enhancement reports, and Fidelity seminar listings for events in your area."

The Hub has a Market News section (see Figure 18-18) that is updated several times a day. You can find the latest stock exchange averages and currency exchange rates, plus U.S. treasury and municipal bond yields. Additionally, you'll see six sections with hyperlinked news stories. The sections are Market Overview, Industry Journal, International, Economy, Debt Markets, and Currency.

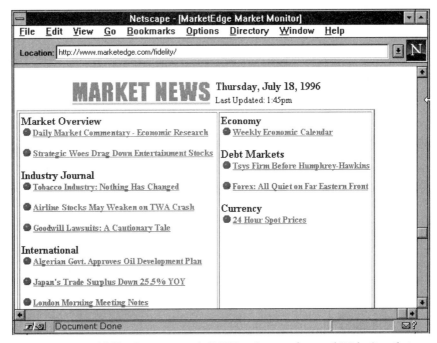

Figure 18-18: *Fidelity Investments's @82Dev is one of several Web sites that carry the syndicated Market News page.*

INDIVIDUAL INC. NEWSPAGE

http://www.newspage.com/

NewsPage can work for you in one of two ways. You can either set up an e-mail subscription service that will send summations of up to 40 new stories on a topic of your choice to your electronic mailbox each morning. Or you can retrieve much of the same information on the Individual Inc. NewsPage Web site. Find a story that you like and you pay a small surcharge to read the full-text version of the article. The amount of the surcharge, if any, depends on the nature of your subscription plan should you have one in place. A subscription plan is not necessary to search the Web site but is required for e-mail. Subscription plans range between $30 and $50 a month.

Each business day, NewsPage's home page menu lists 20 subject categories. As an example, choose Banking, Finance & Real Estate. Linking will, not surprisingly, transport you to the Banking, Finance & Real Estate page (see Figure 18-19).

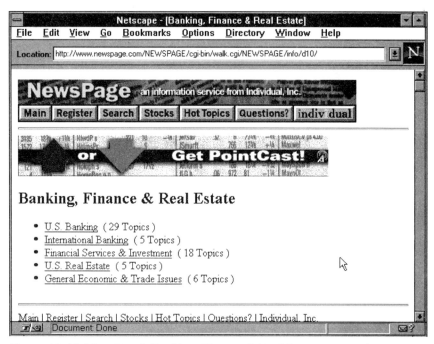

Figure 18-19: *NewsPage's Banking, Finance & Real Estate page topic menu.*

On this page, subdirectories will be available for several classifications. Most days, these classifications are for stories about U.S. Banking, International Banking, Financial Services & Investment, U.S. Real Estate, and General Economic & Trade Issues.

Because the Financial Services & Investment subtopic is most relevant to the mission of this book, I picked out a relatively busy business day and checked to see what types of stories I could find. I found 18 categories in all. Clicking on any launched a link to the page on which the articles were summarized and available for full-text retrieval.

Here are the topics for which I found at least one story:

- U.S. Finance Industry Overview
- Initial Public Offering
- New Bond Issues
- New Stock Issues
- Major Mutual Funds
- U.S. Treasury Bonds
- Currency Markets
- Derivative Markets
- Federal Reserve (Bank)
- Mortgage-Backed Securities
- Securitization
- Real Estate Investment Trusts
- Venture Capital
- Investment Management
- Financial Planning
- Brokerage
- Investment Banking
- Securities & Exchange (Commission)

Clicking on any of these categories launched a link to the page on which the articles were summarized and available for full-text retrieval.

POINTCAST NETWORK

http://www.pointcast.com/

If your morning routine involves reading the newspaper and then turning on your computer to check up on your stocks, a service is now available that lets you do both simultaneously. PointCast is a free, personal news service that, based on the information fields that you specify, delivers news, stock quotes, and other developments right to your desktop. If you specify it, you can also get a running stock and sports ticker that streams a steady flow of information at the bottom of your screen. It will also work with automatic dialers that will access the Network during nonbusiness hours—even in the middle of the night while you are away from your office.

The necessary PointCast software is available for free on its Web site (see Figure 18-20). After you dial in, you'll have access to PointCast via either its proprietary browser or Netscape Navigator, which functions as a plug-in for the PointCast Network. To configure the program, you need Windows 95, Windows for Workgroups, or Windows 3.1. The main and associate files require about 10MB of disk space.

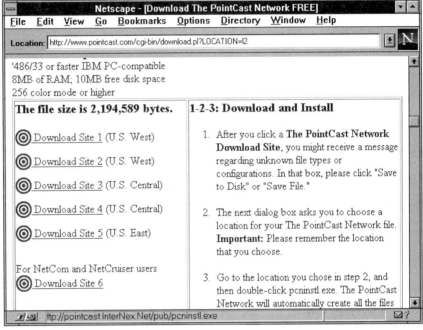

Figure 18-20: *Download the PointCast software that you'll need from here.*

PointCast doesn't refer to subscribers as "subscribers" or "readers," but rather as "viewers." As you learn on the PointCast Web site's Product Fact Sheet page, several content offerings carry business news:

- ■ *News*   Reuters national, international, business, and political news headlines are presented in a compact, easy-to-read format. To view the full text of any story, users simply click on a headline.

- ■ *Companies*   Viewers can instantly access charts with six weeks of stock prices, volume data, and a scrolling stock ticker provided by Standard and Poor's Comstock, along with news from PR Newswire and Business Wire (added with version 1.0) on the companies that interest them. Viewers can change the companies they track at any time.

■ *Industries*   Viewers can track news and information on up to 35 industries, such as advertising, computers/electronics, entertainment, utilities, and software. Current trading prices and volumes for nine major financial indices, including the NYSE, AMEX, NASDAQ composites and Dow Jones Industrials, are displayed. A new index, the Hambrecht & Quist Internet Stock Index, is available with version 1.0. The previous six weeks of trading data are also available for indices in chart format.

You can get sections of the *Los Angeles Times* or *Boston Globe* sent to your PointCast terminal as well.

MOVING ON

As you've learned in this chapter, several news services can be found on the proprietary online networks as well as on the Web. These networks also have their own financial content areas, which include rich reference troves, discussions, and forums. The next chapter takes a look at the leading online services.

The Online Services

Some online services, such as CompuServe, America Online, and Prodigy, have become established reference points in American culture. Chances are that tonight, on at least one of these services, a movie star will be on a chat line plugging his or her new film. Businesspeople and leisure travelers will check what the best airline fare deals are between Denver and Boston, and then will book their tickets online without calling a swamped airline reservations number. A sixth-grader from Charlotte, North Carolina, will go to an online encyclopedia and retrieve an article about the history of railroading in the United States. Electronic mail will zap back and forth across the nation and the world.

Add to this the thousands of investors who will log on to an online service to check on the price of their stocks or read a brokerage research report about a public company in which they're considering investing.

In this chapter, I explore the key differences between online services and Web sites. I also discuss some of the distinctive online trading, news, commentary, and discussion groups that many services offer, and the role that research services and datafeed providers can play to make you a more informed investor.

ONLINE VERSUS THE WEB: HOW DO THEY DIFFER?

The most fundamental differences between online services and Internet Web sites is the way that you access them. The traditional online service model follows these precepts:

1. You get the proprietary service software required by your online service. This software frequently is shrink-wrapped and given away in computer, science, and other magazines.

2. You install the software on your computer, following directions that are printed on the package in which the installation disk or CD-ROM came.

3. The software has a registration option. This usually appears onscreen during the registration process. The software enables your modem to dial a toll-free number. When you are connected, a series of information requests appears on your monitor. You are asked for basic information about yourself, credit-card data, what type of computer you are using, and what subscription plan you would like.

4. During registration, you are also queried on your area code. The software will activate a search of the service's database, and then specify a phone number for your modem to call during all other access attempts. The next time you do so, you're online.

Some online services have not adopted this model, or are moving away from it. A few, such as Delphi and Genie, still allow registration and access via your own telecommunications software package rather than through a customized offering. And, it appears likely that within the next couple of years, several online services will transform themselves into "super" Web sites. When that happens, access will occur not through specialized software but via your Web browser instead. You'll still be charged for most content and services, however.

Much debate has taken place about online services versus the Internet. Many people feel that the online providers turn the potential chaos involved in navigating cyberspace into a comfortable experience. Fans of online services also believe that the nature of the service provider's proprietary environment (you'll usually need special software and a password to get connected) gives the user a more communal field, as opposed to the cold, hard, impersonal world of the Internet and its most popular sector, the World Wide Web.

Such talk is regularly dismissed by Web devotees. What online service fans see as "community," Web fans see as insular and just a bit inbred. This is changing, but content providers building platforms on an online service had to use special presentation elements to make their visuals conform to the technical protocols dictated by the online companies. True, the Web can be a bit chaotic, but it fosters an atmosphere of visual and topical diversity that the closed online world either does not allow or is not equipped to carry.

There is some overlap; all the major online services make it possible to "reach" the Web. Most will carry a To the Web or Internet icon on their Main menu pages. Click there, enter a Web address, and you will then be taken to the specific Web page you requested. When you're there, you won't know the difference. You'll either be using a browser such as Navigator or the provider's own offering. You can spend hours on the Web, forgetting that it was an online service, not an Internet Service Provider, that brought you there in the first place.

You'll encounter some overlap, but these are two distinct models. With an ISP, you usually pay a flat fee of $20 to $30 per month, or a similar amount for a very large dose, such as 100 hours a month. The trend seems to be moving to an "all you can eat" rate, where no additional subscription charges are applied.

Calling up the ISP's dial-in icon on a system such as Windows 95 will tell your modem to call your ISP's Point of Presence. Some of the larger ISPs, such as Netcom, have home pages that exist as pointers to generalized Web content areas and as places for promotional announcements. Unlike CompuServe and AOL, though, there is normally very little "original" content. You might find a financial guru on some AOL chat line next Tuesday, but you aren't going to find an original, non-Web chat area on an ISP such as Netcom or Earthlink.

The pricing model is also different. The online services usually extract a modest fee of $10 or $20 for the first 5 to 20 hours of access per month, and then charge $2 or $3 an hour per month. Some even charge a premium of $2 to $3 an hour for Internet access. With the exception of compulsive chatters or rabid online gamers who may stay on for many hours per session, this arrangement usually favors newer users without compunction or compulsion.

You'll need a separate number to access your online service (a list of 800 numbers through which you can open an account is included at the end of this chapter). This may sound like a pain, but it has its advantages. Web traffic jams can occur at certain times of the day. No matter how fast your modem is or how able your browser, you're at the mercy of the Web's infrastructure and the varying merits of server computers at the site you are accessing. Because online services are closed networks, however, quality assurance is more manageable.

Which is right for you? Do the math. If you'll spend an hour a day checking stock prices and handling electronic mail, you're looking at 30 hours a month. That can be $20 with an ISP but at least double that for an online service. Some online services also charge $2 to $3 extra per hour for Internet access. But what about 10 hours a month? It might be that all the content you'll ever need is there for you on AOL, CompuServe, or Prodigy.

Two good "online vs. ISP" benchmarks:

- Are you new to the online world? Online services probably will be a more comfortable environment for you. It's the equivalent of exploring a city in a tour bus rather than on your own, but the potential confusion factor is abated.

- How much time will you spend online a week? If it's more than five hours a week, and you are relatively experienced in the online environment, a Web account with an ISP wouldn't be a bad idea. I suggest that you keep at least one online service account as a back-up, however. If you need to read news and are pressed for time, online services, because they are in a controlled environment, have ease-of-presentation advantages.

This should be a personal choice, not dictated by fear of the great unknown Web but derived from a knowledge base of what's out there and how best to use it without spending on bills what you hoped to invest in a no-load mutual fund.

WHAT KINDS OF ONLINE SERVICES EXIST?

Four basic types of online services are available. The following sections provide a brief description of each.

CONSUMER ONLINE SERVICES

Consumer online services include America Online, CompuServe, Delphi, Genie, the Microsoft Network, and Prodigy. They are oriented toward a broad range of interests, financial topics among them.

DATAFEED PROVIDERS

Datafeed providers include Bloomberg Terminal, Dow Jones Telerate, and Reuters Integrated Data Network. These are stock quote services, some of which also carry investment-related news. Such companies provide the terminals that your stock broker uses, along with the real-time quotes that he or she needs to make trading decisions. The quotes that you get on the Web or through an online service typically are delayed 15 or 20 minutes. Your broker pays thousands per month for this immediacy; that's where some of your margin money goes. If you are a major investor, you might be able to get such a terminal placed in your own home or office. Counting subscription fees, premium add-ons, and telephone charges, you can expect to pay $2,000 to $3,000 a month for a 2-year lease.

RESEARCH UTILITIES

Research utilities include DataTimes, Dialog, Dow Jones News/ Retrieval, and Lexis/Nexis. With the exception of Dow, these are mainly archival services that hold months or years of content from other providers such as newspapers, newsletters, magazines, and academic research journals.

BULLETIN BOARD SYSTEMS

Of far less importance than the first three categories, bulletin boards often are local or regional. Some are becoming Web sites, but there are still hundreds where a direct modem dial-up is necessary. A fair amount of local BBSes have investment-themed chat areas, where groups of investors can log in and talk about bulls and bears.

WHAT MAKES A GOOD ONLINE SERVICE?

Because price considerations will ensure that you are probably going to be interested in consumer online services or research utilities, I look here at some criteria for each.

The key things to look for are depth of content and navigability. To be worth your time, a consumer online service should have enough topical features not available anywhere else. The subject fields should be named clearly enough so that you know how to get to where you need to be. There should also be a keyword search function that, when you type a word, will send you to the feature or forum that you seek.

The well-designed research utility should allow for plain language searching across multiple databases at once. Looking for information on (the hypothetical company) Seattle Chemicals, which went public last month? How do you know, for example, whether to look in the Chemicals subset tree of the Science section, the Company information area, or under the Seattle Times file in the Publications section?

Research utilities' content areas also need to be updated frequently and speedily. It's not too much to ask that the November version of a journal, which might be published October 25, be input into the database and rendered searchable within two to three days of receipt.

Consumer Online Services

Now I take a look at the investment and financial-related areas of most of the major online services, concentrating on valuable or unique features of each.

America Online

This is the largest, fastest-growing, and, many would say, the most friendly online service. The home page screen shows 20 general-content areas, or channels. Most of the investment-related information that you will want is in the Market News section, which you can access either by typing the keyword phrase **Market News** in the Go To menu or the keyword button on the top toolbar, or by clicking on the home page Personal Finance channel icon.

The Market News page (see Figure 19-1) has six icons, including Company Research, the full-text version of Investor's Business Daily, Business News, Quotes & Portfolios, a link to related Top Internet Sites, and a Search News function.

Figure 19-1: *America Online's main Market News page.*

Unlike *Investor's Business Daily*'s Web site, which requires that you have a subscription to access and search the full range of archived content, America Online's version of IBD is free except for the online time fees charged by AOL itself.

COMPANY RESEARCH

The following is a look at some areas of this site, starting with Company Research. Here's what you'll find on this page:

- *Stock Reports* Comprehensive reports, including key ratios and performance measures.

- *Financial Statements* Detailed balance sheets, income statements, and cash flow statements.

- *Earnings & Estimates* Company earnings performance, plus Wall Street's outlook for the future.

- *Edgar 10Ks and 10Qs* Electronic filings from the Securities and Exchange Commission's Edgar database with both annual 10Ks and quarterly 10Qs. The 10K reports summarize company ownership, business lines, financial performance, and plans.

- *Historical Stock Quotes* Quotes, charts, and downloadable files of historical stock performance.

MUTUAL FUNDS

Another area on this site is the Morningstar Mutual Funds area, which you can reach by typing **Morningstar** in the keyword box (reached from the Go To prompt in the toolbar at the top of the screen). Content on this page, which is provided by one of the largest mutual funds companies, is divided into five basic sections:

- *Top-Performing Funds* The latest data on the 25 best performing funds listed by investment objective and ranked by various time periods (see Figure 19-2).

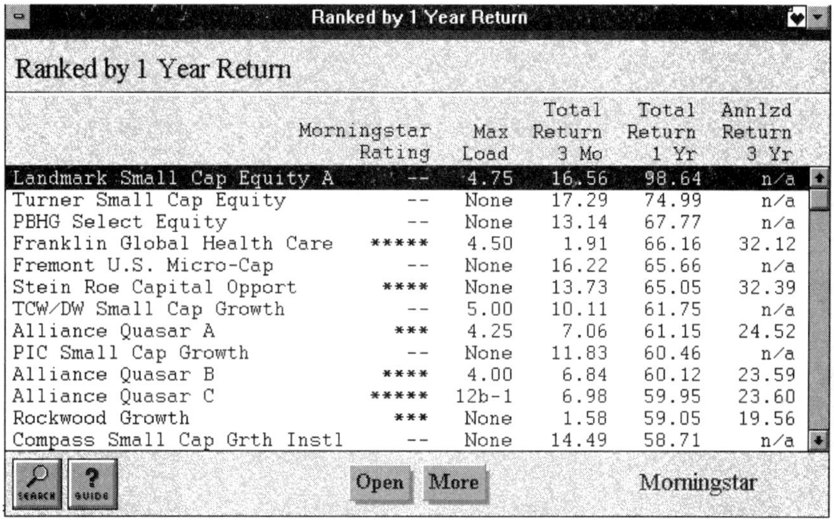
Ranked by 1 Year Return

Ranked by 1 Year Return

	Morningstar Rating	Max Load	Total Return 3 Mo	Total Return 1 Yr	Annlzd Return 3 Yr
Landmark Small Cap Equity A	--	4.75	16.56	98.64	n/a
Turner Small Cap Equity	--	None	17.29	74.99	n/a
PBHG Select Equity	--	None	13.14	67.77	n/a
Franklin Global Health Care	*****	4.50	1.91	66.16	32.12
Fremont U.S. Micro-Cap	--	None	16.22	65.66	n/a
Stein Roe Capital Opport	****	None	13.73	65.05	32.39
TCW/DW Small Cap Growth	--	5.00	10.11	61.75	n/a
Alliance Quasar A	***	4.25	7.06	61.15	24.52
PIC Small Cap Growth	--	None	11.83	60.46	n/a
Alliance Quasar B	****	4.00	6.84	60.12	23.59
Alliance Quasar C	*****	12b-1	6.98	59.95	23.60
Rockwood Growth	***	None	1.58	59.05	19.56
Compass Small Cap Grth Instl	--	None	14.49	58.71	n/a

Figure 19-2: *A list of top-performing mutual funds, found on the Morningstar section of AOL.*

- *Detailed Fund Reports* Data on more than 7,000 funds, including Star Rating, Portfolio Performance, Risk and Fee Information.
- *Editor's Choice Articles* Recent articles and commentaries from Morningstar publications.
- *Morningstar Forum* Calendar of Events, Message Boards, Morningstar Chat Room, and an e-mail facility as well.
- *Morningstar MarketPlace* Mutual fund newsletters and CD-ROMs to facilitate online trading.

PC Financial Network

PC Financial Network, which is also on Prodigy, was one of the pioneers in true online trading. To get to it from AOL's opening Channels menu, you specify Personal Finance. The opening page of this channel shows a matching PC Financial Network icon. Click there or use the pull-down menu on the Personal Finance lead page to get to PC Financial. (If you're having trouble, you can always reach any AOL area from the Keyword choice on the AOL Go To toolbar at the top of every AOL screen.)

When you reach the PC Financial Network area, you'll be taken to a screen with an Apply Online icon (see Figure 19-3). Opening an account takes only a few minutes, requiring basic information such as your name, postal and electronic mail addresses, areas of investment interest, and, of course, a credit card number for premium services.

There is no monthly membership fee on PC Financial Network. The site makes its money in commissions charged to you. A sliding commissions fee is used, with the effect that the more often you trade and the larger your trades are, the less your commission percentage is. For example: for stock trades between $2,501 and $5,000, fees range between $45 and $60. For transactions between $5,001 and $10,000, the fee range increases only to between $60 and $80.

After you register, you'll be able to execute trades in a secured, online environment. The account contract specifies an option that will preclude trading if the stock or stocks reach a price level too low or too high for your tastes.

Many investors like the security aspects involved in trading on a dedicated online network. Recent advances in encryption technology have made Web trading just as safe, but when it comes to safety, the online services got there first.

Figure 19-3: *Use this button to apply for a PC Financial Account on AOL.*

You'll also be able to check on your account status for several factors. These include your cash balance, order status, portfolio value, execution reports, and a historical review of your past trading activities.

The free Quotes & Portfolios area on AOL is also easy to get to, matching the steps that you take to get to PC Financial (home page icon, pull-down menu, or toolbar). Just type the stock symbol, and the display window will show the latest available trading price.

The Motley Fool, another hugely popular AOL feature, can also be reached in the same three-access alternatives manner described for Quotes & Portfolios. This free offering can also be found on its own Web site, which is detailed in Chapter 18.

COMPUSERVE

CompuServe and investing go back a long way. In the early 1970s, long before it became an online service, CompuServe leased its phone network to stockbrokers who needed to connect with each other. For most of its history, it was owned by accounting firm H&R Block. Today, the locus of CompuServe's finance-themed content is its Money Personal Finance Center, which is administered by *Money* magazine. The depth of content here solidifies CompuServe's traditional reputation as the most infocentric of all the online services.

You reach the Money Personal Finance Center by clicking on Finance on CompuServe's main Explore menu (see Figure 19-4). If you have a CompuServe straight-text dial-up account rather than its visually appealing WinCIM software, type **Go Money** at the user prompt.

Figure 19-4: *CompuServe's main Explore menu.*

When you get to the main Money page, you will see three main buttons: News, Investing, and Personal Finance. The next sections discuss each of these forums.

NEWS

As you might suspect, this is the place for financial news, including the following features:

- *Latest Headlines*   Breaking news from Reuters.

- *AP Online*   Summaries from the Associated Press business news wire.

- *Money Daily*   A daily feature written by the editors of *Money* magazine. It's also available on the magazine's Web pages, which are part of the Pathfinder service (see Chapter 18).

- *Fortune Daily*   Several columns from the magazine, as well as the full text of the current issue. Often, this is available before the issue reaches your postal mailbox or the newsstand.

- *Business Wire*   Press releases about companies, usually written by the companies themselves.

- *PR Newswire*   Similar to Business Wire. Both these wires have their own Web sites, which are described in the previous chapter.

- *News & Weather*   Links you back to CompuServe's main News & Weather menu.

- *Personalized News*   Takes you to a menu of all of CompuServe's news services, which include the business wires of AP, UPI, Reuters, and Dow Jones. If you like, you can set up a clipping file that will automatically identify any story that moves across these or other wire services that contain any of seven keywords you specify. These keywords can be investment terms or companies in which you are interested.

INVESTING

These are some of the main content areas that you'll find in Investing:

- *Quotes*   Makes stock quotes available on a 20-minute delayed basis. You can enter up to 75 stock symbols simultaneously. If you're interested in mutual funds, the day's prices and activity reports are updated every trading day at around 6:30 P.M. eastern time.

- *Charts*   Graphs of the current trading day's Dow Jones Industrial, Standard & Poor's 500, American Stock Exchange, and NASDAQ indexes. There is also a link to 30-day graphs of commodity and bond prices.

- *Company Information*   Provides links to several resources of researchers that analyze the performance of publicly traded companies. This is where you will find Thomson MarketEdge, Standard & Poor's Online, Hoover's Company Profiles, and the Disclosure database.

- *Screening Tools*   Two tools, Screen for Stocks and Screen for Funds, are located here. You type a search preference (see Figure 19-5) to look for stocks deemed to have low price-earnings ratios, high dividend yields, or low price-to-book ratios. Also, you can specify mutual funds grouped by the preceding categories, as well as by total return, investment objective, management company, fees and expenses, and other criteria.

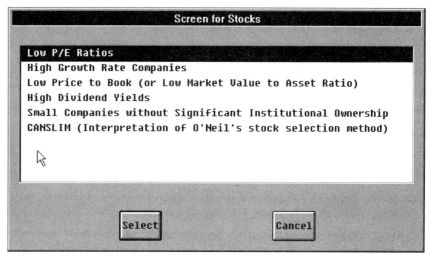

Figure 19-5: *Using Screen for Stocks on CompuServe.*

- *Publications*   Takes you to dozens of publications available on CompuServe. Some of these are valued newsletters chock full of investment advice, such as Capital Markets Publishing IPO Insider, Fabian's Premium Investment Resource, and a library of Kiplinger Newsletters.

- *Brokerages*   This will be a key area for you. From this point, you can apply for and then execute secured environment trading on E*TRADE Securities, Quick & Reilly, National Discount Brokerage, and Max Ule's Tickerscreen. You apply to each via e-mail directly from CompuServe (see Figure 19-6).

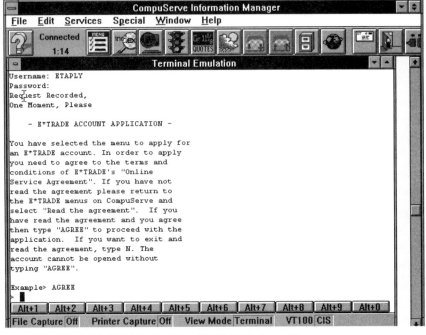

Figure 19-6: *Applying for an online E*TRADE Securities account on CompuServe is done via a Telnet session.*

- *Mutual Funds* Information available here is highlighted by the Mutual Fund Investment Center. This area contains investment kits, prospectuses, and brochures from dozens of mutual fund firms.

- *Global Investing* Has several resources for international investors, such as analyses of foreign companies and markets.

PERSONAL FINANCE

The last of these three icons also has several subareas, including the following:

- *Savings, Borrowing & Credit Rates* Surveys of rates and articles about trends in these areas.

- *Taxes* You can get tax advice here, and you can download more than 500 federal tax forms. No waiting in a long line at the library photocopier!

■ *Answers, Save-On, and Your Goals*   Three separate areas that feature frequently updated contributions from *Money* magazine columnists.

■ *One Family's Finances*   Modeled after the similar *Money* feature, this is a case history of how a given family is planning for its financial future while addressing present-day fiscal concerns.

■ *Money*   This takes you to most of the full content of *Money* magazine. Should you have a question or read something you disagree with, an e-mail letter-to-the-editor link is found here.

CompuServe's other major claim to fame is its forums, which are basically discussion areas on various topics. There are five that you will find useful here: Investors Forum, NAIC Investment Clubs, Tax Forum, Financial Software Forum, and Consumer Forums. You can read the commentaries of experts and talk with other investors or consumers in these forums. Here are the subject areas, or "libraries," of Investors Forum, which is the one most relevant to online investing:

■ Stocks/The Market

■ Bounds/Fixed Income

■ Option Trading

■ Futures/Commodities

■ Mutual Funds

■ Real Estate

■ Financial Planning/Taxes

■ Agribusiness

■ (Investment Software) Demos and Info

■ Newsletters/Theory

■ Charts/Technical Analysis

■ Global Investing

■ Internet Resources

■ The Novice Investor

- Fundamental Analysis
- (Related) Non-Investment (Topics)
- After The Bell Cafe (an investment-related chat area)

DELPHI

Delphi is one of the smaller, lesser-known online services. Its comparatively small user base is fiercely loyal. If you have a text-only communications software package, this is the best service for you by far. You'll find most of the finance-related Delphi areas on other services, but few if any will have the flexible, text-only options that Delphi does. This will also be good for you if you want to download information from the service, print it, and distribute it at a meeting. Because Delphi is text-only, such procedures are easier than on something such as Prodigy, from which downloads are difficult, or Web sites, from which downloads of HTML files into some word processing programs will reveal indecipherable passages of source code.

You access the Delphi business resources through the main Business & Industry menu on the opening page (see Figure 19-7). The $ sign means that the particular subject area carries a surcharge.

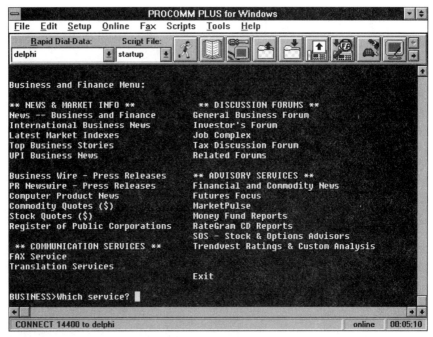

Figure 19-7: *The Delphi main Business & Industry menu.*

Arguably, the most unique offering on this menu is the Executive Desk Register of Publicly Held Corporations. According to the information provided on Delphi, "The Executive Desk Register of Publicly Held Corporations is a continuously updated database that contains all of the approximately 6,200 domestic corporations and financial institutions that are currently trading on the New York Stock Exchange, the American Stock Exchange, and the NASDAQ National Market System. The data in the Executive Desk Register is provided to DELPHI and maintained by Demand Research Corporation, Columbus, Ohio. The EDR is updated daily and published monthly by Demand Research." When you access a company record, you will see the name and address, phone number, ticker symbol, exchange affiliation, and names of key officers.

The most interesting Delphi forum for your purposes might be the Investors Special Interest Group, or SIG. There are discussions in six subject areas, including a General Discussion, Mutual Funds, Stocks, Bonds, Financial Planning, and Investment Software.

The Futures Focus menu under the Advisory Services column has frequently updated trading advice (see Figure 19-8).

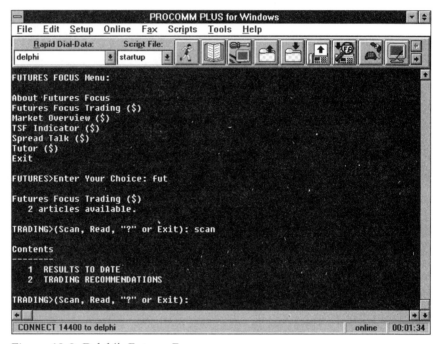

Figure 19-8: *Delphi's Futures Focus menu.*

Genie

Genie was founded by General Electric Corporation, but the conglomerate never made it a high priority. It started out with sufficient momentum, but by the early 1990s, it had become an afterthought as competing services developed more energetic marketing campaigns and a great deal more panache.

In 1996, Genie changed hands twice; its future is uncertain. If Genie went away, though, it would be a shame. Contentwise, it compares favorably to many of its more familiar rivals. Marketing and presentation, not content limitations, have stunted its growth.

Now, as the decade wears on, Genie suffers from giant, twin handicaps. It is the smallest online service in a business environment in which many observers feel that the entire proprietary online service model will be driven into total obscurity by the Web.

Still, Genie survives. I've chosen five areas on Genie that are of interest to investors.

CORPORATE AFFILIATES RESEARCH CENTER

The path to this area is as follows:

1. Upon logging on, you'll see a Top Menu with a Personal Finance & Investing Services choice. There will be a number next to each of these choices.

2. Below the Menu choices, click on the number corresponding to the Personal Finance & Investing Services listing. This will bring you to the main Personal Finance & Investing Table of Contents page.

3. When you're there, you'll see a listing of all finance-related content choices. On the Go To line at the bottom of the page, type the number corresponding to Corporate Affiliates.

This feature is explained by Genie on its Web site: "Quickly locate information on the corporate hierarchy for thousands of companies and their affiliates in the Corporate Affiliates Research Center. All you'll need to know is the name of the company or its ticker symbol and the system will do the rest! Just ask your question . . . the system will quickly search through thousands of company listings and give you a listing of the companies found."

To use this function, you pick a company name from the list of citations and review the results. Genie explains that a company's full record contains a list of all known affiliates, which is shown in a simple indented hierarchy (subsidiaries at the first indent, subsidiaries' subsidiaries at the second indent, and so on). You can search this database to find the relationships among companies with which you're working or are interested in working.

THE INVESTMENT ANALY$T

By following the same route to the Personal Finance & Investing Services Genie menu described previously, and then selecting the number corresponding to the Investment Analy$t, you reach a service that offers Current & Historical Quotes, Stock Performance Analysis, and Stock Screening & Selection. You can use it to track portfolios and note major stock sell-offs by senior company officials or major shareholders. The term for this, as you may have heard, is *strategic intelligence.*

DUN & BRADSTREET PROFILES

As you may have guessed, "D&B Profiles" is the key to the kingdom here. Are you thinking of investing in, or establishing a client relationship with, a company? D&B tracks both public and private companies, placing annual sales, net worth, and number of employees in this area. You can also get all the locations of a given company. You find this feature on Genie's Personal Finance & Investing Services menu as well, echoing the access steps described in the preceding section.

INVESTORS' ROUNDTABLE

This is the most utilitarian of the moneycentric forums on Genie (see Figure 19-9). Typing the keyword **invest** gets you there. When you arrive, you can discuss the merits of individual stocks, ask questions, get answers, and download investment software.

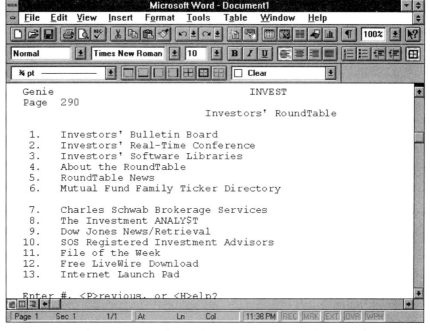

Figure 19-9: *The main page of Genie's Investors' RoundTable, one of the best online investment forums.*

INVESTEXT

As a financial journalist, I've been using Investext for several years. I'm grateful for the opportunity to sing its praises. Essentially, Investext is a compendium of research reports from most of the leading brokerage firms in the nation. If you are thinking of investing in a company, or have some of your money tied up in such, then a periodic visit to Investext will allow you access to research reports. This is a premium service that can be mildly costly, ranging from $3 or $4 dollars for small sections up to $12 for a full report. But it's nowhere near as expensive as taking a hit on a bad investment. Genie's open sesame: the keyword **investment**.

MICROSOFT NETWORK

At this writing, it is unclear exactly when the Microsoft Network (MSN) will make the full transition from an online service to a "super" Web site. Microsoft has announced plans to do so, but indications are it will follow a subscription model. You'll be able to access MSN directly from the Web but will probably pay for a substantial portion of its content. The content doubtless will be much the same as it looks today on the MSN home page.

Most of the areas of interest fall into two realms: data and forums. Data currently available include the following:

- Disclosure Database of company information.

- Dun and Bradstreet's library of company data, including small firms. Useful if you want to check on the size and annual sales of a prospective client or supplier.

- Information Access Company's database of newspaper and magazine articles.

- Thomson Financial Service's MarketEdge, which has reports, commentaries, and news stories about markets, individual companies, and mutual funds. Thomson and *USA Today* also have investment forums in which experts participate.

The Forums area has other specialty forums that feature regular discussions with experts and consultants involved with small businesses or computing. Some useful MSN forums are run by the American Management Association, *Entrepreneur* magazine, *Home Office Computing* magazine, and the Small Business Administration.

PRODIGY

You can reach the Prodigy Business & Finance menu from the home page. This page shows you the latest Dow Industrial, New York Stock Exchange, American Stock Exchange, and NASDAQ composite averages. On the right side of the opening page (see Figure 19-10), you find a list of several content areas. Let's focus on these three: Strategic Investor, Online Trading, and Online Banking.

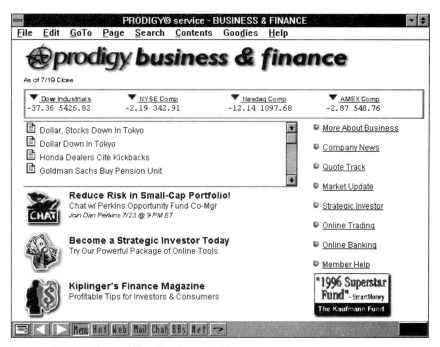

Figure 19-10: *The Prodigy Business & Finance menu.*

Strategic Investor furnishes current prices, historical performance data, and earnings reports on thousands of companies and mutual funds. It also contains investment analytical tools, as well as columns from the editors of *Investor's Business Daily*.

The company reports, which usually run about 12 screens, are prepared by Market Guide. The 6,000 or so reports in the database give analyst earnings estimates, buy/sell/hold recommendations, and an earnings history.

The Mutual Fund Analyst area of Prodigy's Strategic Investor area has performance history, asset composition, and contact information for more than 3,600 funds.

Stock Hunter groups the company reports into eight different classes. According to Prodigy, these are the following:

- *Graham/Dodd*   Recognized value investing model.

- *CANSLIM*   Above-average market performers. These are chosen via guidelines formulated by William O'Neil, founder of *Investor's Business Daily*.

- *One Up on Wall Street*   Based on the principles of earnings growth in financial guru Peter Lynch's book.

- *Wallflowers*   Small caps with growth potential and little institutional ownership.

- *Sustainable Growth*   Firms whose actual growth is less than their sustainable growth.

- *Consistent Dividends*   Stable and increasing dividends.

- *Low Price/Book*   One hundred stocks with lowest price/book ratio.

- *High Price/Book*   One hundred stocks with highest price/book ratio.

Prodigy furnishes Online Banking in two ways. One application, BillPay (available through Prodigy), cuts checks and sends them to your different creditors based on amounts and dispersal dates that you've specified in your application with them. There's also a platform on Prodigy for Wells Fargo Bank, where you can check your account balances and transfer funds between them.

For online trading, Prodigy also has PC Financial Network, which is described in the America Online section of this chapter.

A Word About the AT&T Business Network

Fans of the AT&T Business Network praise the site for its hundreds of links to investment resources and publications. Because it doesn't require a separate dial-in or password and is free over the Web, this offering is not really an online service but a rich aggregate of online content and links to other places. This feature is more like a cyberspace version of an airport or train station. In short, it's a dispatch point to other places. Definitely worth a stop, but an online or research service has to be a destination in itself.

Because most of the content on the AT&T Business Network is available on its own Web sites, I've chosen not to place this handy offering under the microscope in this chapter.

The Research Services

Commercial online services such as America Online and CompuServe are feature-driven, with emphasis on cool graphics and an entertaining user experience. In this way, they are very much like television or the sections of a newspaper. Research services such as Dialog and Lexis/Nexis resemble information vaults, where scores of plain-text, digitized documents from both well-known and obscure content providers sit, waiting for a search. The closest parallel is the reference shelves of a large public or university library.

Thankfully, there has been some improvement in the presentation quality and searchability of these imposing vaults. Dialog, the oldest and quite possibly the most respected of these services, used to have an unfathomable data search process. Now you no longer need an M.S. degree in library science to check on information. Searches are generally directed now by menu prompts, not by arcane codes that have to be memorized. All that is required is a quest for knowledge, some rudimentary searching skills, and a way to access these facilities by modem.

You do this in one of two ways: either by signing up with these services for a direct account, or by reaching elements of them through a handy "side door" provided by CompuServe, Genie, or a telecommunications packager such as MCI Mail.

The following sections survey four leading research services, including what they offer the online investor and how they can be tapped.

DataTimes

DataTimes has more than 5,000 information sources, including several years of newspaper, magazine, newsletter, and broadcast transcripts. You can read citations either as plain text through your telecommunications software program, or via EyeQ, DataTimes's own Windows-based software package provided as part of the subscription package.

You can search major elements of the DataTimes files as plain text on Dow Jones News/Retrieval, which is available directly through Dow, or through a contracted carrier such as MCI Mail (see Figure 19-11). This might the best idea for beginners, but you have to subscribe directly to DataTimes to get the full menu of services. Monthly subscriptions cost $39 a month, and every full-text article that is retrieved costs an additional $3.

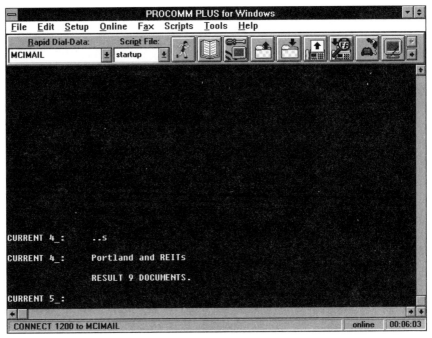

Figure 19-11: *Launching a DataTimes search on Dow Jones News/Retrieval, which can be accessed via MCI Mail.*

When you launch a DataTimes search, you are asked four questions:

- *Who*   The person's name to be searched.
- *What*   The topic to be searched.
- *Where*   The sources in the database that you want to be searched.
- *When*   The date range that should be searched.

EyeQ then shows you a group of headlines from stories that conform to your search. Depending on your subscription arrangements, you may have to pay a small, set price, usually $1 or $2, to read the full-text version of the ones you want.

The EyeQ software is more than just a rote retrieval tool, however. It has three value-added features, including:

- *Private Eye*   A service that tracks your competitors. When it finds stories just added to the DataTimes database mentioning competitors' names that you have previously specified, it sends you these reports via electronic mail, fax, or regular mail.

- *Business Analyst*   Current stock prices and newly received analyst research reports.

- *Today's News*   A daily posting of news headlines from international, national, and U.S. newspapers.

DataTimes Intell.Xx is even more advanced. It's designed for corporate use and can easily be distributed over a Local Area Network. Content groupings are specialized and organized in more than 20 industry fields, including Banking, Telecommunications, Energy, Real Estate, and Insurance. Intell.Xx uses artificial intelligence methods in which new searches, the site explains, "learn searching lessons from" previous ones. Its three main features are as follows:

- *SummaryEXpress*   A daily business summaries update.

- *Intell.XEXpress*   A pared-down version of SummaryEXpress.

- *SourceEXpress*   Updates of requested content from a specific newspaper or magazine.

DataTimes is probably the most user-friendly of the research utilities.

DIALOG

Vaunted Dialog has been around since the mid-1970s. Very few people had modems then. The primitive devices of the time ran at 300 baud, or almost 1 percent the speed of today's 28.8 bps modems. Dialog has changed with the times. It's not pop culture; it can still be intimidating to the inexperienced trover. Yet for those who have grown comfortable with it, Dialog is not only a business tool, it's the closest thing we have to a living archive of our civilization.

You can access dialog directly or through the comprehensive IQuest or Knowledge Index menu choices on CompuServe (see Figure 19-12). The CompuServe–Dialog connection lets you run a search by specific publication or by general topic. You can also do searches and retrievals through Dialog's Knowledge Index.

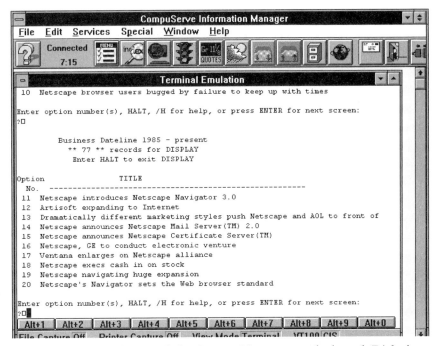

Figure 19-12: *A Dialog search for the term* Netscape *made through Dialog's Knowledge Index on CompuServe pulled up these citations.*

Five of the general topic areas that might serve your needs all fall into the Business category. These are Business & Industry, Business Statistics, International Directories & Company Financials, Product Information, and U.S. Directories and Company Financials.

On the DIALOG Bluesheets pages of the Dialog Web site (http://www.dialog.com), you can find complete content listings for each publication in all the Dialog indexes. Under each name is a description of what topics that publication covers, as well as the date range of issues available in the database.

The list is far too lengthy to reproduce here, but here are highlights from each of the five Business topic areas that I mentioned:

Business & Industry

- Accounting & Tax Database
- Bond Buyer Full Text
- Insider Trading Monitor
- M&A (Mergers and Acquisitions) Filings
- Wall Street Journal Abstracts

Business Statistics

- Cendata: County Business Patterns
- Cendata: Daily Census News
- Econbase: Time Series and Forecast
- EIU: Economist Intelligence Unit
- Knight-Ridder Tribune Business News

International Directories & Company Financials

- Corporate Affiliations (directory)
- FBR Asian Company Profiles
- IAC Company Intelligence
- Moody's Corporate News–International
- Research Centers and Services Directory

Product Information

- Delphes European Business
- IAC Newsletter Database
- Magazine Database
- Thomas Register Online (a listing of business lines and contact information for more than 200,000 public and private companies)
- Time Publications (*Time, FORTUNE, Money,* etc.)
- Brands and Their Companies

U.S. Directories & Company Financials

- Corporate Affiliations (information about the owner of a subsidiary, for instance)
- Disclosure Database
- Standard & Poor's Corporate Descriptions plus News
- TRW Business Credit Profiles

Lots of stuff here, but as I've said before, information is power. With Dialog on your desktop, you can become a powerful, information-equipped heavy hitter.

DOW JONES NEWS/RETRIEVAL

Basic stock price and industry news is available on Dow Jones areas on Genie, Prodigy, and MCI Mail. For the full suite, you have to subscribe to Dow Jones News/Retrieval at either $39.95 or $29.95 a month, and use its software. You can obtain that software via a direct download from the Dow Jones Web site (see Figure 19-13).

DJNR is a cross between an online service and a research utility. Like an online service, much of its news is current, but like a research utility, its archives are formidable. Because it does not have the flair and panache of an offering aimed at consumers, I've decided to group DJNR in the "Research Services" section of this chapter.

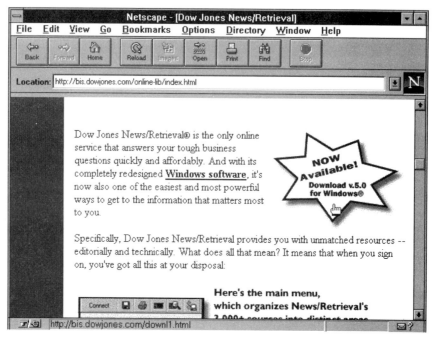

Figure 19-13: *Get Dow Jones News/Retrieval software by clicking here.*

DJNR subscription plans come with one of three software choices. These are the Private Investor Edition, which is strong on news; the Technical Analyst Edition, for both current and historical price quote analysis; and the Technical Analyst Gold Edition, which has elements of both.

On the DJNR Web site (http://bis.dowjones.com/online-lib) you'll see listings of the information sources employed by Dow to bring you Quotes & Market Data as well as Company and Industry information.

Here are the Quotes & Market Data sources used by Dow Jones News Retrieval:

- *Current Quotes* Quotes on stocks, bonds, mutual funds, U.S. Treasury issues, and options. Stock quotes are enhanced with news alerts. Quotes are delayed 20 minutes during trading hours.

- *Real Time Quotes*   Real-time stock quotes on common and preferred stocks on the New York, American, Pacific, Midwest, and NASDAQ Stock Exchanges.

- *Current and Historical Quotes*   Current and historical quotes for commodities and financial futures traded on major North American exchanges, plus daily values for more than 100 selected indexes.

- *Historical Quotes*   Daily high, low, close, and volume for stocks for the past year, and monthly and quarterly stock price summaries.

- *Tradeline Global Security Pricing and Analysis*   Historical information on stocks, bonds, mutual funds, government securities, foreign-exchange rates, options, and indexes (includes both U.S. and global coverage). Tradeline includes screening and reporting features.

- *Historical Dow Jones Averages*   Daily summaries of the Dow Jones Averages back to 1982 and 12-day trading period summaries back one year.

- *Innovest Technical Analysis Reports*   Daily technical opinions on stocks traded on the New York and American exchanges plus over-the-counter issues.

- *Mutual Funds Performance Report*   Comprehensive performance statistics, assets, and background information on mutual funds.

- *MMS Weekly Market Analysis*   Weekly snapshot of expectations from top economists and traders for the world's equity, currency, and debt markets.

- *Wall $treet Week Online*   The four most recent transcripts of this popular PBS television program.

DJNR's Company & Industry data sources are assembled in an all-under-one-roof grouping unsurpassed in the online world for convenience. Here are the sources:

- *Investext Analysts' Reports*   Research reports by investment firms on companies and industries.

- *Dun's Financial Records PLUS* In-depth financial, historical, and operational reports for public and private companies.

- *SEC Full-Text Filings* Full text of 10Ks, 10Qs, annual reports, proxy filings, and 20Fs for more than 6,500 companies listed on the New York, American, or NASDAQ Exchanges.

- *Disclosure Reports Derived From SEC Filings* Detailed business and financial information from 10K and 10Q extracts on publicly held companies.

- *Dun's Market Identifiers* Company and market identification data on public and private companies.

- *Corporate Ownership Watch* Insider transactions of more than 80,000 individuals and 8,000 companies.

- *Zack's Corporate Earnings Estimates* Consensus of securities analysts on earnings-per-share estimates for companies and forecasts for industries.

- *Media General Financial Services* Comparative price, volume, and fundamental data on companies and industries.

- *Standard & Poor's Profiles and Estimates* Profiles of 4,700 companies, including dividend and market figures and outlook.

- *Corporate Canada Online* Business news and financial market information on public, private, and government-owned Canadian companies.

- *Nikkei Telecom Japan News & Retrieval* Japan's largest news source of financial news and corporate information covering Japanese business, the economy, markets, and other political developments.

- *Worldwide Corporate Reports* Comprehensive information on companies from around the world.

- *Saudi 1000* Profiles of the top 1,000 Saudi Arabian companies, including background, financial data, and other company information. You can locate a report by entering a company name.

LEXIS/NEXIS

Lexis/Nexis is actually two services. Lexis is a vast repository of legal information and case law primarily of interest to attorneys. Nexis is similarly structured, but with content areas of broader relevance. Its newspaper archives are quite strong and deep. Journalists consider Nexis the standard bearer for research.

You subscribe to Nexis directly; an application form is available on the Web site. Many subscribers prefer Nexis's Company Quick-Check, a Windows-compatible software program that allows you to search across most Nexis databases, or "libraries." The BUSREF, COMPNY, and MARKET may be of the most interest to you.

Most Nexis business-related content is available elsewhere in some form, but a brief overview is in order. The following sections describe a few of the useful investing and financial-related services that you can find on Nexis.

DIRECTORY OF CORPORATE AFFILIATIONS

In BIZREF, COMPNY, MARKET, and WORLD libraries, this area gives contact and business information for more than 114,000 public and private companies throughout the world.

HOOVER'S COMPANY PROFILE DATABASE

Located in the COMPNY section via the keyword HOOVER, Hoover's has detailed summations and corporate profiles drawn from four of Hoover's publications. Many of the profiles list financial performance and stock price going back several years, the products made by each listed company, and the names of listed companies' major competitors. Publications here include *Hoover's Handbook of American Business*; *Hoover's Handbook of Emerging Companies*; *Hoover's Handbook of World Business*; and *Hoover's Guide to Private Companies*.

IAC INDUSTRY EXPRESS

This is an industry-specific, full-text article database, with articles about computers, electronics, and the telecommunciations industry.

More areas will be added by early 1997. The keyword IACX in the MARKET library gets you to IAC.

LATIN AMERICAN COMPANY DATABASE

If you are considering making an investment in a company south of the border, you'll find this resource to be unsurpassed for timeliness and depth of content. There are details on more than 200 publicly traded companies based in Argentina, Brazil, Mexico, and Venezuela, along with names and contact information for more than 65 money managers and investment advisors in Venezuela and Brazil. You can find this database by typing the keyword **LACDB** in the BUSREF, COMPNY, MEXICO, NSAMER, or WORLD library areas.

THE RED BOOKS

Updated monthly, these books include the Standard Directory of Advertisers, the Standard Directory of International Advertisers, the Standard Directory of Advertising Agencies, and the Standard Directory of International Advertising Agencies. These volumes list virtually all companies who advertise, how much they spend per year on advertising, what type of media they use, and who their advertising agency is. Because well-executed major advertising and marketing campaigns often are linchpins of a corporation's profitability, you may want to use this resource to see what a company that you are thinking of investing in—or already are investing in—is up to. You can find the resources in the BUSREF, COMPNY, and MARKET libraries under the keywords **SDA** (Advertiser Red Books); **SDAA** (Agency Red Books); and **REDBK** (for both).

DATAFEED PROVIDERS

For the last few years, the big three datafeed providers have been Bloomberg Terminal, Dow Jones Telerate, and Reuters Integrated Data Network. Your stockbroker or funds manager almost certainly has at least one of these. If you are willing to pay $2,000 to

$3,000 per month in an airtight 2-year lease for real-time data and stunningly sophisticated information-crunching tools, getting one of these terminals in your home or office just might be practical. Here's a quick look at each.

BLOOMBERG TERMINAL

The Bloomberg Terminal is the only way to get the full text of the Bloomberg news wires. More than 3,000 stories a day move in this fashion. The Terminal is also equipped with multimedia capabilities. If, for example, a CEO is holding a major press conference announcing an acquisition, a subscriber could hear portions of the conference on the Terminal.

On this wire, stories written by reporters for Bloomberg business news are supplemented by feeds from more than 10 other services, including Business Wire, Deutsche Press–Agentur, Futures World News, Billboard Publications, and Phillips Business Information.

Bloomberg is also revered for its cutting-edge price charting and analysis tools, which it integrates with its market-price news feeds.

DOW JONES TELERATE

Telerate (see Figure 19-14) is the main market information datafeed of Dow Jones, the company that publishes the *Wall Street Journal* and *Barron's*. Its flagship is Telerate Workstation, a tool that routes live pricing data, analysis, and breaking news to your terminal and shows this information in a Windows-compatible format. You can also import the information to Excel spreadsheets, where you can incorporate it in a risk or portfolio program that you manage or belong to. Read more about investment-related software in the next chapter.

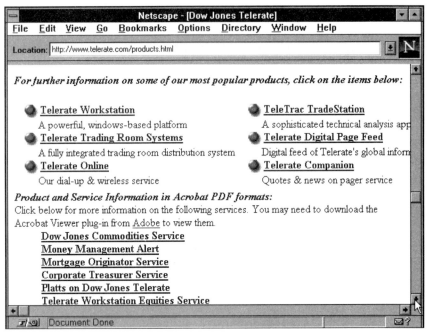

Figure 19-14: *Brief product descriptions are available on the Telerate Web site.*

If you think that Telerate is just a stock ticker, you're wrong. There is a live, real-time stock feed—as opposed to the 15- or 20-minute delayed quotes that you get on a stock wire carried by an online service. Yet Telerate furnishes instantaneous market news on futures and options, money markets, metals, commodities, bonds, and foreign exchange rates.

On its Web site, Telerate identifies seven Telerate Workstation applications:

- *Page Displays* Instant access to more than 60,000 pages of live Telerate data, news, commentary, and financial databases containing pricing, terms, and conditions on Corporate Bonds, Eurobonds, and other bond instruments. Set up hot keys for your favorite pages.

- *Quotes* Data on stocks, ADRs, mutual funds, indexes, bonds, and foreign exchange rates. Customize column headings and color code ticks to monitor market direction with visual ease. Double-click on an instrument and a pop-up window will provide you with a full quote.

- *News* Combine multiple Dow Jones news wires and gain fast access to headlines and stories. Conduct searches on the last 180 days of news, based on keywords, ticker symbols, company names, or geographic locations. Set alarms on headlines that meet specific search criteria. Double-click on a headline and quickly read the related news story.

- *Charts and technical analysis studies* Rich graphic displays to view intraday and historic data in a continuous manner. Several timescales are supported, from one minute to one day. Plot types supported include line, dot, histogram/line, and bar charts showing HLC or OHLC. Studies include RSI, Moving Averages, Oscillators, Momentum, MACD, Spreads, and Stochastics. These charts serve as impressive visual aids for your client or staff presentations.

- *Composite pages* You have the freedom to create and edit your own pages, blending quotes, pages, labels, and bitmaps while customizing colors and fonts to your personal preferences.

- *Dynamic Data Exchange (DDE)* Export live Telerate data to Excel spreadsheets for price/yield calculations, portfolio valuations, or for use in proprietary trading models.

- *Limits, alerts, and scrolling tickers* Display on your screen layouts.

Forget the clattering stock tickers who produced the tickertape that you see in old newsreel footage of parades honoring returning World War II heroes. Thanks to services such as Telerate, today's tickertape is made not from paper but from silicon chips.

REUTERS INTEGRATED DATA NETWORK

If you sign a lease for a Reuters Terminal, you get the choice of customizable news and market price packages appropriate for your sector. Relevant news and market activity reports are then identified and sent to your Terminal.

The sectors for which these packages are provided are Foreign Exchange, Money, Securities, Fixed Income, Commodities, Energy, and Shipping.

You can use an e-mail link on the Reuters Web site information services page (see Figure 19-15) to get more information about the Reuters Integrated Data Network.

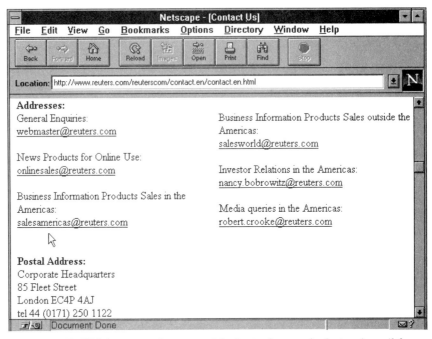

Figure 19-15: *Click here to activate your Navigator browser's electronic mail function. When you do so, you'll be able to write the Reuters Integrated Data Network.*

BULLETIN BOARDS

A number of metropolitan areas have investment clubs that have either set up bulletin board systems (BBSes) or are a feature of a larger BBS, much like a content area on a commercial online service. Little of major input goes on here; these basically are discussion groups.

Here's how you can find an investment bulletin board in your area. Several times a year, *Online Access* magazine puts out a CD-ROM directory of bulletin boards. The directory, which is bundled in an issue (available at major newsstands, bookstores, and computer retail outlets), will group BBSes by area code (from 201, New

Jersey, up to 954, South Florida), areas of interest, and method of access. Some of these boards can also be reached through the Internet, either through a link from a Web site or via a Telnet connection that you can launch from your Navigator browser or telecommunications program. When you get the CD, put it in your CD-ROM drive and load it as you would any new program or feature that you've just acquired.

Boardwatch magazine, a monthly publication, frequently has articles about popular or innovative BBSes. The full text of each issue is available on the Boardwatch Web site (http://www.boardwatch.com).

The 1-800-BBS Directory Web site (see Figure 19-16) lists most of the toll-free bulletin boards in the nation. The listings are grouped by letter, and they mention the primary topic of each board. Because some boards have investment club chat rooms just as a sidelight, you're not likely to find them here, but a few can be located with the help of this resource, which is at http://pages.map.com/~sfinc/bbsdctry/welcome.html.

Figure 19-16: *The 1-800-BBS Directory Web site is your source for a listing of investment-related bulletin boards with toll-free numbers.*

CONTACT INFORMATION

Most of the services described in this chapter are not Web sites. Still, virtually all *use* Web sites to detail their offerings and provide information about how to contact them directly. With this in mind, here is a list of Web URLs and phone numbers for these providers.

Service	URL	Phone Number
America Online	http://www.aol.com	1-800-827-6364
CompuServe	http://www.compuserve.com	1-800-848-8199
Delphi	http://www.delphi.com	1-800-695-4005
Genie	http://www.genie.com	1-800-638-8369
Microsoft Network	http://www.msn.com	1-800-386-5550
Prodigy	http://www.prodigy.com	1-800-776-3449
AT&T Business Network	http://www.bnet.att.com/	1-800-222-0400
DataTimes	http://www.datatimes.com	1-888-328-2846
Dialog	http://www.dialog.com	1-800-354-2564
Dow Jones News Retrieval	http://bis.dowjones.com/	1-800-369-7466
Lexis-Nexis	http://www.lexis-nexis.com	1-800-227-4908
Bloomberg Terminal	http://www.bloomberg.com/	1-212-318-2200
Dow Jones Telerate	http://www.telerate.com/tw.html	1-800-334-3813
Reuters Integrated Data Network	http://www.reuters.com/reuterscom/	1-212-489-5555
1-800-BBS Directory	http://pages.map.com/~sfinc/bbsdctry/welcome.html	
Boardwatch Magazine	http://www.boardwatch.com	

MOVING ON

Whether through an online service, research library, or stock wire, financial information is just statistics and data unless you have ways to harness it. In the next chapter, "Offline Resources, On-Target Tools," I explore some software programs that will help you do so.

Offline Resources, On-Target Tools

Throughout most of this book, I've pointed you to Web sites and other Internet resources from which you can learn about virtually any avenue of available investment opportunity, check the performance of those investments, obtain advice, and stay current on financial sector and "real world" news that may affect their worth.

Now, you know how to a use a modem and a Web browser to get the information you need from the Internet and online services. The next logical step is for you to learn how to organize and harness this data on your own computer.

This skill will be critically important to your future. Information unharnessed is like a mighty, wild river. Tamed, its power can be used to help power a city; but if all you do is stand on the shore and gaze at it, you take nothing tangible from it except an aesthetic sense of wonder.

The analogy should be obvious: you can bookmark and regularly visit every site that talks about bonds, derivatives, commodities, mortgage rates, and tax-planning strategies. That may make you more knowledgeable about finance, but it won't make you richer. The horsepower available on your home computer is the "hydroelectric dam" that can apply and organize this knowledge for your own situation.

There are tens of thousands of software programs and packages, thousands of which might be said to have a significant investment or personal finance component. Even if a book this size were entirely devoted to this material, space limitations would make discussing each one of these programs impossible. This problem obviously is further accentuated when I limit the discussion to one chapter, but I won't let that blur the mission.

This chapter differs somewhat from Chapter 13, "Software," which is largely devoted to meritorious software Web sites. In this chapter, I look at the capabilities of software itself.

I discuss more than a dozen representative programs. Some can be downloaded directly from Web sites, whereas others must be purchased at the computer store, via mail or phone order, or from a CGI-enabled order form from the Web site. A few make all the options available.

Software evaluation is divided into two sections: Investment Software and Personal Finance Software. Despite this chapter structure, please keep in mind that these two types of programs can work on your computer as a digital "team" to manage your money and help it grow as well.

WHAT MAKES A GOOD FINANCIAL SOFTWARE PROGRAM?

In this chapter, we are covering both financial and investment software. At its crux, most investment software has the processing of investment-related information and portfolio management. Financial management software is more generic in scope, integrating information about the performance of your investment portfolio into the tracking of your overall budget, tax situation, and fiscal persona.

Whether we talk about specific investment software or the broader financial management packages, even the best financial software programs are only as intelligent as the information they retrieve.

Here are attributes common to the best financial software offerings:

- The software must be configurable and able to be updated. Financial information is, after all, one of the more volatile, time-sensitive, and mercurial of all resources. For this reason, there can't be hard-and-fast software programs without any configurability.

- The software should have the ability to import statistics from outside sources and then build them into your user profile. This could mean stock prices, maturing CDs, or dates when estimated taxes are due. The main principle at work here is keeping the information fresh.

- An online connection, especially to the Internet, is vital. A bundled browser such as Netscape Navigator 3.0 is a big help. As I've shown you in previous chapters, stock prices can change by the minute and mortgage rates can change by the day. The Internet is full of resources to help you keep up with these changes.

- There should be ways to migrate information across subject fields and, where possible, between one program and another. The capability of relating investment information and personal financial records to each other is absolutely essential. Where feasible, it should also be possible to import records from one area of the software to the other, and then for the record to be updated based on this transferred information.

- Finally, site navigability is critical. Are all the subject fields clearly titled and named? If not, you'll be led down blind alleys.

FINANCIAL SOFTWARE SITES

Here are some sites for investment-related software programs. By no means is this list complete, but I've tried to include most of the well-known offerings that either let you conduct online trading, track the particular price trends for your investments, or both.

FIDELITY ON-LINE XPRESS

http://www.fid-inv.com/
Phone: 1-800-544-9375

Fidelity On-Line Xpress, which is called "FOX" for short, is the PC-based software package trading program used by customers of Fidelity Investments for online trading. See Chapters 10 and 12 for more information on Fidelity services.

FOX, which sells for $49, is a relatively low-tech program that requires only a 2400-baud modem and 640K of RAM (random access memory). That's the amount of memory in all but the most primeval, pre-Windows computers, so unless you are running an ancient Altair or Commodore 64 made before the wheel was invented, you should be fine. Are you a busy investor without too much spare time to learn complicated software navigation routines? No problem. FOX is simple and easy to use.

You have to order the FOX software by phoning Fidelity, but you can receive and test a demo via download from the FOX page on the Fidelity Investments Web site (see Figure 20-1).

If you execute trades with this software rather than call your Fidelity broker directly, you can save 10 percent in stock and option commissions. Only one minor caveat: the minimum commission charged is $38.

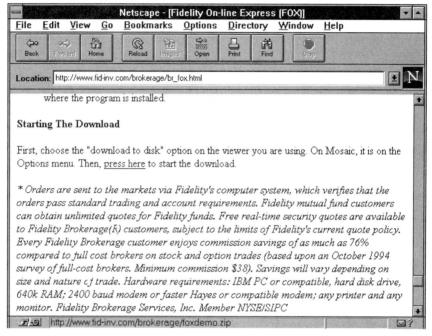

Figure 20-1: *Download a demo of Fidelity's FOX investment software from this page.*

Here's what you can do with FOX's software:

- Trade stock and options via orders sent from your computer system to Fidelity, where they are received, verified, and then executed.

- Buy, sell, or exchange all Fidelity mutual funds.

- Get current balances and transactional histories for all your Fidelity accounts.

- Obtain current stock and mutual fund price quotes.

- For varying but reasonable extra rates, you can subscribe to several sources of market news, such as Telescan, Dow Jones News/Retrieval, and Standard & Poor's MarketScope.

FINANCIALCAD

http://www.financialcad.com/
Phone: 1-800-304-0702

FinancialCAD offers three powerful software packages that, essentially, are sophisticated analytical and predictive tools. FinancialCAD's more than 290 function capabilities make it possible to project cash flows and analyze pricing patterns on numerous financial instruments.

Some of the instruments about which FinancialCAD is capable of processing information include bonds, mortgages, certificates of deposit, commodities, foreign exchange rates, and money market securities.

If you're a single user working from your home terminal, the $395 FinancialCAD for Excel is probably the best product for you. You can register for a demo directly from the FinancialCAD Web site (see Figure 20-2). Besides its powerful analytics, this version also contains a reference library and can convert the data that it crunches into the Excel spreadsheet format.

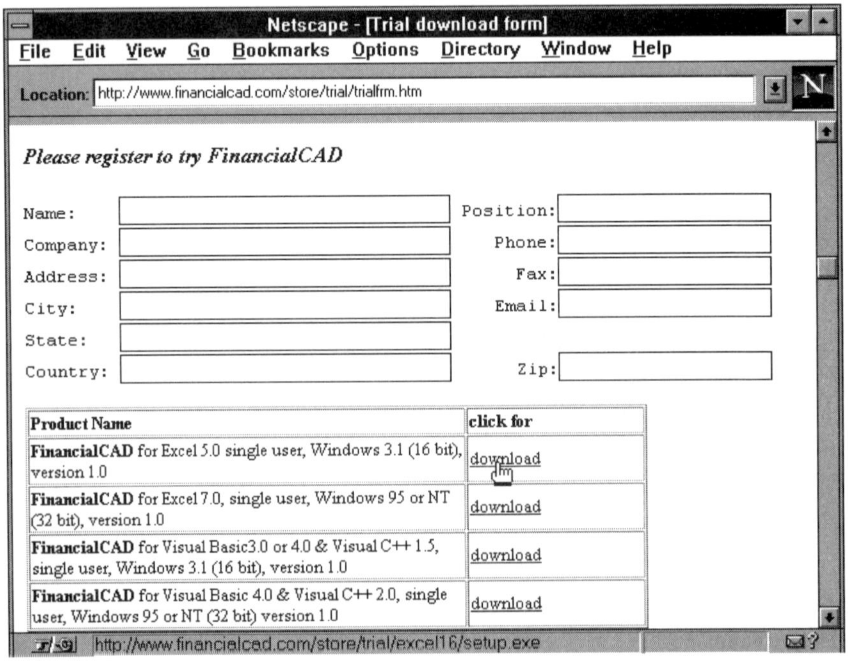

Figure 20-2: *Download a copy of FinancialCAD by clicking here.*

Enhanced programs available include the FinancialCAD for Visual Basic & C, at $529, and the $795 complete FinancialCAD package, which offers both Visual Basic and Excel spreadsheet compatibility.

INVESTORS FASTTRACK MUTUAL FUND PROGRAM

http://www.fasttrack.net/
Phone: 1-800-749-1348 or 1-504-291-4413
Fax: 1-504-291-4811
I've included FastTrack's Mutual Fund Program in this chapter to illustrate the grand possibilities of an integrated stock-management software package with an integrated module able to process same-day stock market data.

This particular program, which costs only $19.95 after a free, 30-day trial, combines analysis capabilities for more than 1,000 mutual funds. The program uses a $24–$36 per month subscription to a funds-price service that sends the day's results to your computer by 7:30 P.M. each business day.

After the data is received, FastTrack's analytical tools go to work. The suggested analysis module contains several ranking tools and can perform assessments of an individual fund's momentum and relative strength. You can specify funds by industry sector, geography, or strategy (such as "balanced" or "growth").

With capabilities more often found in financial software that costs several times as much, FastTrack's Mutual Fund Program can also process daily price information about your own portfolio and assemble the information in a chart.

FastTrack classifies these charts in 10 general areas, including companies that specialize in the following:

- *Health Care*   Biotechnology, medical delivery, and health care, which includes hospital-chain stocks.

- *High Technology*   Multimedia, electronics, computer (hardware) technology, and computer software.

- *Gold and Precious Metals*   Precious metals and minerals and American gold.

- *Financial*   Financial services, regional banks, brokerages, home finance, and insurance.

- *Cyclical Industries*   Automotive, construction and housing, industrial equipment, transportation, consumer products, and retail.

- *Energy Industry*   Chemicals, energy services, industrial materials, natural gas, energy, and paper and forest stocks.

- *Telecommunications*   Developing communications technologies and telecommunications.

- *Social and Environmental Responsibility*   Stocks are screened for corporate standards concerning these issues.

For those companies that don't snugly fit into any of the preceding classes, FastTrack has an Ungrouped category. Firms that fall in this index can be involved in food and agriculture, defense and aerospace, leisure (such as hotels and gaming stocks), and air transportation sectors.

This program requires only 512K of disk space and a relatively unsophisticated VGA monitor. It can be obtained either by downloading directly from FastTrack's Web site for a free, 30-day trial (see Figure 20-3) or by phoning the number listed previously.

Figure 20-3: *Try out Investors FastTrack via a download from here.*

STREETSMART 2.0

http://www.schwab.com/
Phone: 1-800-334-4455 or 1-415-627-7000
As you may have figured out, StreetSmart 2.0 is the proprietary online trading tool provided by Charles Schwab. The $39 program, which can work on Windows or Mac systems, requires you to have a Schwab account. You can purchase it by phoning Schwab directly at the number listed here, or by going to the Schwab Web site and filling out an order form that will be e-mailed directly to Schwab. You can access a free demo version directly from the site (see Figure 20-4).

Hardware requirements vary. For the Windows version, a 486-powered computer running Windows 3.1 or above on at least 8MB of RAM is the minimum. Five megabytes of available hard-drive space will accommodate the basic package, with optional add-ons such as the Reuters Money Network (profiled in Chapter 19) amping up the total space needed to 16MB.

The Mac version requires only 4MB of RAM and 5MB of hard-disk space, along with a computer running Macintosh System 7 or higher.

Some of StreetSmart's capabilities include:

- The ability to buy or sell stocks, mutual funds, or options online (see Figure 20-4).

- A Symbol Lookup database from which you can, via a direct connection with the Reuters Money Network, get current prices on stocks, mutual funds, bonds, and options.

- Creation of transaction and portfolio report spreadsheets.

- The ability to check all your fund balances.

- Research report access and download. Except for access to the Morningstar Mutual Fund Performance Information database, these are premium services. The priciest of these is a connection to the informational treasure trove Dow Jones News/Retrieval database (see Chapter 19). This costs $1.50 for every 1,000 characters (letters or numbers) that you download.

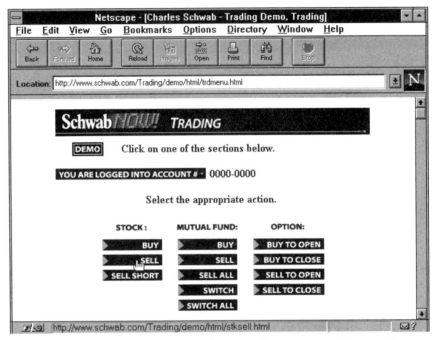

Figure 20-4: *Schwab's trading screen has several options to facilitate online trading.*

TELESCAN ANALYZER & PROSEARCH

http://www.telescan.com:80/
Phone: 1-713-588-9700
Fax: 1-713-588-9750
This $395 system fuses several capabilities not often found with individual programs. Information is freshened every business night via an online subscription to the Telescan System.

Some of Analyzer's and ProSearch's functions include:

■ Access to nearly 25 years of Telescan database information on more than 8,000 stocks, 35,000 options, and 1,800 mutual funds. Data include earnings estimates, company profiles, insider trading histories, and an archive of news stories affecting the companies and funds listed.

■ More than 75 analytical indicator tools such as searching and filtering indicators. These filters permit you to customize your own search and data analysis field to match your stock portfolio. If you like, the chart can contain historical data concerning dividends, earnings, book value, cash flow, capital spending, and sales data for the issues that you specify.

■ A News Menu with three to six months of archived news stories, as retrieved via the Telescan newsfeed.

■ A Quote Menu from which volume, high price, last bid, and closing price (from the most recent trading day) can be requested for up to 50 securities. You can also create a "clipping" file that will retrieve this information automatically.

You gain extra perspective on this raw data by subscribing to one of several Telescan analysis and search services. Here's a quick rundown of Online Pricing Analysis Services:

■ *Protege Pricing Plan* $9.95 a month, including one hour of online access a month.

■ *Premium Pricing Plan* $49.95 a month. For this price, you receive 40 hours of online access, as well as free access to Market Guide Profile Reports and Zack's Estimates Service, as well as a 10 percent discount on Telescan books and seminars.

■ *Platinum Pricing Plan* $99.95 a month for 60 hours, a 25 percent discount on seminars and books, plus the free Market Guide and Zack's reports also available on the premium plan.

■ *Unlimited Pricing Plan* $299.95 a month. This plan gives you unlimited online access plus the other benefits of Platinum Pricing.

Customers on the first three plans who exceed their monthly online time ceiling are charged an additional $4.80 an hour.

If you like, you can also subscribe to customized, historical performance research services that cover stocks, options, and mutual funds. These choices run $12 or $18 per month on an a la carte basis, or can be signed up for as a group for $35 a month. Telescan customers who don't wish to commit to these search plans can perform searches for a $1.25 fee for each search attempt.

Do the math. If you are going to conduct more than 10 searches a month, subscribing makes sense.

Analyzer and ProSearch each require only 8MB of RAM to run. The Web site gives basic information, but doesn't provide a trial run or download capability. You acquire either of these programs by phoning the number listed above.

THOMSON TRADEVIEW

http://investsw.thomson.com/tradview/tradprod.htm
Phone: 1-617-345-2923

I've included this tool as an example of one that your broker or funds manager is likely to use. The PC-based order management system is designed to organize and track trading orders from decision through execution. It is primarily found in large institutional investment firms and brokerage houses. Currently, more than 1,500 of these institutions use this powerful system, which can be configured to the user's specific needs. Like snowflakes, no two TradeView installations are exactly the same.

TradeView comes in Modeling and Compliance models. According to its site, Modeling models, functions include the ability to "monitor cash availability and optionally include cash in modeling calculations," and "evaluate implications of investment decisions on market valuations, cash and security weightings."

The Compliance model acts like a speed-limit governor on a school bus, configuring size of trade limitations into predetermined criteria such as dollar value or share caps on trades. Most models can run on Windows or UNIX platforms.

WALL STREET SIMULATOR FOR WINDOWS

http://www.larax.com/products.htm
Phone orders: 1-800-242-4775 or 1-713-524-6394
Fax orders: 1-713-524-6398
E-mail: 71355.470@compuserve.com
The best description of Wall Street Simulator is as a virtual stock trade manager. The program, which costs only $15 plus $2 shipping and handling, is far less a money manager than it is a fun teaching tool. If you are new to trading and to trading software, this program would be a good one to start with.

Simulated trading can be started by opening your "account" with play money and then, when the mood strikes you, "place trades" with Larax & Co., a make-believe brokerage that is actually Wall Street Simulator's manufacturer.

Because Simulator's Security Conversion Utility lets you import "real world" stock prices from online services such as America Online, CompuServe, and Prodigy, it can keep the database that you use to assess the advisability of "trades" current.

Wall Street Simulator can be ordered via phone, fax, e-mail, or directly from the Larax Web site (see Figure 20-5).

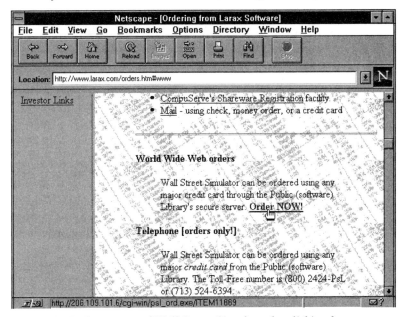

Figure 20-5: *Get a copy of Wall Street Simulator by clicking here.*

Personal Finance Software

After you've gotten your investment software up and running, you'll be so pleased with the order that these tools can bring to your financial life that you'll want to bring similar organizational and processing standards to your personal finance record-keeping and planning, too.

Several leading personal finance software packages are described in Chapter 13, "Software," or in Chapter 14, "Taxes." But because I fashioned those chapters as a broad overview of financial software and tax Web sites, I couldn't possibly get into specifics on many leading programs. Some of the ones not included in earlier chapters are covered here.

Kiplinger TaxCut

http://kiplinger.com
Phone: 1-800-457-9525, operator 347
You already know the name Kiplinger from the monthly *Kiplinger's Personal Finance* magazine, one of the leading magazines that imparts financial advice to consumers.

Now you can avail yourself of Kiplinger's expertise not only by reading its magazine but also by using its tax-preparation software. TaxCut has all the federal tax forms and spreadsheet-delivered computational capabilities that you could ever want. Only an onscreen icon click away, value-added advice features in the software include a deductions reminder and suggestions about last-minute tax-saving tips.

If it's the morning of December 31, the run to the store for New Year's Eve party supplies can wait; boot up TaxCut and see what it recommends. If it's the morning of April 15, you may still have time to apply at least a few of the lessons TaxCut imparts.

The package, which is published by Block Financial Software, is available in one of three general edition categories. The Federal Edition is $29.95; the planning-oriented (no tax forms included) Head Start Edition is $11.95; and any one of the 23 State Editions, which contain state income tax forms, costs $24.95. The state editions let you import the federal tax information that your state may require for you to complete the form.

TaxCut comes in Windows, Windows CD-ROM, or Mac versions. It is available in local computer, office supply, and warehouse club stores as well as by phoning the toll-free number furnished here.

MICROSOFT MONEY FOR WINDOWS 95

http://www.microsoft.com/moneyzone/more.htm
Order by phone: 1-800-426-9400 or 1-206-882-8080
Microsoft Money for Windows 95 is available at prices that range from around $24 to $35. You can get it from your local retailer or direct order from Microsoft or a licensed distributor (see Figure 20-6).

When you boot up the program, you see an opening screen whose Go To icons can take you to these main areas:

- *Report and Chart Gallery*   Contains more than 45 reports and charts, including ones that will process aspects of and print records of your investment portfolio and tax records.

- *Account Register*   The Payment Calendar is the highlight here. Primarily, it is a bill planning, tracking, and payment resource. You can configure this section by entering specifics about your regular payments (such as a mortgage or car loan), deposits, and money transfers. The Payment Calendar then draws up a chart for you indicating when each payment is due and how each payment will affect your checking account balance. The Calendar also has a retirement savings calculator.

- *Online Services*   This function allows 24-hour direct online banking with more than 20 U.S. banks. Participating banks will, via Microsoft Money access, let you check your account balances, transfer funds, send e-mail to the bank, and pay bills.

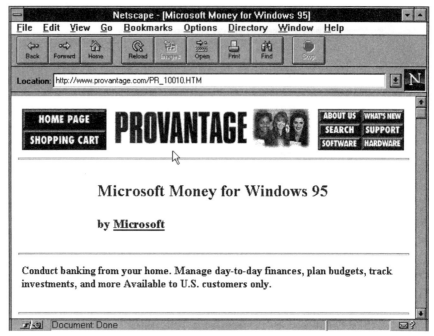

Figure 20-6: *Software distributor Provantage lets you order Microsoft Money for Windows 95 from this page on their Web site (http://www.provantage.com/).*

To run Microsoft Money for Windows 95, you need 10MB of hard drive space and a minimum 4MB of RAM. As you may have guessed, Windows 95 is required.

QuickBooks Pro 4.0

http://www.intuit.com/int-marketplace/quickbooks-pro/index.html
Order by phone: 1-800-224-0991, ext. 500482
QuickBooks Pro 4.0 is accounting software designed for small businesses. Even if you run a small business out of your home, you would probably find many uses for the program, which is listed at $189.95 and comes in PC, Mac, and CD-ROM versions. You can get a copy at retail, or download a free, 60-day trial copy from the Web site of Intuit, Inc. (see Figure 20-7).

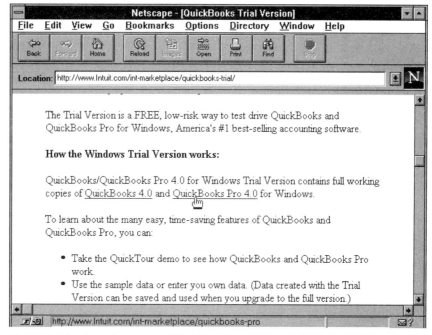

Figure 20-7: A trial version of QuickBooks Pro 4.0 can be obtained by clicking on this link.

Here are some highlights:

- *Graphs*   Income and expenses, sales, accounts receivable, accounts payable, net worth, and budget variance.

- *Advanced project reports*   Job administration, job profitability, job estimates vs. actuals, and time reports classifiable by name, item, and activity.

- *Profit and loss reports*

- *Accounts receivable balance sheets*   Aging, collections, and open invoices reports, as well as charts of pending invoices and customer balances.

- *Inventory reports*   Stock status, open-purchase orders, inventory valuation, and price list.

- *Accountants' reports*   General ledger, trial balance, and audit trail.

Cash flow forecasts, payroll, and tax reports are also available. To run QuickBooks Pro 4.0, you'll need Windows 3.1 or higher, and at least 4MB of RAM (8MB recommended). The disk version takes up 21MB of space, but the CD-ROM product needs 27MB plus an additional 10MB for the optional U.S. Zip Code Directory.

QUICKEN DELUXE FOR WINDOWS

http://www.intuit.com/int-marketplace/quicken-deluxe/win.html
Order by phone: 1-800-224-0991, ext. 500482
This $59.99 package is widely praised for its powerful suite of online banking, portfolio-tracking, and budget-planning capabilities. Quicken Deluxe is also a superb teaching tool. Best yet, it can run on either Windows 95 or Windows 3.1. (Slimmed-down Mac and DOS versions are also available for the same price.)

You access these services via HomeBase, an opening screen setup like a home page on a Web site. Then, by clicking the Deluxe Gateway icon, you come to a page called Finance 101. In the CD-ROM version, you can choose from a list of questions to ask such prestigious investment experts as syndicated columnists Jane Bryant Quinn and Marshall Loeb. Depending on your question, they deliver prerecorded answers to you, right on your computer terminal.

If you'd rather do your own online research, Quicken Deluxe now comes prebundled with a handy copy of Netscape Navigator 2.0.

Quicken Deluxe also furnishes electronic funds-transfer and bill-pay capabilities via an interface with more than 20 banks. On average, these banks charge a flat $3 per month for a subscription. This is added to Quicken Deluxe's $5.95 a month subscription rate for online banking. This rate entitles you to 20 bills paid per month. Each batch of 10 additional bills will cost you $2.95.

To run the Windows-compatible CD-ROM version of Quicken Deluxe, you must have Windows 3.1 or higher, 8MB of RAM, soundboard and speakers, 24MB of free disk space on your hard drive, and, of course, a CD-ROM drive.

The floppy disk version is less demanding, needing only 4MB of RAM and 20MB of available hard drive room. The Macintosh version will work with 8MB of RAM and 12MB of available real estate on your hard disk.

As with other Intuit, Inc., products, you can purchase a copy of Quicken Deluxe at retail or through the "buy now" icon on the Quicken Deluxe home page. Hitting this area takes you to an Order Now page, where your online request for a copy is transmitted to Intuit and encrypted with Netscape's Secured Sockets Layer security (see Figure 20-8).

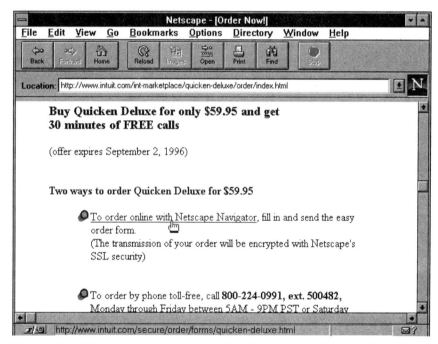

Figure 20-8: *The quickest way to order Quicken Deluxe is through this page on its Web site, as shown here.*

QUICKEN FINANCIAL PLANNER

http://www.intuit.com/int-marketplace/quicken-financial-planner/about/new.html
Order by phone: 1-800-224-0991, ext. 500482
As its name indicates, Quicken Financial Planner is a financial planning program that analyzes budgetary data either typed in by you or imported from your companion Quicken for Windows program. It can then advise you on whether your self-defined financial plan (such as having a given amount of money on hand when you want to retire at a certain age) is on track. This information is displayed on a QuickPlan option screen (see Figure 20-9).

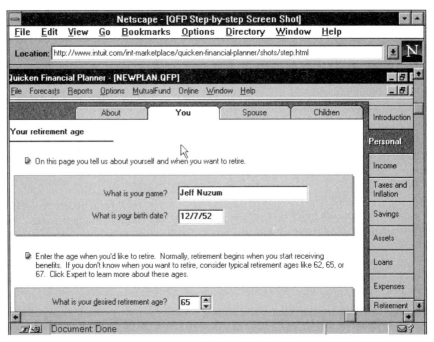

Figure 20-9: *Quicken Financial Planner asks you to configure a personal and financial profile, which it will use as a guidepost to advise you about your financial plans and goals.*

QFP next takes this initial set of data and asks for additional details, such as life insurance and college expenses. After it absorbs everything, it prints a personalized financial plan along with recommendations about specific investment and money-management strategies that you might use to reach these goals.

Arguably the most powerful set of features in QFP is the ability to obtain price-trend information about more than 4,400 mutual funds from the Web, and then, should you so specify, integrating this information into the software's financial planning and recommendations modules.

QFP costs $29.95. As with other Intuit products, it can be purchased at computer, office supply, or warehouse stores, or ordered directly from the Intuit Web site.

CONCLUSION

I hope that you are now well on the way to becoming a sophisticated and knowledgeable online investor. Still, you may have questions. This is understandable. Online trading, financial management software technology, and related fields are changing fast. A new acronym may appear, a new technology may be enabled, an old one may become obsolete. Plus, you may have specific questions about issues that I couldn't cover exhaustively in this book.

The following appendices and glossary will either give you the information you may still need or point you to resources from which you can obtain it.

In the meantime, may all your books balance and may all your trades be profitable!

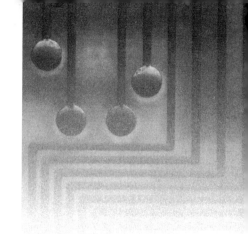

SECTION IV:

Appendices

Appendix A

About netscapepress.com

Netscapepress.com is where you will find the most up-to-date information about Netscape Press. Please visit the site at **http://www.netscapepress.com/**. Netscapepress.com features a catalog of other Netscape Press titles, technical support information, and updates to the book as needed.

Netscapepress.com is the home of *Navigate!*, the official electronic publication of Netscape Press. *Navigate!* is a monthly online publication that offers a wide range of articles and reviews aimed at Netscape users. *Navigate!* features interviews with industry icons and experts, as well as articles excerpted from upcoming Netscape Press titles. Learn how to improve your Web site or to use the best search engines online. Stay abreast of the latest technological innovations and impress your friends with your intimate knowledge of the world's most popular Internet browser.

Netscape Press is a joint effort between Ventana Communications Group, Inc., and Netscape Communications Corp., and serves as the publishing arm of Netscape.

Appendix B

Frequently Asked Questions About Online Investing

What exactly is online investing?

The narrow definition is the execution of trades for investment instruments, such as stocks, bonds, commodities, and mutual funds, from your computer to another computer at your brokerage or at a trading exchange. The broader definition is to use online informational tools not only to make trades but also to stay informed about and better facilitate the decisions necessary to make all types of investments.

What types of financial sites are available on the Internet?

We've just described more than 100 of them in this book, but here are some financial topics where the selection of sites is especially comprehensive: stocks, mutual funds, venture capital sources, banking information, real estate, taxes, and breaking financial and general business news. I've devoted chapters to each of these topics and more. The Introduction will tell you where to find these resources.

What are the benefits of online investing vs. "regular" investing?

Online investing is fast, inexpensive, and secure. It also is a great time-organizer. You can find out news about companies in your portfolio at the same time your broker does. You may even be able to execute your own trades, and save on margins. It also helps lessen at least a few of life's annoying frustrations. If you've ever played telephone tag with your broker, or had your cell phone wink out while you were getting details about a rumored two-for-one stock split or a canceled dividend, you'll know what I mean.

So many sites, so little time. How do I know which sites are worth my time?

I knew you were going to ask! That's why, in this book, I've stayed away from the clunkers and have tried to point you to quality sites. To help you further, I've included a "what makes a good site" section in most of the topic chapters.

Say I want information about a particular company. How do I find its site?

I hope that after reading Chapter 3, "How Do I Find the Information I Need," you will have learned some useful lessons about how to search the Internet, and especially, the World Wide Web.

What are the tools that I need to get online?

You need a computer with at least an Intel 486 or equivalent Macintosh-compatible chip. A 28,800 bps modem and a telecommunications software program are necessary to access the online world. Because so much of the information that you process will be delivered in visual media rather than just straight text, your computer should be running on Windows 3.1, Windows NT, Windows 95, or a Mac 7.5 operating system. You should also have a printer, preferably either laser or late-model ink-jet, so that you can print out the informational materials you receive online.

Last but certainly not least, you need a powerful Web browser such as Netscape Navigator 2.0 or above so that you can access the features of the World Wide Web described in much of this book. You will also need an account with an Internet Service Provider or an online service. In Chapter 1, I've included tips about finding an Internet Service Provider. I've devoted all of Chapter 19 to the online services, and have provided phone numbers for each.

What are the tools that I need to do online investing?

You certainly must have all of the tools described in the previous answer. It also helps to have financial spreadsheet capability and up-to-date tax software. The most compelling reason is that information retrieved from Web sites or online or news services is only raw information. You still need a way to harness this information and relate it to your own investing goals. I've described some necessary programs in Chapter 20.

What types of online investing exist?

As you've discovered by reading this book, you can execute stock trades, review your mutual fund portfolio, e-mail your broker, check your bank balances, apply for a credit card or certificate of deposit, obtain tax advice—and much, much, more.

Are there limits to what I can do online? If so, will those limits change?

We live in exciting times. The year 1996 saw the first substantial incidents of online trading executed by individuals. The first platforms to enable this type of commerce were the online services. Due to the proprietary nature of their networks, they were the pioneers in striking up alliances with forward-looking brokerages planning to test the online waters. In the latter part of 1996, technology advances rendered encryption and other electronic transactional protocols virtually impervious to interception. This watershed development has made direct online investing possible. The number of brokerage-run Web sites through which you can make trades (using their proprietary software for access) is increasing weekly.

Is online investing safe?

Yes, it is. The number of arithmetic calculations that even the most skilled hacker would need to intercept your transaction would take decades to perform even on today's most powerful mainframe computers. The handful of security violations that do occur happen because of human transgressions, such as an illicitly sold password, rather than through a flaw in encryption security.

I own a business. After reading this book, I'm thinking of putting up my own Web site that might be equipped with electronic ordering capability for my key customers. What type of safety features does Netscape Navigator have that can safeguard the security of transactions?

Transactions delivered via Netscape browsers use something called RC4 128-bit encryption technology. The amount of computer power necessary to intercept and decrypt such a message would be 309,485,009,821,345,068,724,781,056 times greater than earlier encryption technologies. Netscape uses this technology with its Secure Sockets Layer protocol, which uses digital technology to create unique online "signatures" for each person accessing a given network. That's why companies such as Security First Network Bank and Wells Fargo Bank (see Chapter 7) are fervent believers in and deployers of Netscape-enabled encryption. Security First Network Bank, the world's first Internet-only bank, has no physical branches but provides virtually all the services of a regular bank, via its Netscape-secured Web site (http://www.sfnb.com).

I read about a major computer hacker incident last week. Was this an isolated crime? I'm excited about the possibilities of secured electronic commerce, but what can you tell me to reassure me that break-ins will never happen? The last thing I need is for one of my customers to have a credit card number intercepted, stolen, and then used for illegal purposes.

Most credit card violations of this type don't happen due to some superhacker intercepting a credit card number. The few such violations (out of tens of billions of transactions) that occur each year are almost always traceable to transgressions committed by a human—such as that rare department store sales-clerk that takes charge receipt carbons out of the trash and sells the credit card numbers on the black market.

I've just read an investment offer on a Web site. It sounds too good to be true. Can you point me to any resources on the Internet that can counsel me about whether to believe certain offers I see?

I have two sites you can check. The Federal Trade Commission (http://www.ftc.gov/) has several pages of advice about investment scams and crooked schemes. The National Fraud Information Center (http://www.fraud.org/), which is a partnership of the FTC, the National Consumers League, and the National Association of (state) Attorneys General, updates its fraud watch files every business day with new incidents. These unfortunate occurrences reflect not only greed at its worst, but also avarice at its tackiest.

What is SET?

This stands for Secure Electronic Transaction standards. SET's primary and most proactive backers have been Visa and MasterCard. Briefly, the guiding principle behind SET is public key cryptography. SET software will "reside" in your computer as well as in the merchant's network computer and the bank's. Your computer's SET software will have a coded sequence, or a "key," unique to you, that will be recognized as such by the SET-equipped computer on the other end. The SET standards are expected to be relatively commonplace by the first quarter of 1997.

How do I know if the company I'm doing business with adheres to SET standards?

Throughout 1996, companies intending to conform their online transactional capabilities to the SET standard realized the importance of these initiatives. They used their Web site to tout their intent. You can be confident that SET-enabled companies will tout this on their home page. If you don't see it, call the company and ask whether they are SET-compliant.

What is the future of electronic commerce and investing?

Virtually boundless. With faster modems, more people online, and even more sophisticated security regimes in place, the holdouts almost surely will be converted. At the same time, the Web sites on which electronic commerce will be conducted will be more enthralling and more intuitive.

What do you mean by "more enthralling"?

Faster data retrieval and advanced multimedia production elements, to name two reasons. In a year or so, you'll be able to log on to an investment Web site and a voice will say something like, "Hello, Mr. Jones. Would you like to check your portfolio?" Next, a voice will "read" the real-time price of each stock to you. If Internet-delivered telephone applications continue to progress, you will be able to converse with your broker through a plug-in application on your browser, rather than over the phone as you do now.

What do you mean by "more intuitive"?

Investment Web sites will use "intelligent agents." No, these are not humans who secure $9 million-a-year contracts for .245 hitters, but software programs that will be able to respond to your informational requests. These programs will be on investment-related Web sites (and others as well). A typical case-use scenario: you will activate the agent, and, via a typed command, ask it something along the lines of, "find me information about all the high-tech sector IPOs (Initial Public Offerings) announced so far this month." The software will search the Web for a data depository, or depositories, that contain this info. You'll get the information in seconds and be an even more informed investor.

Where can I get more information on the topics you covered in this FAQ?

Besides the hundreds of sources cited in this book, you'll want to bookmark the Netscape Communications home page (http://home.netscape.com). The site is updated daily and contains information in an understandable, mature tone. Unlike at least a few of the sites I've seen, the language used on the site isn't geek for geek's sake, nor does it underwhelm you with carnival-atmosphere hustle. It treats you as the learner and striver that you are.

Appendix C

Other Resources

This appendix is divided into two parts: first, a look at timely resources that can keep you up-to-date on the world of online investing; and second, a list of books that discuss in greater detail some of the topics I've explored.

 ## TIMELY RESOURCES

Most of the best resources are on the Web itself. Many of them have been described in this book. Four others are widely available. They are as follows:

- *Internet World* magazine   Points to interesting Internet sites and coverage of trends. URL: http://www.ix.com

- *NetGuide* magazine   Covers trends in Internet site development and content. URL: http://www.netguide.com

- *Online Access* magazine   Thoroughly discusses places to go and things to do on the Web. URL: http://oamag.com

- *Wall Street & Technology* magazine   Examines the confluence of technology and finance, including periodic articles about online trading. They don't yet have a Web site, but this publication can be found on many newsstands.

Two other magazines, *The Red Herring* and *Upside*, cover Internet technologies from a company-analysis standpoint. If you are interested in investing in Internet-related or other high-tech stocks, these magazines will be invaluable to you. They both have Web sites as well: http://www.herring.com (*The Red Herring*) and http://www.upside.com.

I'd also like to suggest four Web-based site review services. New sites that will have debuted after you buy this book likely will be reviewed on these services, which include:

- iGuide   http://www.iguide.com/

- McKinley   http://www.mckinley.com/

- Point   http://www.point.com/

- Yahoo! Computing   http://www.zdnet.com/yahoocomputing/

There's also a Web site heavily devoted to online investing news and trends. It's called Web Finance, and can be found on the WWW at http://nestegg.iddis.com/webfinance/.

Books

What's your reason for going online? Playing a game on America Online, checking the news on a Web site, or maybe putting up your own site and making money from it? There are several books under the Netscape Press or Ventana imprints that will give you all the information you need.

Other Netscape Press Books

Other Netscape Press titles explore some of the topics I've covered, but in greater detail. Here are two you will find useful:

- *The Official Online Marketing With Netscape Book*, by Greg Holden, shows how to use Netscape's tools to create, process, and distribute electronic newsletters and promotional materials.

- *Official Netscape Navigator 3.0 Book*, by Phil James, is available in Windows and Mac editions.

VENTANA BOOKS

Here are some Ventana books that you might find helpful as well:

- *News Junkies Internet 500*, by David Haskin, details the top sites for information addicts.

- *The Official America Online Membership Kit & Tour Guide*, by Tom Lichy, comes in Windows 95, Windows 3.1, and Macintosh editions.

- *The 10 Secrets for Web Success*, by Bryan Pfaffenberger and Dave Wall, explains what it takes to do your site right.

- *The Windows 95 Book*, by Richard Mansfield and Charles Brannon, is a guide on how to use the service.

Appendix D

URLs for Sites
Described in This Book

CHAPTER 1

The Academ Consulting Services Gopher **gopher://
gopher.academ.com**
The main menu of the **misc.invest** Usenet newsgroup.

CHAPTER 2

Netscape   **http://home.netscape.com/**

CHAPTER 3

Yahoo!   **http://www.yahoo.com**
Excite   **http://www.excite.com**
Deja News   **http://www.dejanews.com**
AltaVista   **http://www.altavista.digital.com/**
InfoSeek   **http://www.infoseek.com/**
Lycos   **http://www.lycos.com/**
Open Text   **http://www.opentext.com/**
WebCrawler   **http://www.webcrawler.com/**

CHAPTER 4

Yahoo!   http://www.yahoo.com
The main menu of the **misc.entrepreneurs** Usenet newsgroup.

CHAPTER 5

National Directory of Mortgage Brokers   **http://206.86.104.2:80/
loans**
AccuComm   **http://www.he.net/~accucomm/**
Appraisal Institute   **http://www.realworks.com/**
ERC   **http://www.erc.org**
Financenter   **http://www.financenter.com**
Golden Appraisal Services   **http://www.GoldenGroup.com**
Homebuyer's Fair   **http://www.homefair.com**
Mortgage Market   **http://www.interest.com**
Mortgage Resource Center   **http://www.mortgageselect.com**

CHAPTER 6

Accel Partners   **http://www.accel.com/**
American Venture Capital Exchange   **http://
www.businessexchange.com**
America's Business Funding Directory   **http://
www.business1.com/**
Commercial Finance Online   **http://www.cfonline.com/**
Corporate Finance Network   **http://www.corpfinet.com**
Draper Fisher Associates   **http://www.drapervc.com**
FinanceHub   **http://www.FinanceHub.com/**
Olympic Venture Partners   **http://product.com/olympic**
Price Waterhouse LLP National Venture Capital Survey   **http://
www.pw.com/**
RLS, Inc.   **http://iplex.com/rls**
Sierra Ventures   **http://www.sierraven.com**

CHAPTER 7

Advanta National Bank   http://www.edvance.com/
AT&T Universal Card   http://www.att.com.ucs/
Bank of America   http://www.bankamerica.com/
Credit Scoring   http://pages//prodigy.com/ID/vcr/Score.html
First Consumers National Bank   http://www.FCNB.com/
First Union Bank   http://www.firstunion.com/
MasterCard Information Center   http://www.mastercard.com
RAM Research Group   http://www.ramresearch.com
TRW Information Services   http://www.trw.com/
U.S. Bankruptcy Code   http://www.law.cornell.edu/uscode/11/
Visa Worldwide   http://www.visa.com
Wells Fargo Bank   http://www.wellsfargo.com

CHAPTER 8

American Management Association   http://www.tregistry.com/
ttr/ama.htm
Birmingham Business Assistance Network   http://www.
tech-comm.com/customer/bban
Cedar Consulting   http://www.cedarconsulting.com/
CEO Resource   http://www.ceoresource.com/ceo/
Ernst & Young   http://www.ey.com
MC 100, Inc.   http://www.mc100inc.com/
McKinsey & Company   http://www.mckinsey.com/
Personal Profiling for Career Planning   http://www.win.net/
~comp1/
SMI Consulting Services   http://www.xmission.com/
Small Business Advisor Newsletter   http://www.smartbiz.com/
sbs/pubs/n7a.htm
Wilson Internet Services   http://www.wilsonweb.com/

CHAPTER 9

AccuQuote   http://www.accuquote.com
Aid Association for Lutherans   http://www.aal.org
CNA Insurance Companies   http://www.cna.com
Gary and Tony's Online Insurance   http://
   www.studentinsurance.com/
Illinois Department of Insurance   http://www.state.il.us/ins
Independent Insurance Agents of America   http://
   www.iiaa.iix.com/
ITT Hartford Group, Inc.   http://www.itthartford.com
Prudential Insurance Company of America   http://
   www.prudential.com
State Farm Insurance   http://www.statefarm.com
Travelers Insurance   http://www2.pcy.mci.net/bin/travelers/
   autohome.cgi

CHAPTER 10

BanxQuote   http://www.banx.com
Cannon Trading Co., Inc.   http://www.cannontrading.com/
Charles Schwab   http://www.schwab.com
CompuTel Securities   http://www.rapidtrade.com
E*Trade   http://www.etrade.com
Fidelity Investments   http://www.fid-inv.com
Jack Carl Futures   http://www.jackcarl.com/
MarketEdge   http://www.marketedge.com/join.htm
MarketGuide   http://www.marketguide.com
NASDAQ   http://www.nasdaq.com
National Discount Brokers   http://www.pawws.secapl.com
OLDE Discount Brokers   http://www.oldediscount.com
Zacks Investment Research   http://aw.zacks.com

CHAPTER 11

A+ On-line Resumes   **http://ol-resume.com/**
All-Internet Shopping Directory   **http://www.webcom.com/
~tbrown**
America II Job Seeker Services and Career Corner   **http://
www.americaiidirect.com**
Auto Connection   **http://www.automart.com**
CareerMosaic   **http://www.careermosaic.com**
Covey Leadership Center   **http://www3.pcy.mci.net/market-
place/covey**
DealerOnline   **http://www.dealeronline.com**
Industry.Net   **http://www.industry.net**
MarketPlace 2000   **http://www.market2000.com**
OfficeMax   **http://www.officemax.com/**
TravelWeb   **http://www.travelweb.com**

CHAPTER 12

Dynamic Mutual Funds   **http://www.dynamic.ca**
Alger Fund   **http://networth.galt.com/www/home/mutual/alger/
alger.htm**
Benham Funds   **http://networth.galt.com/www/home/mutual/
benham/benham.html**
Charles Schwab & Co.   **http://www.schwab.com/**
Dreyfus Online Information Center   **http://www.dreyfus.com**
Fidelity Investments   **http://www.fidelity.com**
Gabelli Funds   **http://www.gabelli.com**
Kemper Money Funds   **http://www.kemper.com/**
Vanguard Mutual Funds   **http://www.vanguard.com/**

CHAPTER 13

ChartPro   http://www.fastlane.net/homepages/wallst/
    c-pro.html
The Collector System   http://www.colubs.com/
Financial Freedom Billing Manager   http://www.winmag.com/
    library/1995/0395/3worrex.htm
Hotel Carousel   http://www.hotel-carousel.com
Investor Insight   http://www1.qfn.com/investorinsight/
Monnet Financial System   http://www.monnet.com/
Smart Business Plan   http://www.smartonline.com/
Smart Home Manager   http://www.surado.com/
Time & Profit   http://www.bytepro.com

CHAPTER 14

Ernst & Young   http://www.ey.com/
Hale & Dorr's Family Business Report   http://
    www.haledorr.com/
Idea Cafe   http://www.IdeaCafe.com/
Internal Revenue Service   http://www.irs.ustreas.gov/prod/
    forms_pubs
Mercury Center Tax Guide   http://www.sjmercury.com/
    business/tax
Merrill Lynch: Minimizing Your Taxes   http://www.merrill-lynch.
    ml.com/personal/taxes
Tax Analysts   http://www.tax.org
The Tax Prophet   http://www.taxprophet.com/
TurboTax   http://www.intuit.com/turbotax

CHAPTER 15

American Business Information Business Credit Service   http://
    www.lookupusa.com/
American Law Institute/UCC   http://www.law.cornell.edu/ucc

Art of Smart Automobile Leasing **http://www.mindspring.com/ ~ahearn/lease/lease.html**
Charter Media Briefing.com **http://www.briefing.com**
CommerceNet **http://www.commerce.net**
Financial Services Technology Consortium **http://www.fstc.org**
NetExchange **http://www.tradeguide.com**
Stern Management Consulting **http://www.stern.nyu.edu**

CHAPTER 16

Newsgroups discussed in this chapter:
alt.invest.penny-stocks
alt.business.misc
   alt.misc.invest
biz.marketplace.services.discussion
   comp.os.ms-windows.apps.financial
misc.invest.funds
   misc.invest.futures
misc.invest.stocks
misc.invest.technical

CHAPTER 17

Gopher sites discussed in this chapter:
Bureau of Labor Statistics Consumer Price Index **gopher:// ftp.SHSU.edu:70/00/Economics/bls/doc/cu.doc**
The Holt Report **gopher://wuecon.wustl.edu:671/00/holt/ holt.current**
Insurance Information Institute **gopher://infx.infor.com:4200/**
Pennsylvania Department of Agriculture **gopher:// psupena.psu.edu:70/**
Role of Luck in Strategic Performance **gopher:// ursus.jun.alaska.edu:70/00/working_papers/davis1**
SBA Online **gopher://www.sbaonline.sba.gov/**

CHAPTER 18

American Banker Online   http://www.americanbanker.com
American City Business Journals   http://www.amcity.com/
Investor's Business Daily   http://ibd.ensemble.com/
Money Magazine: Pathfinder   http://pathfinder.com/
    @@VrPxQAYAQPYo5YCM/money/
    The Motley Fool   http://fool.web.aol.com/
Mutual Funds Online   http://www.mfmag.com/
New York Times Business Section   http://www.nytimes.com/
USA Today Money Section   http://www.usatoday.com/money/
Wall Street Journal Interactive Edition **interactive4.wsj.com/**
    edition/current/summaries/front.htm
Associated Press Financial Wire available on CompuServe.
Bloomberg Personal   http://www.bloomberg.com/
Business Wire   http://www.businesswire.com/
Dow Jones News Service available on CompuServe, Genie, and
    Prodigy.
PR Newswire   http://www.prnewswire.com/
Reuters Business Alert   http://inwp.reuters.com/default.htm
United Press International Financial wire available on
    CompuServe and Delphi.
ClariNet accessed through the Usenet **clari-biz.** area.
CNNfn   http://www.cnnfn.com/
Fidelity Investments @82 Dev   http://www.fid-inv.com/82DEV/
    index.html
Individual Inc. NewsPage   http://www.newspage.com/
PointCast Network   http://www.pointcast.com/

CHAPTER 19

Web sites for online services covered in this chapter:
America Online   http://www.aol.com
CompuServe   http://www.compuserve.com
Delphi   http://www.delphi.com
Genie   http://www.genie.com
Microsoft Network   http://www.msn.com

Prodigy   **http://www.prodigy.com**
AT&T Business Network   **http://www.bnet.att.com/**
DataTimes   **http://www.datatimes.com**
Dialog   **http://www.dialog.com**
Dow Jones News/Retrieval   **http://bis.dowjones.com/**
Lexis-Nexis   **http://www.lexis-nexis.com**
Bloomberg Terminal   **http://www.bloomberg.com/**
Dow Jones Telerate   **http://www.telerate.com/tw.html**
Reuters Integrated Data Network   **http://www.reuters.com/ reuterscom/**

CHAPTER 20

Web sites for financial software programs reviewed in this chapter:
Fidelity On-line Xpress   **http://www.fid-inv.com/**
FinancialCAD   **http://www.financialcad.com/**
Investors FastTrack Mutual Fund Program   **http:// www.fasttrack.net/**
StreetSmart 2.0 (Charles Schwab)   **http://www.schwab.com/**
Telescan Analyzer and ProSearch   **http://www.telescan.com:80/**
Thomson TradeView   **http://investsw.thomson.com/tradview/ tradprod.htm**
Wall Street Simulator for Windows   **http://www.larax.com/ products.htm**
Kiplinger TaxCut   **http://kiplinger.com**
Microsoft Money for Windows 95   **http://www.microsoft.com/ moneyzone/more.htm**
QuickBooks Pro 4.0   **http://www.intuit.com/ int-marketplace/quickbooks-pro/index.html**
Quicken Deluxe for Windows   **http://www.intuit.com/ int-marketplace/quicken-deluxe/win.html**
Quicken Financial Planner   **http://www.intuit.com/ int-marketplace/quicken-financial-planner/about/new.html**

Glossary

You may be fluent with investment-related alphabet soup but relatively new to the online world. As your teacher once told you, never be afraid to ask questions. For you, part of the initial learning curve is mastering the technical jargon that all users must know.

Here's a beginner's level glossary of some common Internet terms.

ASCII   Stands for American Standard Code for Information Interchange. Every uppercase and lowercase letter in the Latin, or Western, alphabet, is represented by a seven-digit number with various sequences of 1s or 0s. When it receives a text message from a remote computer, your modem translates these binaries into words that appear on your screen.

backbone   In this reference, an **Internet** network pathway.

baud rate   How fast a modem is, or how many **bits** of data it can process per second. A 28,800-baud modem can process up to 28,800 **bits** per second (**bps**), although, in practice, the amount can fluctuate depending on the integrity of the phone connection and the way the text and graphics are presented on the site you're reading.

BBS   A bulletin board system. A BBS can also be a Web site, but many with specialized interests are dial-up only. In turn, some BBSes can be accessed through an **Internet** connection via **Telnet**. Others require you to dial their modem directly.

bit   A single number in a binary code sequence, either 1 or 0. One of these binary numbers is a bit, or *binary digit*. This means, for example, that the letter "c" will have 7 bits, or binary components.

bps   Stands for **bits** per second and is another indicator of modem speed. Because a letter has 7 **bits**, a 14,400 bps modem will handle up to 1800 bytes per second. Because there are spaces between words and modem line quality can fluctuate, however, the actual figure is somewhat lower.

browser   A software utility such as Netscape Navigator 3.0 that reads and then "translates" an Internet page on a user's computer screen. Depending on how the page was written and on the capabilities of the browser program, the page may come across as straight text, as a Web page with graphics, or as a graphic Web page with additional sound and motion video presentation capabilities.

bytes   A collection of **bits** that form one letter or punctuation mark. There are usually 8 **bits** to a byte. The word *frequently* would contain 10 bytes, for example.

client   A software program that lets a user access a remote computer. A user linking to your Web site, for example, would use a client such as the Navigator 3.0 **browser** to reach your **server**.

Common Gateway Interface   Also called CGI, this is an electronic mail or other utility that, when accessed, pulls up a screen that allows the user to transfer information to your Web site. CGIs can be used for everything from polling customers to requesting specialized data.

cyberspace   This was once a cool term to describe the universe of electronic communication and information retrieval. Still applies, but now is a cliché.

domain name   Your **newsgroup** or Web site address. Two hypothetical examples are www.widgetworks.com and www.stateleg.gov.

electronic commerce   A range of transactional capabilities possible through **cyberspace**. Examples are ordering software directly from a Web site and checking your bank balance online.

e-mail   Stands for electronic mail; messages of text or graphical components sent from one computer to another either over the **Internet** or proprietary network such as an online service or dial-up connection.

encryption   The process of coding sensitive data so that they cannot be read except by authorized users. Frequently used in electronic commerce to shield sensitive information, such as credit-card numbers, from being intercepted by unauthorized third parties.

FAQ   Stands for Frequently Asked Questions, a collection of questions and answers describing the site's purpose, content, and how users can navigate around the site. Some FAQs also contain basic information about **Internet** or **World Wide Web** issues that directly affect the site's functionality.

firewall   One of the main technologies that helps secure **electronic commerce**. A software program that protects a collection of computers from general access by unauthorized users. In a bank setting, for example, the Web site will be "outside" the firewall but individual customer account records will be "inside" the firewall and won't be accessible to people visiting your site.

Gopher   A text-only **Internet** site. Gopher appeared several years before the Web's emergence, and was used primarily by sites with large volumes of archived material. It's still viable as a text-based repository of information. Now, many Web sites "mirror," or copy, data stored on Gopher servers.

host   Can mean a company that houses and makes accessible the information and utilities on a Web site. Hosting services frequently rent a given amount of space per month. Some even design and prepare content for Web sites. A machine on the **Internet** is also called a host.

HTML   Stands for HyperText Markup Language, the type of commands inserted in Web documents to specify how a site should look and where a link might be included. Unless you ask your **browser** to read the source code of a Web document, an HTML command will not appear on a user screen.

HTTP   HyperText Transfer Protocol, a communications sequence for transferring **World Wide Web** documents across the **Internet**.

hypertext   A word or phrase linked to another Web site, **Gopher** page, or **newsgroup**. On some Web **browsers**, this appears as an underlined section, such as, http://www.att.com (which means, put hyperlink here).

Internet   The full range of interconnected **World Wide Web**, **Usenet**, **Gopher**, **listserv**, and other sites.

ISDN   Integrated Services Digital Network, a high-speed data transfer system using specially configured phone lines. Some Web sites that are rich in content are designing special applications that these 128,000 **bps** connections will be better able to handle than slower 28,000 **bps** modems can.

InterNIC   A central registry where new Web sites are registered.

ISP   An Internet Service Provider. These can be national, regional, or local companies that, for a monthly fee, make **Internet** access possible.

Java   A programming language that allows Web sites to transfer mini-programs, or *applets*, to customer **browsers**. Java applets are appearing all over sites. Common examples might be stock price tickers streaming across the bottom of your computer screen via a Web site you're accessing, or a brief animation of someone writing a check on the Web site home page of a company that can perform this service for you.

listserv   A mailing list, often for a specialized topic. Usually free, these lists require a simple online registration process. Then, unless the list is moderated for the quality of posts, most e-mail messages received by the listserv are posted and electronically e-mailed to subscribers' computers.

mail-to   A hyperlink at the end of a Web page that triggers a Web **browser**'s electronic mail program. The program then comes up on the screen. Users who have configured their **browser**'s mail server properly can upload a message directly to an address on your site. A typical mail-to might prompt an electronic mail message to customer service.

MIME   Multipurpose Internet Mail Extensions. These can be graphics files sent by a Web **browser**'s electronic mail utility.

newsgroup   Discussion groups on **Usenet**. Doesn't necessarily mean that the content is newsworthy, however!

POP   Point of Presence. If you're in Portland, Oregon, and are using an Internet Service Provider such as Netcom to log on to the Web and visit a site, you've probably configured your software to dial a local Netcom number, or POP.

posting A message received and archived by a **newsgroup** or Web site.

Secure Electronic Protocols (SET) An **encryption** technical standard used to safeguard transactions made over the **Internet** with a credit card.

server In **Internet**-speak, a computer and/or software program that contains information stored on your Web site. A site visitor's computer uses **client** software to read the Web page information stored on your server. Servers are sometimes referred to as **hosts**.

spamming One of the more irritating aspects of online life. Certain programs let a user with a commercial or ideological message access hundreds of **newsgroups** with a few keystrokes. These result in simultaneous postings, most of which are despised by conscientious Netizens.

streaming (audio and video) Sound and video that are broadcast over a Web site in real (actual as opposed to delayed) time, rather than you downloading and playing these back only after download is complete. An example of streaming audio might be a real-time broadcast of stock market commentaries sent over a Web site that you are accessing. This broadcast is then played with the help of your computer's sound card.

Telnet A command used to transfer from one site to another. Users often use Telnet to read their electronic mail when they are on the road.

URL Uniform Resource Locator, or **Internet** site address. On a Web site for the hypothetical Dakota Debentures, the URL could be: http://www.dakdeb.com/.

Usenet The area of the **Internet** for **newsgroups**.

World Wide Web The group of **Internet servers** and pages that enable text, graphics, sound, and moving images to be transferred between computers and presented in an integrated fashion.

Index

Y

Z

the online magazine for Netscape™ users

Empower

yourself with up-to-date tools for navigating the
Net—in-depth reviews, where to find them and
how to use them.

Enhance

your online experience—get to know the latest
plug-ins that let you experience animation, video,
virtual reality and sound...live, over the Internet.

Enliven

your Web pages—tips from experienced Web
designers help you create pages with punch, spiced
with multimedia and organized for easy navigation.

Enchant

your Web site visitors—learn to create interactive
pages with JavaScript applets, program your own
Internet applications and build added functionality
into your site.

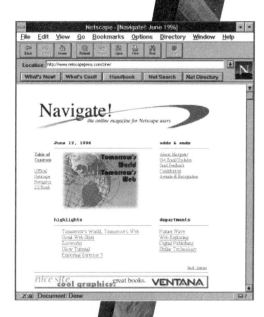

http://www.netscapepress.com/zine

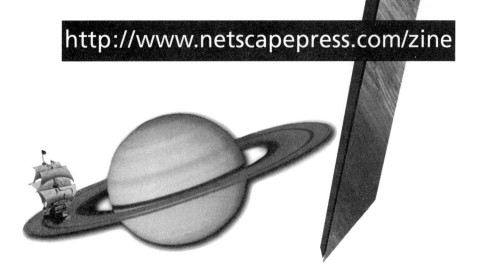

Follow the leader!

250,000+ in its first edition!

ot on the heels of the
unaway international
bestseller comes the
mplete Netscape Press
ine—easy-to-follow
torials; savvy, results-
ented guidelines; and
geted titles that zero in
your special interests.
All with the official
scape seal of approval!

**Official Netscape
Navigator Gold 3.0 Book**
$39.95
Windows 420-0
Macintosh 421-9

956 pages

**Official Netscape
Navigator 3.0 Book**
$39.99
Windows 500-2
Macintosh 512-6

696 pages

"Destined to become the bible to the
world's most popular browser."
—*PC Magazine*

OFFICIAL

Netscape Navigator 3.0 BOOK

The definitive guide to
the world's most popular
Internet navigator

BY PHIL JAMES
FOREWORD BY MARC ANDREESSEN

*International Bestseller!
More than 250,000 in print!*

Add Power to Web Pages

Official Netscape JavaScript Book

$29.99, 520 pages, illustrated, part #: 465-0

Add life to Web pages—animated logos, text-in-motion
sequences, live updating and calculations—quickly and
easily. Sample code and step-by-step instructions show how
to put JavaScript to real-world, practical use.

Java Programming for the Internet

$49.95, 806 pages, illustrated, part #: 355-7

Create dynamic, interactive Internet applications. Expand
the scope of your online development with this
comprehensive, step-by-step guide to creating Java
applets. Includes four real-world, start-to-finish tutorials.
The CD-ROM has all the programs, samples and applets
from the book, plus shareware. Continual updates on
Ventana's *Online Companion* will keep this information
on the cutting edge.

The Comprehensive Guide to VBScript

$34.99, 408 pages, illustrated, part #: 470-7

The only encyclopedic reference to VBScript and HTML
commands and features. Complete with practical examples
for plugging directly into programs. The companion CD-
ROM features a hypertext version of the book, along with
shareware, templates, utilities and more.

Make it Multimedia

Macromedia Director 5 Power Toolkit 🌐

$49.95, 800 pages, illustrated, part #: 289-5

Macromedia Director 5 Power Toolkit views the industry's hottest multimedia authoring environment from the inside out. Features tools, tips and professional tricks for producing power-packed projects for CD-ROM and Internet distribution. Dozens of exercises detail the principles behind successful multimedia presentations and the steps to achieve professional results. The companion CD-ROM includes utilities, sample presentations, animations, scripts and files.

Shockwave! 🌐

$49.95, 400 pages, illustrated, part #: 441-3

Breathe new life into your web pages with Macromedia Shockwave. Ventana's *Shockwave!* teaches you how to enliven and animate your Web sites with online movies. Beginning with step-by-step exercises and examples, and ending with in-depth excursions into the use of Shockwave Lingo extensions, *Shockwave!* is a must-buy for both novices and experienced Director developers. Plus, tap into current Macromedia resources on the Internet with Ventana's *Online Companion*. The companion CD-ROM includes the Shockwave player plug-in, sample Director movies and tutorials, and much more!

The Comprehensive Guide to Lingo 🌐

$49.99, 700 pages, illustrated, part #: 463-4

Master the Lingo of Macromedia Director's scripting language for adding interactivity to presentations. Covers beginning scripts to advanced techniques, including creating movies for the Web and problem solving. The companion CD-ROM features demo movies of all scripts in the book, plus numerous examples, a searchable database of problems and solutions, and much more!

Web Favorites

Looking Good Online 🌐
$39.99, 400 pages, illustrated, part #: 469-3

Create well-designed, organized web sites—
incorporating text, graphics, digital photos, backgrounds
and forms. Features studies of successful sites and design
tips from pros. The companion CD-ROM features samples
from online professionals; buttons, backgrounds, templates
and graphics.

News Junkies Internet 500 🌐
$24.99, 500 pages, illustrated, part #: 461-8

Quench your thirst for news with this comprehensive listing
of the best news and most useful sites and sources on the
Web. Includes business, international, sports, weather,
law, finance, entertainment, politics and more. Plus rated
reviews of site strengths, weaknesses, design and
navigational properties.

Walking the World Wide Web, Second Edition 🌐
$39.95, 800 pages, illustrated, part #: 298-4

More than 30% new, this book now features 500 listings
and an extensive index of servers, expanded and
arranged by subject. This groundbreaking bestseller
includes a CD-ROM enhanced with Ventana's exclusive
PerpetuWAVE technology; updated online components that
make it the richest resource available for web travelers;
Netscape Navigator; and a hypertext version of the book.

TO ORDER ANY VENTANA TITLE, COMPLETE THIS ORDER FORM AND MAIL OR FAX IT TO US, WITH PAYMENT, FOR QUICK SHIPMENT.

TITLE	PART #	QTY	PRICE	TOTAL

SHIPPING

For all standard orders, please ADD $4.50/first book, $1.35/each additional.
For software kit orders, ADD $6.50/first kit, $2.00/each additional.
For "two-day air," ADD $8.25/first book, $2.25/each additional.
For "two-day air" on the kits, ADD $10.50/first kit, $4.00/each additional.
For orders to Canada, ADD $6.50/book.
For orders sent C.O.D., ADD $4.50 to your shipping rate.
North Carolina residents must ADD 6% sales tax.
International orders require additional shipping charges.

SUBTOTAL = $ _____
SHIPPING = $ _____
TAX = $ _____
TOTAL = $ _____

Or, save 15%–order online. http://www.vmedia.com

Mail to: Ventana • PO Box 13964 • Research Triangle Park, NC 27709-3964 ☎ 800/743-5369 • Fax 919/544-9472

Name _____

E-mail _____ Daytime phone _____

Company _____

Address (No PO Box) _____

City _____ State _____ Zip _____

Payment enclosed ___VISA ___MC ___ Acc't # _____ Exp. date _____

Signature _____ Exact name on card _____

Check your local bookstore or software retailer for these and other bestselling titles, or call toll free: **800/743-5369**

**All technical support for this product is available from Ventana.
The technical support office is open from 8:00 A.M. to 6:00 P.M. (EST) Monday through
Friday and can be reached via the following methods:**

World Wide Web: http://www.netscapepress.com/support

E–mail: help@vmedia.com

Phone: (919) 544-9404 extension 81

FAX: (919) 544-9472

America Online: keyword **Ventana**